PETER SINGER AND CHRISTIAN ETHICS

Interaction between Peter Singer and Christian ethics, to the extent that it has happened at all, has been unproductive and often antagonistic. Singer sees himself as leading a "Copernican revolution" against a sanctity-of-life ethic, while many Christians associate his work with a "culture of death." Charles C. Camosy shows that this polarized understanding of the two positions is a mistake. While their conclusions about abortion and euthanasia may differ, there is surprising overlap in Christian and Singerite arguments, and disagreements are interesting and fruitful. Furthermore, it turns out that Christians and Singerites can even make common cause, for instance in matters such as global poverty and the dignity of non-human animals. Peter Singer and Christian ethics are far closer than almost anyone has imagined, and this book is valuable for those who are interested in fresh thinking about the relationship between religious and secular ethics.

CHARLES C. CAMOSY is Assistant Professor of Theology at Fordham University, New York. He is author of *Too Expensive to Treat? Finitude, Tragedy and the Neonatal ICU* (2010).

PETER SINGER AND CHRISTIAN ETHICS

Beyond Polarization

CHARLES C. CAMOSY

CAMBRIDGE
UNIVERSITY PRESS

CAMBRIDGE UNIVERSITY PRESS
Cambridge, New York, Melbourne, Madrid, Cape Town,
Singapore, São Paulo, Delhi, Mexico City

Cambridge University Press
The Edinburgh Building, Cambridge CB2 8RU, UK

Published in the United States of America by Cambridge University Press, New York

www.cambridge.org
Information on this title: www.cambridge.org/9780521199155

First published 2012

Printed in the United Kingdom at the University Press, Cambridge

A catalog record for this publication is available from the British Library

Library of Congress Cataloging in Publication data
Camosy, Charles Christopher.
Peter Singer and Christian ethics : beyond polarization / Charles C. Camosy.
p.   cm.
Includes bibliographical references and index.
ISBN 978-0-521-19915-5 (Hardback) – ISBN 978-0-521-14933-4 (Paperback)
1. Singer, Peter, 1946–   2. Christian ethics.   I. Title.
B5704.S554C36 2012
170.92–dc23
2011042774

ISBN 978-0-521-19915-5 Hardback
ISBN 978-0-521-14933-4 Paperback

Contents

Acknowledgements

Given that my first serious interaction with Peter Singer's work began in their courses, I need to begin by thanking three important mentors at the University of Notre Dame: Jean Porter, Maura Ryan, and Todd Whitmore. This project would probably not have been put forward at all without the encouragement of Robin Gill and Franklin Harkins, and so special thanks goes to them. I also find myself in great debt to graduate assistants Monica Pierce, who tirelessly graded homework so that I could complete two chapters for initial peer review, and Ian Jones who did a full edit of the manuscript and updated the quotes to the new edition of Singer's *Practical Ethics*. My editor at Cambridge University Press, Hilary Gaskin, has also been extremely helpful every step of the way.

Two grants from Fordham's Office of Sponsored Programs supported my research for this book, which included travel to Oxford for the 'Christian Ethics Engages Peter Singer' conference. An invaluable resource for the project (most of Chapter 6 comes directly from insights gathered at the conference), I want to thank the conference hosts, Nigel Biggar and the McDonald Centre for Theology, Ethics and Public Life, for inviting me to present. Special thanks go to John Perry, organizer of the conference, who generously led a manuscript colloquium for me from which I also received invaluable feedback. I'd like to thank everyone who attended the colloquium, and particularly David Albert Jones who gave me detailed notes on two draft chapters.

I'd be totally remiss if I didn't thank Fordham's Center for Ethics Education for allowing me access to three of their best graduate students – Sigourney Giblin, Stefanie Juell, and Angelique Rivard – in a semester-long independent study of the manuscript. The book would not have been the same without their insights. I want to personally thank Stefanie and Angelique for putting together the charts in the appendix, and especially Sigourney for doing a final edit and heroic work on the footnotes, bibliography, and index down the stretch.

I'm most grateful to five people who read full drafts of the manuscript and gave me detailed written comments: David Gushee, Agata Satan, Peter Wicks, Sydney Callahan, and Peter Singer. Singer was also incredibly generous in making sure I had access to his most recent work throughout the writing process. Gilbert Meilaender, Christiana Peppard, Hilary Hammell, Elizabeth Johnson, Susan Kopp, Tito Carvalho, Travis Timmerman, and Tim Mulgan gave me helpful written feedback on individual chapters as well. I also want to thank the following individuals who contributed to the project by pointing me in the direction of an important text or thinker, sharing their own work with me, or helping me with a specific problem: Jacaranda Turvey, David Clough, Morwenna Ludlow, Christine Hinze, Barbara Andolsen, Maureen O'Connell, Maureen Tilley, Richard Viladesau, Aristotle Papanikolaou, Christopher Kaczor, Helen Alvare, Donald Kyle, Robert George, John Finnis, Jay Hammond, Oliver Putz, William Mattison, David Hollenbach, Kenneth Himes, Lisa Cahill, Stephen Pope, John Rivera, Dan Sulmasy, Eric Gregory, and John Hare.

Finally, an important thank you goes to Amy Uelmen and others I've met from the Focolare movement (especially in New York, Toronto, Trento, and Rome) for living out an amazing example of the spirituality of unity. Their capacity for dialogue inspired the spirit in which this book was written. Let me also make special mention of my father, a man who not only taught me how to make an argument, but who encouraged me to live my life boldly.

Introduction

> The patching could go on, but it is hard to see a long and beneficial future for an ethic as paradoxical, incoherent and dependent on pretense as our conventional sanctity of life ethic has become ... It is time for another Copernican revolution. It will be, once again, a revolution against a set of ideas we have inherited from the period in which the intellectual world was dominated by a religious outlook.
>
> Peter Singer, *Rethinking Life and Death*

> Singer's support of infanticide, euthanasia, and bestiality shows the consistency of an anti-Christian, ultimately antihuman philosophy. A true Christian humanism thus shines in stark relief, affirming the correct intuitions of others that all creatures have worth for their own and God's sake, not mere utility.
>
> Gordon Preece, *Rethinking Peter Singer*

There is a time-honored strategy for young people at an academic conference: peruse the publishers' tables while hoping that a conversation breaks out with a really important thinker with whom you've always wanted to exchange. Not that long ago, I was fortunate enough to have this strategy pay off with one of my favorite distinguished Christian ethicists. I had read all of his books, and was anxious to get his reaction to a book I was writing on Peter Singer and to the fact that I was going to meet with Singer personally to discuss my project. He responded with a worried glance and said, "Be careful, Charlie, you're going to like him."

The more I have thought about this reaction, the more interesting and revealing it has become. Imbedded in it are several assumptions: (1) it would be surprising for a Christian ethicist to like Singer, (2) liking Singer might make one be more open to his ideas, and (3) being open to Singer's ideas is something about which we should "be careful." For some, this care might be about an academic disagreement or worry.[1] But for other Christians there is a strong sense that, if they take Peter Singer at all seriously as a thinker, his views are more dangerous by an order of magnitude than the other thinkers to whom we might expose our students.[2] I know colleagues, for instance, who will refuse to assign him in classes, dismiss him as a 'popularizer,' and who will take just about any tactic possible to marginalize his point of view. To the extent they even engage his arguments at all, many do so without reading him carefully or broadly, and instead respond to caricatures of his views.

But in its 2000-year-old quest for moral wisdom, the Church[3] has acknowledged both the historical point that its ethical theory has developed "in critical dialogue with the wisdom traditions that it encountered" and its continuing "desire to invite experts and the spokespersons of the great religious, sapiential and philosophical traditions of humanity"[4] to dialogue on such matters. Given that Singer is probably the world's most influential living philosopher,[5] and the likelihood that at least some Christians were eventually going to examine his views in a way that is consistent with the Church's intellectual tradition, it might not be surprising that some small cracks are starting to form in the intellectual wall separating Peter Singer and Christianity. The Christian ethicist Eric Gregory, Singer's colleague at Princeton, has attempted to engage Singer charitably on our duties to the poor.[6] Gerard Maguiness wrote a remarkable dissertation while at the Pontifical Lateran University's Institute for Moral Theology, which charitably and carefully engaged Singer on the issue of assisted suicide.[7] The distinguished Christian ethicist at Yale, John Hare, has also engaged Singer seriously in several contexts. And in an attempt to make this kind of engagement more systematic, Nigel

---

[1] Garth Hallett suggests that the "vogue of virtue-centered ethics among contemporary Christian ethicists" helps explain the neglect of approaches which have a Singer-like focus on casuistry, analytic reasoning, and utility. *Priorities and Christian Ethics* (Cambridge University Press, 1998), 13.

[2] This seems to be the motivating concern of the book quoted in the epigraph above. Gordon R. Preece, *Rethinking Peter Singer: A Christian Critique* (Downers Grove, IL: InterVarsity Press, 2002).

[3] This book will engage multiple Protestant authors, but I approach this project as a Roman Catholic theologian. More about my methodology follows below.

[4] The International Theological Commission, "The Search of a Universal Ethic: a New Look at Natural Law," 9, 116. Translation by Joseph Bolin, www.pathsoflove.com/universal-ethics-natural-law.html (Accessed March 27, 2011).

[5] Consider that one of his many books, *Animal Liberation*, has been translated into more than twenty languages, including Chinese, Hebrew, Croatian, and Turkish.

[6] Eric Gregory, "Agape and Special Relations in a Global Economy: Theological Sources," in Douglas Hicks and Mark Valarie (eds.), *Global Neighbors: Christian Faith and Moral Obligation in Today's Economy* (Grand Rapids, MI: William B. Eerdmans Publishing Co., 2008).

[7] Gerard H. Maguiness, "Assisted Suicide, Self-Love, and a Life Worth Living," Dissertation (Rome: 2002).

Biggar and John Perry invited Singer and several of his utilitarian students to engage with Christian ethicists like Gregory, Hare, and myself at *Christian Ethics Engages Peter Singer: Christians and Utilitarians in Dialogue*, a conference held at Oxford University's McDonald Centre for Theology, Ethics and Public Life in the spring of 2011.[8]

But perhaps some Christians can be forgiven for reacting to Peter Singer in a less than charitable way. After all, as we saw from the quote above, Singer's basic project claims to be one designed to undermine the foundations supporting our view of the world. It's not just that Singer can't imagine a God who allows all the suffering that exists on this earth,[9] but he holds that our culture has a hangover in our ethics from a period, long past its prime, where we mistakenly took Christian religious belief seriously – and we need to purge this last remaining vestige of its religiosity from the way we think about how we should live our lives. At times Singer seems unable or unwilling to do anything other than dismiss Christian sources of scripture and tradition, and will also resort to sloppy caricature when critiquing Christian positions.[10] Indeed, one might reasonably conclude that he simply has a dismissive skepticism toward religious belief itself as a *prima facie* reaction. In a recent debate he had with Singer, John Hare had the following response to such skepticism:

Why would we want to remove that power from people's lives, or spread skepticism about it? Especially for a utilitarian, a belief should be welcomed that makes people happy, unless it can be shown to be false or is itself productive of harm. Why can't Singer accept religious believers who have the same goals as he does, many of them? Why can't he accept them as allies and welcome the additional motivation that their faith gives them? I have noticed, recently, he is starting to be more generous in his appreciation. And I think that is to be welcomed.[11]

Singer does claim that religious belief causes a lot of harm, but is that really the whole story here?[12] Especially in a postmodern world where

---

[8] http://mcdonaldcentre.org.uk/peter-singer-conference/ (Accessed July 31, 2011).
[9] This, as we shall see below, is Singer's primary reason for rejecting belief in the Christian God.
[10] We will see this take place several times in this book, but it happens in particular with his interpretation of scripture and of important intellectual figures like Thomas Aquinas.
[11] Dallas Willard (ed.), *A Place for Truth: Leading Thinkers Explore Life's Hardest Questions* (InterVarsity Press, 2010), 170–171, 182.
[12] His supporting example, though it really doesn't speak much to Christian ethics, is that of the Middle East. Willard, *A Place for Truth*, 187. Some might be tempted to suggest that religion in general, and Christianity in particular, is somehow especially prone to violence and war. But in a recent book that devastates this position, William Cavanaugh shows how such a view is historically inaccurate and philosophically imprecise. See William T. Cavanaugh, *The Myth of Religious Violence* (Oxford; New York: Oxford University Press, 2009), 285.

academics are more aware than ever of the faith-filled traditions and narratives which undergird the meaning that even atheists like Peter Singer believe are present in our lives, my view is that his reasons for rejecting religious (and specifically Christian) ethics are far more complex. And to see the complexity we need to learn a bit more about him. There are several texts written on his background and that of his family, but in this context I am primarily interested in biographical information which impacts on his view of religion and specifically of Christianity.[13]

WHO IS PETER SINGER?

For someone whose views are constantly being compared to those of the Nazis, it might surprise some readers to learn that three of Singer's four grandparents were killed in the Holocaust.[14] One of those to meet such a horrible fate – his maternal grandfather, David Ernst Oppenheim – was of such interest that Singer wrote a book about him.[15] Remarkably, this particular line of Singer's family has at least seven Rabbis all by itself, including another David Oppenheim, who became the chief Rabbi of Prague in 1702. It is interesting to learn that Singer's maternal grandfather was also an academic who interacted with Sigmund Freud and Alfred Adler. And in a dramatic revelation that foreshadowed an important aspect of his grandson's academic career, we learn that David Ernst Oppenheim was careful to distinguish "between the 'genuine philosopher' who aims to integrate his teaching and his life, and the 'theoretical professor' who is concerned only with his professional standing and personal reputation."[16]

Singer's parents escaped the Holocaust and moved from Vienna to Australia, the country in which he was raised. According to his own

---

[13] Maguiness' dissertation, Preece's book, and Dale Jamieson, *Singer and His Critics*, Vol. 8 (Oxford; Malden, MA: Blackwell Publishers, 1999), 368, all have important biographical information. As we will soon see, Singer himself writes a detailed intellectual autobiography in the introduction to Jeffrey A. Schaler, *Peter Singer Under Fire: The Moral Iconoclast Faces His Critics*, Vol. 3 (Chicago, IL: Open Court, 2009), 571 and quite a lot on his family background in Peter Singer, *Pushing Time Away: My Grandfather and the Tragedy of Jewish Vienna*, 1st edn. (New York: Ecco, 2003), 254.

[14] As we will see in Chapter 2, Singer has been banned from speaking in various German-speaking areas because his views are seen by some as Nazi-esque. Other times he has been shouted down such that he could not continue with his presentation. At one event, a protester ripped Singer's glasses from his face and stomped on them.

[15] The previously cited *Pushing Time Away*.   [16] *Ibid.*, 4.

account, neither of his parents was religious (understandable given what they had just experienced), and both were eager to assimilate Peter and his sister Joan into Australian life.[17] He refused a bar mitzvah at age 13 and apparently fitted well with what he describes as the Australian "independent spirit." Singer's secondary school was in the Presbyterian Christian tradition, but he claims that this "exposure to Christianity had an effect on me that was opposite of what the school's founders presumably intended." During morning assembly he would peruse the Bible and find passages ('the cursing of the fig tree' gets particular attention as problematic) that "seemed difficult to reconcile with the idea that this was a truthful account of the doings of a benevolent and omnipotent being." Perhaps more importantly, after reading about Jesus' claims that it was difficult for a rich man to get into heaven, the young Singer "wondered how that squared with the fact that the most expensive car in the school parking area was the chaplain's shiny black Mercedes."

While at university, Singer was exposed to Plato in a philosophy class, and from then on it was always ethics and political philosophy that most interested him. He joined the Rationalist Society and "was soon familiar with all the fallacies in all the usual arguments for the existence of God." But one problem stood out for him in particular:

The real clincher, however, was the argument from evil. How could the kind of god Christians describe – omnipotent, omniscient, and omnibenevolent – have allowed something like the Holocaust to take place? . . . Wouldn't an omnipotent and omnibenevolent god have at least given us a less erratic climate, and a more stable surface to build on? While one might have doubts about the existence or non-existence of different gods, variously defined, for me the fact of evil removed any reasonable possibility that the world could have been created by the kind of God Christians worship.[18]

While still an undergraduate, Singer also started an activist path from which he was never to stray – even as a chaired professor at Princeton. In

[17] All biographical material from now until Singer's graduate studies at Oxford will be taken from his own 'intellectual autobiography' in *Peter Singer Under Fire*, 1–9.

[18] Much of Singer's skepticism about belief in God seems to assume the kind of Platonic god for which the classic problem of evil does indeed seem to be a serious problem. Though the kind of evil Singer is concerned about is the source of real tension in the Christian tradition, it is perhaps less problematic when one attempts to look at it through the lens of Christian scripture and tradition purged of this Platonic influence. At any rate, both Singer and the Church share a dramatic concern for suffering, and the Church's intellectual tradition is full of thousands of texts reflecting on it in serious ways.

response to the Vietnam War, he became president of an organization called Melbourne University Campaign Against Conscription. Despite abortion still being illegal in Australia, Singer became convinced that the law should change and served as the treasurer of the Abortion Law Reform Association of Victoria. He also relates a story which, as we will see in Chapter 1, would foreshadow one of the most important philosophical moves of his career. When pressed during a public debate on why his support of abortion rights wouldn't also lead to support for the right to infanticide, he recalls how the question made him realize "how difficult it is to draw a sharp line at birth" when determining moral status at the beginning of human life.

Singer would do his graduate study in philosophy at the University of Oxford. Once there, he decided to work with R.M. Hare – an interesting and important ethicist who was at once a utilitarian and a Christian. As we will see in some detail in Chapter 5, he would go on to incorporate his mentor's ethical theory, but not his explicit religious faith. This is not at all surprising given that nothing in Singer's background up to that point had exposed him to anything like a sophisticated take on theological method. Indeed, in the aforementioned debate with John Hare, and in response to moderator Eric Gregory's question probing his views about the life and teachings of Jesus, Singer said the following:

That is the incident of the Gaderene swine, when Jesus took out devils and cast them into a herd of swine, and the swine ran down the hill and drowned themselves. Why did he do that? If he could cast out devils, why couldn't he make them vanish into thin air rather than drowning the poor pigs, not to mention the people who presumably owned the pigs and were now bereft of a means of livelihood.

And in response to Gregory playfully teasing him by pointing out that in articulating this literalist view of scripture Singer shared much in common with the Protestant fundamentalist Jerry Falwell, he said:

You see, the questions is, if we don't take these as true accounts, then what do we take? Then we're in the business of distilling the essential message, while leaving out the little stories. It's hard, then, to work out what exactly the essential message is . . . If we're going to talk about some version which doesn't deal with these details, we obviously need a lengthy discussion as to what we do take from it, and I'm not even quite sure where we'd begin and end.[19]

---

[19] Willard, *A Place for Truth*, 192–193.

Had Singer been around any sort of even mildly sophisticated scriptural analysis in his formative years, he might have known at least where to begin. From its beginnings, important figures like St Augustine have explained how Christians should interpret scripture in ways which go beyond the simplistic approach of Singer and Falwell. Indeed, innumerable texts have been written which interpret various biblical texts in light of history, sociology, psychology, feminism, and much more.

THESIS AND METHOD OF THIS BOOK

I want to argue that Singer's sweeping rejection of Christian ethics comes largely from the same place as does the Christian rejection of his point of view: a kind of ignorance which comes from defining oneself by opposition to another. This has led to misreadings and caricatures which have further limited serious engagement. And this book is a systematic attempt to break this unfortunate cycle. My basic thesis is that if Christians and those who take Peter Singer's approach engage each other in the spirit of intellectual solidarity, rather than defining by opposition, we will find (1) that our disagreements are actually quite narrow and interesting, and (2) that we can work together on many important issues of ethics and public policy.

The Roman Catholic ethicist David Hollenbach helpfully defines intellectual solidarity as an orientation of mind that regards differences among traditions as stimuli to intellectual engagement across religious and cultural boundaries. Such an orientation

leads one to view differences positively rather than with a mindset marked by suspicion or fear. It starts from a posture that welcomes foreign or strange understandings of the good life in a spirit of hospitality, rather than standing guard against them. This receptive orientation expects to be able to learn something valuable by listening to people who hold understandings of the good life different from one's own. It also expects to be able to teach something valuable to those who are different by speaking to them respectfully about one's own understanding of the human good ... It is a disposition based on the hope that we can actually get somewhere if we decide to listen to what others think a good life looks like and in turn tell them why we see the good the way we do. Differences of vision are not so total that we are destined to remain eternal strangers to one another.[20]

---

[20] David Hollenbach, *The Common Good and Christian Ethics*, Vol. 22 (Cambridge, UK; New York: Cambridge University Press, 2002), 269, 138.

And the teaching of the Church agrees, claiming that being in solidarity with our fellow human beings means that we are to seek "points of possible agreement where attitudes of separation and fragmentation prevail."[21] For some, and perhaps especially for those who see Christianity as closed-minded and not open to serious engagement with those who think differently, this might seem like a new thing for the Church. But for those who know the Church's history, it will not be strange at all. Indeed, perhaps the most important Christian theologian in the Church's history, Thomas Aquinas, spent his entire career in intellectual solidarity with the thought of the pagan philosopher Aristotle. And Christianity was forever changed as a result.[22]

Peter Singer and the Church, in part because they share some similar lenses through which they look at the world,[23] have the possibility of interesting exchange on many ethical issues which, unfortunately, cannot receive sustained attention in this book: war, the death penalty, the role of international law and international organizations, ecological and environmental concerns, allocation of healthcare resources and healthcare reform, the moral and legal status of migrants and immigrants, and the practical nature of ethics. In the interest of drilling down into the complexity of some crucial ideas, I will limit sustained attention to the following topics: abortion, euthanasia and end-of-life issues, non-human animals, duties to the poor, and ethical method. For each topic I plan to (1) map out significant and non-trivial agreement, (2) map out the surprisingly narrow disagreement, and (3) make an argument about how Singer and/or the Church should push each other with regard to (2). What I hope will become obvious, however, is that this book is only the starting point for what must be a continuing discussion – with regard to both the topics it considers and those that must be saved for another time and context.

---

[21] Catholic Church, Pontificium, *Compendium of the Social Doctrine of the Church*, 194. www.vatican.va/
      roman_curia/pontifical_councils/justpeace/documents/rc_pc_justpeace_doc_20060526_compendio-
      dott-soc_en.html (Accessed February 27, 2011).

[22] Indeed, some Christians criticize the significant influence that Thomas Aquinas has had on
      Christianity precisely because of how much Aristotle influenced both him and the Church that
      would come after him.

[23] Most striking is a common skepticism of our secular culture's worship of autonomy and
      consumerism. Though it will be clear how this skepticism functions in several specific contexts
      throughout the text, more systematic reflection on this overlap will come in the conclusion to
      the book.

A NOTE ABOUT MY APPROACH AS A CHRISTIAN

When I refer to the views of 'the Church' throughout this book, though I hope it will be clear from the context, I will most often mean the current teaching of Roman Catholicism.[24] This might raise the eyebrows of some readers, and for different reasons, so let me be clear about two things up-front. First, this is merely a shorthand way of referring to a particular approach to Christian ethics, and not meant to be part of a larger argument that, say, other Christian churches do not count as real churches or that other Christians do not count as real Christians. Indeed, many Protestants (John Hare, Andrew Linzey, C.S. Lewis, Nigel Biggar, Stanley Hauerwas, Robert Wennberg, Joseph Fletcher, Eric Gregory, Gilbert Meilaender, David Clough, etc.) appear in these pages as important and at times essential representatives of Christian ethics, and Orthodox Christian thought does important work as well. Furthermore, many of the official documents I will cite are written to appeal to 'all those of good will' and not just Roman Catholics. But despite these considerations, it goes without saying that Roman Catholics are also Christians, and therefore Roman Catholic ethics are Christian ethics.

Second, this move is not meant to imply that the current teaching of the Church is the only legitimate answer for all Christians. Indeed, both Thomas Aquinas and the theologian Joseph Ratzinger (before becoming the current Pope) argue for the primacy of a well-formed Christian conscience in doing moral discernment and ultimately making moral choices. Roman Catholics do consider the current teaching to be normative, but what this means in any given situation (especially for the work of academic theologians) is difficult to describe in the abstract, and this book is certainly not making an argument about this complicated matter.

Let me also briefly address non-Christian and secular readers. You may come to this book skeptical of what the Church claims, simply because you do not share its theological presuppositions and foundations. This might be especially likely when it comes to doctrine – or tradition-specific theological principles about things like who Jesus was, what the Bible is, the nature of revelation in general, etc. However, I predict that many of you will be surprised to discover that you actually agree with many of

---

[24] Many Roman Catholic theologians are aware that there are tensions pulling in various directions throughout the tradition, and sometimes even within the current teaching, but it goes beyond the scope of this book to get into these nuanced and complex arguments. My method will simply highlight major aspects of the tradition and current teaching insofar as it aids an examination of Singer's and Christian ethics.

the Church's 'thin' theological claims about the nature of human persons and the broader ecological world, avoiding violence, the pitfalls of consumerism, having a special concern for the most vulnerable, and more. This would not be surprising to Christians who believe that our God is a God of reason and love, and that both have been "written on the hearts" of every human person. Indeed, this belief forms the basis for the Church addressing many of its teachings not just to Christians, but also to all those of good will.

Armed with this good will, then, let us begin an exchange between Peter Singer and Christian ethics. And let us begin with perhaps the most difficult and complex issue of them all: abortion.

CHAPTER I

Abortion

A week-old baby is not a rational and self-aware being, and there are many nonhuman animals whose rationality, self-awareness, capacity to feel and so on, exceed that of a human baby a week or a month old. If . . . the fetus does not have the same claim to life as a person, it appears that the newborn baby does not either. If these conclusions are too shocking to take seriously, it may be worth remembering that our present absolute protection of the lives of infants is a distinctively Christian attitude rather than a universal ethical value.

Peter Singer, *Practical Ethics*

For God, the Lord of life, has conferred on [humanity] the surpassing ministry of safeguarding life in a manner which is worthy of man. Therefore from the moment of its conception life must be guarded with the greatest care while abortion and infanticide are unspeakable crimes.

Bishops of Vatican Council II, *Gaudium et Spes*

INTRODUCTION

If one is after productive exchange between Peter Singer and Christian ethics, it might seem that abortion is an odd place to begin.[1] In his important and comprehensive work *Practical Ethics*, Singer suggests that

we accord the fetus no higher moral status than we give to a nonhuman animal at a similar level of rationality, self-consciousness, awareness, capacity to feel and so on. Because no fetus is a person, no fetus has the same claim to life as a person.[2]

---

[1] By 'abortion' here, I am not referring to ending pregnancies via drugs which cut off the pregnancy hormone to the fetus or which may refuse the embryo implantation into the uterine wall. Such examples bring complexities with them such as (1) the moral status of the early embryo (which, unlike the fetus, can twin and recombine and prompt questions about whether it is an individual substance) and (2) the difference between directly killing and refusing to sustain (without aiming at death) that go beyond the scope of this chapter. Instead, I am referring to *surgical* abortions, which directly kill a fetus.

[2] Peter Singer, *Practical Ethics*, 2nd edn. (Cambridge; New York: Cambridge University Press, 1993), 136, 395.

He believes that the overwhelming majority of abortions are justified because a woman's preferences will almost always outweigh the (at best) rudimentary preferences of a fetus. And as we will soon see, Singer notoriously goes further and argues that the right to an abortion also implies a right to *infanticide*, because a newborn infant, like a fetus, has few valuable preferences. Contrast this point of view with Pope John Paul II in *Evangelium Vitae*:

I declare that direct abortion, that is, abortion willed as an end or as a means, always constitutes a grave moral disorder, since it is the deliberate killing of an innocent human being.[3]

And not only fetuses and infants, but even the early embryo deserves a special level of moral and legal protection due to its vulnerability, and their killing is described as "an unspeakable crime" by the bishops of Vatican Council II.[4] John Paul II's *Veritatis Splendor* would cite Vatican II and go even further, putting abortion in the same category as torture, genocide, and slavery by calling it "intrinsically illicit."[5] It looks not only as if abortion should be something other than the focus of the opening chapter, but as if, given the goals of this book, perhaps it should not be treated at all. The disagreement seems wide-ranging, fundamental, and intractable.

But I argue that this understanding of the abortion debate comes from a combination of three factors: (1) entrenched tribalism and a need to see the identity of one's self or group in opposition to 'the other', (2) a growing fatigue with such a divisive topic that seems hopelessly polarized, and (3) general confusion with regard to which issues are at stake and even which ones are actually being contested. In order to avoid this kind of confusion, one must intellectually and perhaps artificially separate three kinds of issues that often get lumped together when discussing abortion: the moral status of the fetus, whether it is ever morally acceptable to kill or refuse to sustain a fetus, and complications surrounding whether any of this could ever be enacted in a public policy – including whether abortion restrictions harm the moral and legal status of women. In this chapter

---

[3] Pope John Paul II, *Evangelium Vitae, Issues in Law & Medicine* II, no. 4 (Spring, 1996), 62, 443–453.

[4] National Catholic Welfare Conference and Donald R. Campion, *Pastoral Constitution on the Church in the Modern World: Gaudium et Spes, December 7, 1965* (Washington, D.C.: National Catholic Welfare Conference, 1976), 138, 51.

[5] Pope John Paul II, *Veritatis Splendor* (Vatican: The Holy See), August 6, 1993. www.vatican.va/holy_father/john_paul_ii/encyclicals/documents/hf_jp-ii_enc_06081993_veritatis-splendor_en.html (Accessed July 31, 2011), 80.

I will dispel confusion which leads to thinking that Peter Singer and the Church have wide-ranging, interminable disagreement on the issue of abortion. Indeed, I will show that the narrow disagreement between them is about the moral status of the fetus; and even more narrowly, about whether 'potential' should count when determining such status. I will also make an argument which shows that the Church's position on the moral value of the fetus' potential is more convincing – an argument that I think, especially in light of his current theoretical shift, Peter Singer could in principle accept.

Before I begin, however, let me emphasize what this chapter is not doing. It is *not* designed to do anything like comprehensively address the issue of abortion. I limit the focus to comparisons of Singer and the Church on this topic. Some will likely find it frustrating that both approaches do not give the moral status of women enough sustained attention to make a fruitful comparison.[6] Some pro-choice feminists argue, for instance, especially in light of the history of men dominating women's bodies and reproductive capacities, that taking broad abortion choice away from women sends our culture back to a place we don't want to go. However, a diverse group of feminists argues that true freedom for women cannot be seen as mere legal choice and, ironically, widely available legal abortion actually serves the interests of men and reduces the autonomy of women.[7] Indeed, the conclusion of this book will highlight that both Singer and the Church, with regard to each of the main ethical issues this book considers, have a radical suspicion of a hyper-emphasis on mere individual choice.

ISSUES ON WHICH SINGER AND THE CHURCH AGREE[8]

Public policy

At a very basic level, it is clear that both Singer and the Church believe that, all things being equal, it is seriously wrong (both morally and legally)

---

[6] Some feminists find it difficult to imagine how one can consider the fetus (given her place inside a woman's body) without also considering the moral status of women. But perhaps because Singer and the Church have strongly related issues in mind which do not involve this bodily relationship (how we treat embryos in the laboratory, for instance), they do not focus as much as they should on this question.

[7] This group includes not only pro-life feminists like Sidney Callahan and Rachel MacNair, but also pro-choice feminists like Andrea Dworkin and Catherine MacKinnon.

[8] Let me make another caveat about what is being done in this section. To the extent that it deals with arguments, it does so *only to show the overlap* – both in premises and conclusions – between Singer's approach and that of the Church. I am not trying to make the argument for Singer and the Church against their opponents as doing so would go well beyond the scope of the chapter.

to kill a person. Singer, as we will discuss at various points throughout this book, is a utilitarian who believes that the moral life is about maximizing preference satisfaction, but his theory also provides for a general rule against killing persons:

> [A]n action contrary to the preference of any being is wrong, unless this preference is outweighed by contrary preferences. Killing a person who prefers to continue living is therefore wrong, other things being equal ... [T]aking the life of a person will normally be worse than taking the life of some other being.[9]

The *Catechism of the Catholic Church* also claims that direct and intentional killing of persons is "gravely sinful" and this even forbids forming the intention to bring about a person's death indirectly.[10]

But when we apply this principle to abortion public policy, doesn't the complexity of the moral status of the fetus (and other questions) mean that we should leave it to the private choices of individuals? This seems to have been the argument of the majority in the United States Supreme Court Decision *Roe* v. *Wade*, which claimed that abortion rights are part of a broader right to privacy. Peter Singer rejects this position and claims that this reasoning works only with regard to "acts that do not harm others," but those who make privacy arguments implicitly "take it for granted that abortion does not harm an 'other' – which is precisely the point that needs to be proven before we can legitimately apply the principle to the case of abortion."[11]

The Church, as we will see many times throughout this book, agrees with Singer. Though the state "must sometimes tolerate, for the sake of public order, things which it cannot forbid without a greater evil resulting ... the inalienable rights of the person must be recognized and respected by civil society and the political authority."[12] Pope John Paul II claimed that in an inordinate focus on privacy "lies the ethical relativism which characterizes much of present-day culture," but "it is precisely the issue of respect for life which shows what misunderstandings and contradictions, accompanied by terrible practical consequences, are concealed in this position." And therefore the legal toleration of abortion "can in no way

---

[9] Singer, *Practical Ethics*, 3rd edn. (New York: Cambridge University Press, 2011), 80.

[10] Catholic Church, *Catechism of the Catholic Church* [Catechismus Ecclesiae Catholicae], 2nd edn., Vol. 5–109 (Citta del Vaticano; Washington, D.C.: Libreria Editrice Vaticana; distributed by United States Catholic Conference, 2000), 904, 2268, 2269. This will become important in later chapters – and especially Chapter 4, which explores how Singer and the Church view a decision not to aid those in absolute poverty.

[11] Singer, *Practical Ethics*, 131.

[12] Congregation for the Doctrine of the Faith, *Donum Vitae* (Libreria Editrice Vaticana, 1987), III.

claim to be based on respect for the conscience of others, precisely because society has the right and the duty to protect itself against the abuses which can occur in the name of conscience and under the pretext of freedom."[13]

Another argument about public policy, however, asks us to consider the unintended consequences of laws restricting abortion. Perhaps such laws would merely send us back to a time when abortion was 'underground', with unqualified people doing abortions that threatened the health and even the very lives of many women, especially the poor and vulnerable who might not be able to pay for a trained physician. But Singer maintains that without meeting the argument that abortion is the killing of a person, one could reasonably argue that the focus should instead be on changing the social situation which would drive mothers to have an illegal abortion and also on getting "the law properly enforced."[14] The Church is in agreement:

The gravity of the problem comes from the fact that in certain cases, perhaps in quite a considerable number of cases, by denying abortion one endangers important values to which it is normal to attach great value, and which may sometimes even seem to have priority. We do not deny these very great difficulties ... but we proclaim only that none of these reasons can ever objectively confer the right to dispose of another's life, even when that life is only beginning.[15]

A final issue to be considered[16] is perhaps the most talked-about public policy of all (at least in the United States): a constitutional approach to regulating abortion, as in the legal decision of *Roe* v. *Wade*.[17] Speaking on a panel at a recent conference at Princeton University, Peter Singer also rejected this point of view on the basis of his broader political philosophy[18]:

---

[13] Pope John Paul II, *Evangelium Vitae* (Vatican: The Holy See), www.vatican.va/holy_father/john_paul_ii/encyclicals/documents/hf_jp-ii_enc_25031995_evangelium-vitae_en.html (Accessed July 31, 2011), 70–71.

[14] Singer, *Practical Ethics*, 130.

[15] Congregation for the Doctrine of the Faith, *Declaration on Procured Abortion* (Libreria Editrice Vaticana, 1974), 14.

[16] Again, it is certainly a limitation of this chapter that the moral status of women and other feminist arguments were not considered. But both Singer and the Church do not give the matter enough sustained attention to make a fruitful comparison.

[17] And the follow-up decision of *Planned Parenthood* v. *Casey*.

[18] All quotes transcribed from video of *Open Hearts, Open Minds, Fair-Minded Words: A Conference on Life and Choice in the Abortion Debate.* "Abortion in America: Should it be a Constitutional Question?" (October 15, 2010) http://uchv.princeton.edu/Life_Choice/program.html (Accessed January 22, 2011).

I think the overwhelming majority of abortions at least are not morally wrong. I also think that abortion, when performed by a licensed medical practitioner, should never be a criminal offense. At the same time, I believe that abortion should not be a constitutional matter. I believe that it should be left to the legislatures.

And to abortion constitutionalists he said the following:

To those who say that this is a matter of fundamental rights that should be protected, I say that those rights are contested . . . and why should the resolution to that difference of views come from judges appointed for life rather than the majority in the normal political process?

And in a moving moment of empathy and even compassion for pro-lifers, Singer said the following:

If I put myself in the position of someone who is opposed to abortion . . . I would be enraged by the fact that even if I could get a clear majority of congresspeople thinking the way that I do . . . I could not get change on that issue.

Of course, one group who has been just so enraged is the United States Conference of Catholic Bishops, a group that has been articulating arguments against *Roe* v. *Wade* for decades. In what many (in America, at least) will no doubt find a stunning example of overlap, both Peter Singer and the Roman Catholic Church believe that *Roe* v. *Wade* is bad law and both would prefer a legislative approach to the current public policy.[19]

Killing a fetus acknowledged to be a person

Another question, one that can be separated from public policy and moral status considerations, is whether someone could morally kill or refuse to sustain a fetus we acknowledge to be a person with full moral value.

---

[19] Interestingly, Singer objects to the Supreme Court's reason not only as a matter of political philosophy, but on moral principle as well. In another example of common ground with the Church, Singer rejects fetal viability as a morally significant dividing line. In his updated version of *Practical Ethics* (126–127) he points out that the court "gave no indication why the mere capacity to exist outside the womb should make such a difference to the state's interest in protecting potential life." Furthermore, viability is problematic because it varies so much in different time periods and social situations. Though variables such as the time and place in which a fetus is living can change her potential for living outside the womb, they do not "change the nature of the fetus, so why should [they] remove its claim to life?" Singer also rejects the argument that a fetus' total dependence on her mother means that she has no rights independent of her mother's wishes. He offers multiple counter-examples where one person is totally dependent on another (an infant and her mother, an elderly mother and her adult son caretaker, a hiker with a broken leg and his hiking companion) in which we reject the idea that the one with the power has the right to kill the one who is dependent.

This question is engaged by the famous argument of Judith Thomson and her successors such as F. M. Kamm.[20] They begin simply by assuming, for the sake of argument only, that a fetus is a person and nevertheless conclude that abortion is morally permissible. In defending their point of view, though complex arguments are made,[21] their basic claims are: (1) that becoming pregnant is analogous to being hooked up, against your will, to the body of a person you do not know (in Thomson's well-known example the person is a "famous violinist") who requires your body in order to live, and (2) that abortion is analogous to removing yourself from that person.

Thousands of pages have been written attacking and defending Thomson's argument on various grounds,[22] but Peter Singer claims that "the consequences of disconnecting myself from the violinist are, on balance and taking into account the interests of everyone affected, worse than the consequences of remaining connected."[23] Singer believes that if we actually do think that the older human and the fetus are both persons, "to disconnect oneself is wrong," and "it would be wrong to refuse to sustain a person's life for nine months if that was the only way the person could survive."[24]

Although official Church teaching hasn't addressed this kind of argument directly, it has obviously done so implicitly in arguing that direct abortion is always wrong. It also lays the groundwork for a more direct response by claiming that the moral law "prohibits exposing someone to mortal danger without grave reason, as well as refusing assistance to a person in danger."[25] This principle is very similar to the central point of Singer's argument above. In addition, Brian Parks argues in the *National Catholic Bioethics Quarterly* that the primary reason we may not have a duty to sustain life in Thomson's case is because of a natural/artificial distinction.[26] If we were to consider a

---

[20] Judith Jarvis Thomson, "A Defense of Abortion," *Philosophy and Public Affairs* 1, no. 1 (Autumn, 1971), 47–66 and F. M. Kamm, *Creation and Abortion: A Study in Moral and Legal Philosophy* (New York: Oxford University Press, 1992), 227.

[21] All of the arguments in this section are complex, but doing justice to their complexity goes beyond the scope of the chapter. Again, all I am trying to do in this section is to show how Singer and the Church agree in their final evaluations of such arguments.

[22] Many, for instance, reject (1) the idea that pregnancy as a result of voluntary sex is analogous to being hooked up against one's will to someone's body, and (2) that direct surgical abortion is analogous to removing oneself from another person. Singer, however, attacks Thomson's argument from another point of view.

[23] Singer, *Practical Ethics*, 134.   [24] *Ibid.*, 134.

[25] Catholic Church, *Catechism of the Catholic Church*, paragraph 2269.

[26] Brian D. Parks, "The Natural-Artificial Distinction and Conjoined Twins: A Response to Judith Thomson's Argument for Abortion Rights," *National Catholic Bioethics Quarterly* 6, no. 4 (Winter 2006).

similar case of dependence, but the players were instead conjoined twins, Parks argues that our intuitions would fit with those of Singer and the Church. At any rate, both Singer and the Church end up rejecting the argument that it is not morally required to support a fetus with one's body for nine months. For them, our moral duty to sustain human persons requires significant sacrifice.[27]

Given how famously and energetically Peter Singer and the Church are opposed on the issue of abortion, it might be surprising that they agree on so many of the major issues in the debate. Indeed, it turns out that the single issue about which they disagree is the moral status of the fetus. But it takes some careful analysis to figure out precisely where the disagreement lies even here. And in exploring this topic we will discover *even more* that the two approaches have in common on abortion.

THE MORAL STATUS OF THE FETUS

Connecting abortion and infanticide

Interestingly, both Peter Singer and Roman Catholicism are unafraid to explicitly connect their positions on abortion to their logical implications for infanticide, and both have been well known for doing so. Singer acknowledges, quite plainly, that his arguments about the moral status of the fetus also apply to the newborn baby. The view that the life of a newborn baby is sacred may be widely accepted, but he claims that such views need to be challenged:

In attempting to reach a considered ethical judgment about this matter, we should put aside feelings based on the small, helpless and – sometimes – cute appearance of human infants ... If we can put aside these emotionally moving but strictly irrelevant aspects of the killing of a baby, we can see that the grounds for not killing persons do not apply to newborn infants.[28]

Singer explicitly connects his view of abortion and the moral status of the fetus with infanticide and the moral status of the infant. We will look

---

[27] This view, especially if it applies in the case of pregnancy following non-consensual sex (as the Church currently believes that it does), has dramatic implications for what we are required to do to sustain other persons. Perhaps not surprisingly, both Singer and the Church articulate quite radical requirements for sustaining the vulnerable in other contexts as well. Much more will also be said about this duty to aid another in the chapter on duties to the poor.

[28] Singer, *Practical Ethics*, 152.

carefully at this argument in more detail below, but for now it suffices to quote him here to make the point:

Now we have to face the fact that these arguments apply to the newborn baby as much as to the fetus. A week-old baby is not a rational and self-aware being, and there are many nonhuman animals whose rationality, self-awareness, capacity to feel and so on, exceed that of a human baby a week or a month old. If . . . the fetus does not have the same claim to life as a person, it appears that the newborn baby does not either.[29]

Singer's notorious support of infanticide is at first shocking to most people and has contributed to his becoming an internationally and popularly known figure. This position alone is enough for some to reject him outright, but Singer responds by saying that if

these conclusions are too shocking to take seriously, it may be worth remembering that our present absolute protection of the lives of infants is a distinctively Christian attitude rather than a universal ethical value.[30]

Indeed, the Church has been connecting abortion and infanticide virtually since its beginnings. Even in the contemporary West, when infanticide is not a clear public policy issue, the Church still makes the connection. Consider the following statement from the Bishops of Vatican Council II:

For God, the Lord of life, has conferred on men the surpassing ministry of safeguarding life in a manner which is worthy of man. Therefore from the moment of its conception life must be guarded with the greatest care while abortion and infanticide are unspeakable crimes.[31]

The connection is an ancient one. *The Didache,* one of the earliest Christian manuals for converts,[32] specifically mentions them together: "You shall not murder a child by abortion nor kill that which is born."[33] Unlike today, the prohibition of infanticide at this time would have had significant counter-cultural bite considering how widespread the practice was in ancient Greece and Rome. Indeed, we have evidence of

---

[29] *Ibid.*, 151.

[30] *Ibid.*, 153. It is probably worth mentioning that Jews and other ancient peoples also held this view for some time, and well before Christianity, and in that sense it is not distinctively Christian.

[31] National Catholic Welfare Conference and Donald R. Campion, *Gaudium et Spes,* 51.

[32] It was certainly known by the third century, but some scholars claim it dates to 70 CE.

[33] J. Armitage Robinson (trans and ed.), "Didache," *Barnabas, Hermas and the Didache,* D.ii.2c (New York: The MacMillan Co., 1920), 112.

the practice being so common that it dramatically skewed the female/male population ratio. From inscriptions belonging to ancient Delphi, for instance, we can reconstruct 600 families – and remarkably only one of these had more than one daughter.[34] Rodney Stark claims that it was widespread female infant abandonment and infanticide on the part of pagan Romans and Greeks, coupled with a Christian refusal to do the same, which shifted the demographics in favor of Christianity becoming the dominant religion of the Empire – a shift that was underway long before Constantine's conversion.[35]

The practice of infanticide and abandonment was a socially open one, and often the infants died horrible deaths. Here is a description of the practice from Pliny the Elder:

Some of them do the deed with their own hands; with monstrous cruelty and barbarity they stifle and throttle the first breath which the infants draw or throw them into a river or into the depths of the sea, after attaching some heavy substance to make them sink more quickly under its weight … others take them to be exposed in some desert place, hoping, they themselves say, that they may be saved, but leaving them in actual truth to suffer the most distressing fate. For all the beasts that feed on human flesh visit the spot and feast unhindered on the infants … Carnivorous birds, too, come down and gobble up the fragments, that is, if they have not discovered them earlier, for, if they have, they get ready to fight the beasts of the field for the whole carcase [sic].[36]

In response to a practice which today seems unthinkable, Will Durant notes that "in many instances Christians rescued exposed infants, baptized them, and brought them up with the aid of community funds."[37] This emphasis on refusing to abandon and even saving infants – especially females – became an object of mockery, ridicule and scorn for the ancient Roman and Greek pagans.[38] So despite drawing different ultimate conclusions, the long tradition of the Church agrees with Singer about the logical connection between abortion and infanticide.

[34] Jack Lindsay, *The Ancient World: Manners and Morals* (London: Weidenfeld & Nicolson, 1968), 312, 168.
[35] Rodney Stark, *The Rise of Christianity: A Sociologist Reconsiders History* (Princeton University Press, 1996), 246, 95–128.
[36] Adele Renihartz, "Philo on Infanticide," *Studia Philonica Annual* 4 (1992), 46–47.
[37] Will Durant, *Caesar and Christ: A History of Roman Civilization and of Christianity from their Beginnings to A.D. 325*, Vol. 3 (New York: Simon and Schuster, 1944), 751, 598.
[38] Cornelius Tacitus and D. S. Levene, *The Histories* [Historiae.] (Oxford; New York: Oxford University Press, 1997), 310, 5.5.

A first disagreement?

Though many treat the Church's position on abortion with similar mockery, ridicule, and scorn today, Peter Singer is one of the few who reject their position against infanticide as well. He laments the historical development in the West of the Christian "sanctity of life ethic" which supposedly works from the presupposition that life is sacred. For Christians who make such claims "almost never mean what they say."[39] While they do think that all *human* life is sacred, they wrongly ignore or discount the interests of individuals that are not members of the species *Homo sapiens*. This "speciesist" attitude gives "greater weight to the interests of members of their own species when there is a clash between their interests and the interests of those of other species. Human speciesists do not accept that pain is as bad when it is felt by pigs or mice as when it is felt by humans."[40]

Singer argues that discrimination on this basis is similar to sexism or racism. All three might be 'natural' to human beings, but that does not make them justified. Women and men, whites and blacks, we all have the same kinds of interest in many things – such as participating in the political process of one's community. It is therefore wrongful discrimination to deny voting rights based on something insignificant like race or sex. Singer asks us to extend this kind of reasoning when the category of species is insignificant as well. Consider pain: we have no reason to think that a chicken does not feel pain when, say, its beak is cut off without anesthetic by a worker at a factory farm. Our discounting such pain (often by financially supporting factory farms which engage in these kinds of practices), simply because chickens are not *Homo sapiens*, is also wrongful discrimination. Instead of being speciesists, the comparable interests of non-human animals should factor equally into our moral decisions.

One major upshot of such a critique, and we will spend much more time with this in Chapter 3, is that it is wrongful discrimination to dine on the flesh of sentient and mentally sophisticated animals like pigs while considering the lives of human fetuses and infants sacred. For when it comes to morally relevant interests, the pig is far more morally valuable than the fetus or infant – at least if one agrees that species membership has no moral value. Indeed, if it were not for Christianity

---

[39] Singer, *Practical Ethics*, 71.   [40] *Ibid.*, 50–51.

becoming dominant in the West, Singer says, we would find little wrong with infanticide because infants would not be seen as members of the moral community simply by being *Homo sapiens*. Although he thinks that the theology which has undergirded Christian speciesism is no longer generally accepted by our culture,[41] "the ethical attitudes to which they gave rise fit in with the deep-seated Western belief in the uniqueness and special privileges of our species; these ethical attitudes have survived."[42]

Avoiding speciesism does not necessarily mean, however, treating other animals as morally equal to human persons. Singer admits that "the greater the degree of self-awareness and rationality and the broader the range of possible experiences, the more one would prefer that kind of life," and thus "it would not necessarily be speciesist to rank the value of different lives in some hierarchical ordering."[43] But things get complicated when we start attempting to justify such a ranking.[44] Singer spends quite a bit of time considering the moral status of a 'person': that is, a self-conscious being that is aware of itself as a distinct entity, with a past and a future.[45] Persons, because they can have plans for the future and are aware of themselves existing over time, would have their interests violated by being killed in ways that non-persons would not. According to Singer's view, the Church rightly claims that infants and fetuses are human beings, but this is a *biological* claim and doesn't lead to the *moral* claim that fetuses are persons. Claiming that this is so only because they are *Homo sapiens* is blatant speciesism.

Do we finally have our first disagreement between the two traditions? No, because it turns out that the Church's definition of 'person' is not speciesist and, in fact, it even has important similarities with Singer's own definition. Fetuses are not persons because they are *Homo sapiens*, but rather because of what membership in this biological species *indicates*: their possession of a rational nature.

[41] In one of the weakest places in his argument, Singer tries to claim that this goes back to a theological anthropology which was built on the wrongness of killing human beings as somehow connected to their immortality and their being God's creatures – and that non-humans were merely under "man's" [sic] dominion. As we will see below this is a misunderstanding of the Christian tradition, which is shared not only by Singer and those with similar concerns, but by many Christians as well.

[42] Singer, *Practical Ethics*, 76.   [43] *Ibid.*, 91–92.

[44] This is especially true, as we will see in more detail in Chapter 5, if one does not accept the existence of objective goods and objective method by which to rank them. Until very recently, this kind of metaphysical talk was something that Singer consistently avoided.

[45] Singer, *Practical Ethics*, 76.

The Church's definition of 'person'[46]

One of the best-known early Christian thinkers, Boethius (*c.* 480–524 AD), developed a very important and influential definition of personhood.[47] Both for him, and for the Church today,[48] a person is simply "an individual substance of a rational nature."[49] This definition, quite plainly, is not speciesist and actually uses Singer's category of rationality. Any biological species, not just *Homo sapiens*, could theoretically indicate the presence of a rational nature. Boethius' definition, in its non-speciesist form, is also appropriated by the great medieval theologian, Thomas Aquinas,[50] who even uses it to describe angels as persons. What could be a more clear example of a non-speciesist, and yet very Christian application of personhood?[51]

So perhaps, for Christians, *personhood is not limited to human beings*, but what about the Church's view that *all human beings are persons*? Isn't this speciesism of a different kind? John Paul II, perhaps the last Christian Singer would suspect of doing so, admits to the non-speciesist possibility that there are some human non-persons. Consider this fascinating quote from *Evangelium Vitae* in which he discusses the moral status of the human embryo:

Even if the presence of a spiritual soul cannot be ascertained by empirical data, the results themselves of scientific research on the human embryo provide "a valuable indication for discerning by the use of reason a personal presence at the moment of the first appearance of a human life: how could a human individual not be a human person?" Furthermore, what is at stake is so important that, from the standpoint of moral obligation, the mere probability that a human person is

[46] The treatment of this question in this chapter will be quite brief, but look for a robust analysis in a following chapter on the moral status of non-human animals. There I argue that certain animals do, in fact, count as a kind of person in the traditional Christian sense of the term.
[47] Indeed, some think that his definition set the standard for future debate over the concept. Clement Charles Julian Webb, *God and Personality: Being the Gifford Lectures Delivered in the University of Aberdeen in the Years 1918 & 1919, First Course*, Vol. 1918–19 (London; New York: Allen & Unwin; Macmillan, 1918), 281, 54.
[48] In fact, the International Theological Commission's recent document on natural law uses this very definition in paragraph 67. The International Theological Commission, "The Search of a Universal Ethic: a New Look at Natural Law," 67. Translation by Joseph Bolin, www.pathsoflove.com/universal-ethics-natural-law.html (Accessed March 27, 2011). However, look to Chapter 3 for an understanding of rationality in the Christian tradition which goes beyond an Enlightenment concept to one which indicates the capacity for loving relationships.
[49] Boethius, H. F. Stewart and Edward Kennard Rand, *The Theological Tractates* (London; New York: W. Heinemann; G.P. Putnam's Sons, 1918), 420, 85.
[50] Thomas and Dominicans. English Province, *Summa Theologica*, Complete English edn. (Allen, TX: Christian Classics, 1981), 3057, Q 29, art 1.
[51] See *Summa Theologica* QQ 50–64, especially Q 50, art 4, Q 54, art. 1–4, and Q 58.

involved would suffice to justify an absolutely clear prohibition of any intervention aimed at killing a human embryo. Precisely for this reason, over and above
all scientific debates and those philosophical affirmations to which the Magister-
ium has not expressly committed itself, the Church has always taught and
continues to teach that the result of human procreation, from the first moment
of its existence, must be guaranteed that unconditional respect which is morally
due to the human being in his or her totality and unity as body and spirit: "The
human being is to be respected and treated as a person from the moment of
conception; and therefore from that same moment his rights as a person must be
recognized, among which in the first place is the inviolable right of every
innocent human being to life."[52]

What is the 'precise reason' that the Church commits itself to the
proposition that the human embryo should be treated as a person?
Interestingly, it is the *mere probability* that an embryo is a person. The
Church doesn't commit itself to any of the scientific and philosophical
positions that inform the debate – nor does it even commit itself to
the position that the embryo has a rational soul.[53] What the Pope *does*
claim is that there is a very strong probability that an embryo is a person
and, given that what is at stake is so important, the embryo should
be treated *as* a person. This opens up at least the logical possibility that
the embryo is *not* a person. And when one combines this insight with the
Church's definitive claim that the embryo has "the life of a new human
being," we have Pope John Paul II implicitly acknowledging the logical
possibility of a member of the species *Homo sapiens* that is not a person.
Of course, this should not be surprising to us now, given that the
Church's definition of 'person' is not speciesist in the first place.

And, tragically, there have been multiple times in history where Christians
went beyond the theoretical in making this distinction. Indeed, in what
I believe to be one of the most beautiful moral rebukes in human history, the
Dominican Friar Antonio de Montesinos called out sixteenth-century Spanish
colonizers for treating certain human beings as if they were not persons:

In order to make your sins known to you I have mounted this pulpit, I who am
the voice of Christ crying in the wilderness of this island; and therefore it
behooves you to listen to me, not with indifference but with all your heart and
senses; for this voice will be the strangest, the harshest and hardest, the most
terrifying that you ever heard or expected to hear ... This voice declares that you

---

[52] Pope John Paul II, "*Evangelium Vitae*," 60.
[53] This position of the Church was confirmed most recently in the Vatican's latest bioethics
document: Congregation, *Instruction Dignitas Personae*. www.vatican.va/roman_curia/congregations/
cfaith/documents/rc_con_cfaith_doc_20081208_dignitas-personae_en.html, 5. (Accessed May 10, 2011)

are in mortal sin, and live and die in it by reason of the cruelty and tyranny that you practice on these innocent people. Tell me, by what right or justice do you hold these Indians in such cruel and horrible slavery? By what right do you wage such detestable wars on these people who lived mildly and peacefully in their own lands, where you have consumed infinite numbers of them with unheard of murders and desolations? Why do you so greatly oppress and fatigue them, not giving them enough to eat or caring for them when they fall ill from excessive labors, so that they die or rather are slain by you, so that you may extract and acquire gold every day? And what care do you take that they receive religious instruction and come to know their God and creator, or that they be baptized, hear mass, or observe holidays and Sundays? Are they not men? Do they not have rational souls? Are you not bound to love them as you love yourselves?[54]

But for many Christians of the day, the answers to these questions were not at all obvious. They had inherited an intellectual tradition from Aristotle, through Thomas Aquinas, which accepted the metaphysical claim that certain human beings were slaves *by nature*. That is, certain human beings did not have the rational capacity to govern themselves and needed others to do it for them. Consider the description of the Dominican friar Tomis Ortiz, who said:

The Indians were "like asses, stupid-looking, reckless, mad ... did not hold to the truth unless it was to their benefit ... inconstant ... ungrateful ... they were incapable of doctrine [Christianity] ... About the age of ten or twelve years it appears they are going to turn out with some education and virtue, but from then on they become like brute beasts."[55]

A systematic debate on whether violence could be used against the natives – hinging on whether the kinds of views offered by Ortiz or de Montesinos were correct – was joined. Perhaps the most famous public debate on the matter occurred in the city of Valladolid, Spain between Bartolome de Las Casas and Juan Gines de Sepúlveda in 1550. Though Las Casas' position ended up winning the day[56] (and with its victory came a

---

[54] Lewis Hanke, *The Spanish Struggle for Justice in the Conquest of America* (Boston, MA: Little, Brown, 1965), 217, 17.

[55] Patricia Seed, "'Are These Not Also Men?': The Indians' Humanity and Capacity for Spanish Civilisation," *Journal of Latin American Studies*, Vol. 25, No. 3 (Oct., 1993), 642.

[56] It is perhaps best exemplified in the work of theological giant Francisco de Vitoria, who claimed that "The Indians clearly are rational, since they have an ordered society, cities, marriage, magistrates, laws, artisans and markets, all of which require the use of reason. Since the distinctive characteristic of human beings is reason, the Indians are human beings and no one has the right to deprive them of their property. Vitoria furthermore adds the important point that rights reside not in the exercise of reason, but in the possession of a rational nature, whereby even children who have not yet attained the use of reason are capable of ownership." Thomas D. Williams, "Francisco de Vitoria and the Pre-Hobbesian Roots of Natural Rights Theory," 57. www.upra.org/archivio_pdf/a07103-williams.pdf (Accessed April 23, 2010).

first declaration of international human rights – a full century before
Hobbes started his ground-breaking work), the philosopher and theologian Sepúlveda claimed that the Indians were a barbarian race whose
natural, inferior condition entitled the Spaniards to wage war on them.
He argued that their passions ruled over whatever reason they had, and
they were therefore slaves or servants by nature.

And this point of view was to remain mainstream opinion for several
centuries. Later Christians, and even those normally thought of as heroic
supporters of the values of enslaved peoples, also rejected a speciesist
version of the claim that all humans are persons. In the late eighteenth
century the outspoken evangelical Christian, William Wilberforce, was
leading a crusade against the English slave trade, but he constantly had to
battle against the narrative of a slavery lobby, which tried to show that
equality with whites was where Wilberforce's struggle was leading. "They
were closet revolutionaries, fomenting unrest with their talk of rights,
justice and equality."[57] Consider also what American politician and future
President Abraham Lincoln (a man who consistently invoked the providence of God and the authority of the Bible) would claim about this
question a half-century later in his famous senatorial debates with Stephen
Douglas. On a hot August day in Ottawa, Illinois in 1858, Lincoln made
the following unfortunate response to Douglas, a skilled rhetorician who
was pressing him in much the same way the English slavery lobby was
pressing Wilberforce:

I have no purpose to introduce political and social equality between the white
and the black races. There is a physical difference between the two, which in my
judgment will probably forever forbid their living together upon the footing of
perfect equality, and inasmuch as it becomes a necessity that there must be a
difference, I, as well as Judge Douglas, am in favor of the race to which I belong,
having the superior position ... I agree with Judge Douglas he is not my equal in
many respects – certainly not in color, perhaps not in moral or intellectual
endowment.[58]

The speciesist version of the claim that "all *Homo sapiens* are persons,"
simply *by virtue of their being human beings*, is clearly not one that has

---

[57] Stephen Tomkins, *William Wilberforce: A Biography* (Grand Rapids, MI: William B. Eerdmans
Publishing Co., 2007), 238, 93. www.loc.gov/catdir/toc/ecip0710/2007004652.html
[58] Abraham Lincoln and Stephen A. Douglas, *Political Debates between Hon. Abraham Lincoln and
Hon. Stephen A. Douglas, in the Celebrated Campaign of 1858 in Illinois: Including the Preceding
Speeches of each at Chicago, Springfield, etc., also the Two Great Speeches of Mr. Lincoln in Ohio, in
1859, as Carefully Prepared by the Reporter of each Party and Published at the Times of their Delivery*
(Columbus: Follett, Foster and Company, 1860), 268, 390.

unequivocal support throughout the Christian tradition.[59] No, the disagreement between Singer and the Church on the moral status of the fetus is about something other than speciesism.

A DISAGREEMENT OVER POTENTIAL

What, then, is the actual disagreement between Peter Singer and the Church over the public policy issue of surgical abortion?[60] For Singer, either the human fetus is a person with the actualized capacities he deems necessary for this kind of moral status, or, if not, she should be treated as having no greater value than the life of a non-human animal at a similar level of capacity. Anything else is going to be speciesism. But must the moral value of the fetus be located in her actualized capacities? A human fetus may not be any more rational or self-aware than a snail, but there is an obvious distinction to be made between a snail and a fetus, and that distinction lies in the *potential* of the fetus. The snail can only develop as a snail does: never able to love or feel love, never able to have projects of its own, never able self-consciously wonder about its place in the universe, etc. The fetus, if she is permitted to actualize her potential, will experience all of these things.

And here, finally, we have found our disagreement. Peter Singer and the Church disagree about the moral value of the potential of the fetus. Singer thinks it is of no moral value, while the Church's view entails that such potential (properly understood) separates it morally from non-human animals at similar levels of sentience, rationality and self-awareness. The remainder of the chapter will explore the complex issues surrounding the argument from potential. What follows is a fairly technical philosophical argument, but given that it encapsulates the foundational disagreement between Peter Singer and the Church on abortion (along with central points of contention in the next two chapters as well), it is important to be precise and careful in our reasoning about these matters. Let us begin, then, by taking a look at an argument often cited in support of considering the future of a fetus in evaluating her moral status.

---

[59] It is also worth noting the sorry history that the Christian tradition has (along with almost all cultures throughout history) in treating women as less than full persons as well.

[60] This section of the chapter builds on an argument I made in "Common Ground on Surgical Abortion? – Engaging Peter Singer on the Moral Status of Potential Persons," *The Journal of Medicine and Philosophy* (January 2009) 33(6), and also an argument I made about infants in *Too Expensive to Treat? – Finitude, Tragedy, and the Neonatal ICU* (Grand Rapids, MI: William B. Eerdmans Publishing Co., 2010), 29–61.

Don Marquis and "a future like ours"

Don Marquis is well known for his attempts to account for how the future potential of a fetus might be morally relevant. To do this, he starts with what he thinks is an unproblematic assumption: "it is wrong to kill *us*" because "the loss of one's life deprives one of all the experiences, activities, projects, and enjoyments that would otherwise have constituted one's future."[61] In addition, there are most probably goods in one's future that, while I do not currently value them, will "come to be valued by me as I grow older and as my values and capacities change." Therefore, what makes killing "*any* adult human being"[62] seriously wrong is the "loss of his or her future."[63] Marquis uses this basic insight to draw several conclusions, including that is it "*prima facie* seriously wrong to kill fetuses because they have a future like ours."[64] He then articulates the potential of the human infant and fetus as their capacity to have "a future like ours," and locates not only *their* moral status in this potential, but also *everyone's* moral status in this potential. It is an intuitively convincing argument, but not one, I think, without important problems.

Marquis moves the debate in the proper direction – toward the moral value of the potential future of the infant and fetus (and *all* those with full moral status) – but he needs to be pushed further. A key question is who *counts* as 'us' in his assumed dictum: *it is wrong to kill us.* Apparently because it would be "difficult" and "controversial," Marquis admits that he has no "additional account of just what it is about my future or the futures of other adult human beings, which makes it wrong to kill us."[65] He sees this question as only related to specific questions regarding whether certain animals have a future like ours, but it is not clear why this is the case. Suppose that *just what it is* that is morally valuable about my future (that which makes it wrong to kill me as opposed to another being without a future like mine) is the fact that I will be rational and self-aware – Singer's definition of personhood. This allows for not only the abortion and infanticide of many thousands of mentally disabled human beings, but also the killing of such human beings as older children or adults. Did former President Ronald Reagan, as a victim of mental

---

[61] Don Marquis, "Why Abortion is Immoral," *Journal of Philosophy* 86 (AP, 1989), 189.
[62] One might ask here what Marquis means by this phrase. Does he mean literally *any* adult human being? What about an adult human in a permanently comatose state? In point of fact, he does not mean to include such a being – and the fact that he is not more specific creates a problem for his project.
[63] Marquis, "Why Abortion is Immoral," 189–190.   [64] *Ibid.*, 190–192.   [65] *Ibid.*, 191.

illness such that his future would never be rational or aware of himself, have a future like ours? If the answer is no, then we end up denying full moral status to Reagan and all those with similarly profound mental illness (those with advanced Alzheimer's disease or other severe dementia, for instance), but if the answer is yes, then what other non-human animals *wouldn't* qualify for full moral status? On what basis would one deny dogs, chickens or even snails full moral status? No, Marquis needs to say more about what precisely it is about our futures which makes denying them morally problematic.

It seems that one may accept Singer's definition of an actualized person, but argue that this is not the only way to talk about the kind of moral status that Singer wants to reserve only to actualized persons. I argue that *potential persons* – that is, to use Singer's categories, those beings that are potentially rational and self-aware – have the same moral status as beings with actualized rationality and self-awareness.[66] This is what accounts for our moral intuitions regarding not only fetuses and infants, but also many other adult human beings. The enraged, the extremely intoxicated, the asleep, the insane and the temporarily comatose are all human beings which fail to meet Singer's actualized criteria for personhood – but virtually no one denies these beings moral status. This is because of their potentiality for rationality and/or awareness of themselves in time at some point in the future.[67] And it is precisely for this reason that moral status should also be extended to fetuses.

OBJECTIONS TO THE ARGUMENT FROM POTENTIAL

As Massimo Reichlin notes in "The Argument from Potential: A Reappraisal," the argument from potential (AFP) is not a popular one in today's academic abortion debate.[68] Even Don Marquis, who as we just saw

---

[66] Singer's categories are perhaps not the best way to think about personhood – both in the modern era of feminist critical theory and from the standpoint of the Roman Catholic tradition. Both emphasize relationality as related to personhood in a way that Singer's definition does not. (More will be said about this in Chapter 3.) However, none of this really matters for the argument that I am making here – fill in any trait or traits that constitute personhood and it's still going to be the potential for that trait which counts.

[67] Certainly many proponents of theories like Singer's 'interest' view disagree and try to locate rationality, etc. in such beings in light of their having had rational interests (and the like) in the past. But this chapter will show that such arguments are fundamentally flawed.

[68] Massimo Reichlin, "The Argument from Potential: A Reappraisal," *Bioethics* 11, no. 1 (Jan, 1997), 1.

makes an argument very similar to the AFP, calls its basic inference invalid.[69] Those who object to the AFP seem to make two general kinds of arguments:

1. If only those with the proper interests can have moral status, then a potential person cannot have moral status because it has none of the relevant interests. Indeed, many kinds of things might be 'potential persons' but do not have the interests proper to persons and therefore cannot have moral status. (NI)
2. If every potential person has moral status, then this leads us to questions about the relationship between probability and possibility. Is any being which has a probability greater than zero of becoming a person a 'potential person'? If the answer is yes, this may lead us to absurd conclusions about what counts as having moral status. If the answer is no, then we have a problem with deciding what level of probability of becoming a person grants something 'potential person-hood' and therefore full moral status. (PP)

I will treat the "no interest" (NI) and "problems with probability" (PP) arguments in turn.

Do fetuses have interests?

Peter Singer, Ronald Dworkin, and Michael Tooley all make different versions of NI argument. Singer claims that "the fact that the embryo has a certain potential does not mean that we can really harm it, in the sense that we can harm a being who has wants and desires or can suffer."[70] Indeed, if it is claimed that destroying an embryo does it harm because of the loss of its potential, "why should we not say the same about an egg and sperm?"[71] Would we consider a laboratory technician blameworthy for rinsing spare ova and sperm down a drain and causing the loss of potential personhood?[72] A sperm–egg pair, considered jointly, is surely a potential person – but it cannot have interests and therefore cannot have moral

[69] Marquis, "Why Abortion is Immoral," 192.
[70] Peter Singer, *Rethinking Life and Death: The Collapse of our Traditional Ethics* (New York: St. Martin's Griffin, 1996), 97.
[71] Singer, *Ibid.*, 99.
[72] Depending on what part of Singer one is currently reading, he speaks about either potential life, potential human, or potential person as if they were interchangeable. I use 'personhood' here because I assume this is what he must respond to in order to answer AFP as presented in this book.

status. In the same way, a newborn infant is a potential person, but because it cannot have interests it also cannot have moral status.

Dworkin makes a version of NI argument very similar to Singer's. He claims that "it is very hard to make sense of the idea that an early fetus has interests of its own," for, in order to have interests, it is not enough that it *might* grow or develop into a human being.[73] He asks us to consider an assemblage of body parts on the laboratory table of Dr Frankenstein. Suppose that just as he is about to throw the lever which would give the assemblage the life of a rational and self-aware creature, someone rushes in and smashes Dr Frankenstein's machine. We would not, of course, consider the individual blameworthy for harming the assemblage of body parts. Dworkin claims that if the assemblage is a potential person, then the AFP insists that it *has* been harmed. But this is absurd because the assemblage clearly has no interests of its own.

Michael Tooley, another supporter of both abortion and infanticide, gives perhaps the most interesting version of NI argument considered.[74] Tooley asks us to imagine that in the future it will be possible to inject kittens with a chemical that will enable them with the capabilities consistent with human personhood. These injected kittens would then have full moral status because they would be rational and aware of themselves in time. But would we think a person was seriously wronged if someone, upon finding a stray kitten, refused to inject the kitten, and instead handed it over to animal control to be euthanized? The kitten does not have the morally relevant interests (she is not rational or self-aware) to be wronged as a person, but given the injection technology it appears that the kitten is a potential person. Given the AFP, it then also appears that the kitten should have the same moral status as a person, and would be wronged by the person who did not inject her. But this is absurd.

An obvious first move in response to these arguments is to point out again that a friend of NI must have answers to questions about our moral intuitions regarding the enraged, the extremely intoxicated, the insane, the temporarily comatose and even those who have simply fallen asleep. It looks as if, because NI requires that a being is currently actualizing the relevant traits in order to have full moral status, regardless of its potential to have them in the future, the above examples are beings which a friend

---

[73] Ronald Dworkin, *Life's Dominion: An Argument about Abortion, Euthanasia and Individual Freedom* (New York: Alfred A. Knopf, 1993): 16.

[74] Michael Tooley, *Abortion and Infanticide* (Oxford; New York: Clarendon Press; Oxford University Press, 1983), 191–193.

of NI must claim are not persons. Some have attempted to respond to this move by claiming that in each example above, the human being in question has had personal interests *in the past* and, on the basis of this, should still be considered a person. Daniel Dombrowski and Robert Deltete, for instance, point out that a car mechanic who is not currently fixing cars can still legitimately be called a car mechanic.[75] In the same way, a person who currently does not have interests that are personal can still legitimately be called a person.

What follows are simple forms of the argument:

1. Joe is not now acting as a car mechanic.
2. Joe has acted as a car mechanic in the past.
3. Therefore, Joe can still be considered a car mechanic.

1. Joe is not now acting as a person.
2. Joe has acted as a person in the past.
3. Therefore, Joe can still be considered a person.

Joe has actualized certain interests in the past which indicate something about his status now, but a fetus has had no such past.

But how far do we want to take this line of reasoning? Consider the following argument:

1. Charlie is not now acting as the third baseman for St Joseph's High School.
2. Charlie has acted as the third baseman for St Joseph's High School in the past.
3. Therefore, Charlie can still be considered the third baseman for St Joseph's High School.

Of course, this conclusion is absurd. I am now many years removed from having been St Joseph's third baseman and I have *no potential* to ever be again. My past is wholly irrelevant to the question of whether or not it is legitimate to consider me the third baseman for that school. The same can be said of Joe. If Joe never again fixes a car, and is now not currently fixing cars, in what sense is it legitimate to still call him a car mechanic?

A thought experiment might help clarify this point. If Michael Tooley can speak of injecting cats with a drug that turns them into rational creatures, then perhaps I can speak of a *Star Trek* 'replicator machine.' Let us take Joe, a human being in a temporary coma, put him into the

[75] Daniel A. Dombrowski and Robert Deltete, "A Brief, Liberal, Catholic Defense of Abortion," *American Journal of Theology and Philosophy* 22, no. 3 (S, 2000), 78.

replicator and throw the switch. Now we have Joe 1 and his identical 'clone,' Joe 2, both comatose, and both exactly the same in every other respect. Before replication, Joe 1 had interests and full moral status and he has them after replication as well. But it looks as if those who support NI must argue that Joe 2 does not have moral status and may be killed without wronging him. After all, Joe 2 (like a fetus) has not had personal interests in his past which can be said to be operative while he is currently comatose. If it is the past that matters and not the future, then Joe 2 may be killed without killing a person. But Joe 2 is indistinguishable from Joe 1 – except for his past. Someone wanting to defend the dignity of Joe 1 would undoubtedly argue that his coma is temporary and that his future potential for personal interests grants him the moral status of a person. But the same thing is true of Joe 2 and of the human fetus. For both, it is the *future* that matters, not the past.

But one might object here and say that some backward-looking considerations are a necessary condition for Joe 1's having personal interests such that it would be wrong to kill him. Perhaps he must have been connected to his past through memory. Or perhaps he must have integrated his past with his present *prior* to his current unconscious state – and in so doing integrate his current self with a previous desire to live. Both are considerations, obviously, which fail to apply to Joe 2 and the fetus.

But consider, say, a car accident victim who (while rational and self-aware) is diagnosed with total amnesia and then suddenly falls unconscious into a light coma. Certainly we would wrong her personal interests if we were to kill her, but it would not be in light of any backward-looking considerations like these. She is not connected to her past through memory, nor has she integrated her past in a way that could possibly connect it to her comatose state. Or consider a 20-year-old pre-medicine student who has just failed a third-straight organic chemistry exam. After realizing that he is likely never going to fulfill his life-long dream of becoming a physician, suppose he decides that no other life is worth living and overdoses on painkillers. Suppose also that the suicide attempt fails and he is left in a light coma. But then his roommate, upon discovering his comatose body, decides that he didn't like the pre-med student anyway and smothers him with a pillow. The roommate is both morally and legally guilty of murder, of course, but it cannot be because of backward-looking preferences (he actually preferred to die rather than live) in the pre-med student.[76] Rather, we recognize that,

---

[76] Especially if this person has despaired of living for quite a long time.

despite this person's current preference not to live, the roommate has the responsibility to honor the objective goodness and value of the pre-med student's current and future existence.[77]

Indeed, we now see that there are several counter-examples to show that it is the future, and not the past, which accounts for the moral status of those who are not currently rational and self-aware. And it is for this reason that the fetus should be considered a person with a right to life.

Problems with probability?

But a different kind of argument against the AFP is one that raises questions about probability. Someone who makes an interesting version of PP is R. Alta Charo in "Every Cell Is Sacred: Logical Consequences of the Argument from Potential in the Age of Cloning."[78] Charo points out that, given the possibility of cloning, *every single human cell* is now a potential person – though the probability of a particular cell becoming a person is vanishingly small. If one is not just as worried about killing our skin cells as many of us are about killing infants or fetuses, we need to deal with the problem of probability. What level counts and what level does not? Roy Perrett explores this question in some detail and cites John Noonan's 80 percent mark (which Noonan believes is the average probability of an early-term fetus becoming a person) as an example of one answer.[79] This number appears to contrast with the probability that a body cell will become a person to such a degree that it is reasonable to say that the fetus should count as a potential person, and the body cell should not. But Perrett argues that this marker will not work for fetuses before week six gestation because "more recent research has altered our best estimate of the real probabilities" and, before week six, a fetus has less than an 80 percent probability of becoming a person.[80] So, suppose we consider the following:

---

[77] Chapter 6 will detail several examples that will push this concept of 'objective goods' for persons much further. I think this conclusion follows from Singer's increasing willingness to see the good of human beings over the course of their life and beyond whatever they happen to prefer in the present moment.

[78] In Paul Lauritzen, *Cloning and the Future of Human Embryo Research* (Oxford; New York: Oxford University Press, 2001), 291. Charo's argument is most persuasive as a defense of destruction of human fetuses outside of a mother's womb, but it is worth bringing up in this context as well.

[79] Roy W. Perrett, "Taking Life and the Argument from Potentiality," *Midwest Studies in Philosophy* 24 (2000), 189.

[80] Indeed, if the research Perrett cites is correct, before week six (but post-implantation) the probability is anywhere from 46–60 percent.

3 zeros = thousands, 9 zeros = billion, 15 0's = quadrillion
6 zeros = million, 12 zeros = trillion, 18 = quintillion
21 = sextillion, 35 = ...

Objections to the argument from potential

1. A body cell with a 0.0000000000000000000001 percent probability of becoming a person.
2. A fetus at 16 weeks' gestation with an 80 percent probability of becoming a person.
3. A fetus at 5 weeks' gestation with a 55 percent chance of becoming a person.
4. A fetus at 10 weeks' gestation which a physician, due to complications in the pregnancy, gives a 10 percent chance of becoming a person.

On what basis, those who make Perrett's argument ask, can one claim that (2), (3) and (4) above should count as having moral status, but (1) should not?[81]

This is an important challenge, but appears to conflate the concept of potentiality with probability. Reichlin points out that

> a correct understanding of the embryo's potentiality shows that by progressively acquiring new capacities – including the capacity to perform rational operations – the human individual develops and perfects the human nature it already possesses.[82]

An absolutely crucial point for our discussion is the Aristotelian distinction between *active* and *passive* potential.[83] A tree, in its passive potential, is a *possible* table (it has a certainly probability of being cut down and turned into something else) – however, this does not mean in any sense that a tree is *already* a table. Active potential, by contrast, is "inherent to the very nature of the being, whose principle of actualization is the very nature of that being." No external agent is necessary, and the potentiality is "the capacity to express and actualize inherent potentialities towards which the being in question has a natural tendency – i.e., a tendency which is dependent on its very nature."[84] A fertilized acorn, then, is a potential oak tree; but because this potential *is part of its very nature*, this means that the acorn is already an oak tree.

This argument, in addition to answering PP (which we will consider below), provides us with another reason to reject some versions

---

[81] Alternatively, (2) and (3) should count as having moral status, but (1) and (4) should not.
[82] Reichlin, "The Argument from Potential: A Reappraisal," 12.
[83] Thomas Aquinas, not surprisingly, also adopts the distinction: "[A]n object is said to be something *potentially* in two ways: in one way when it does not possess the principle of its operation; in a second way when it does possess that principle but is not functioning in accord with it." Saint Thomas Aquinas, *Sentencia Libri de Anima*, Commentary on Aristotle's De Anima, English, Translated by Kenelm Foster and Silvester Humphries, (Notre Dame, IN: Dumb Ox Books, 1994), II.2.107–12.
[84] Perrett, "Taking Life and the Argument from Potentiality," 16–17.

of NI. With regard to a move like Singer's to consider a 'sperm and egg jointly,' Perrett says that

> [a] gamete is not even a potential embryo, but rather depends essentially on external causes. The human sperm does not just need a proper place wherein to develop its inherent potentialities, but needs an external event which is going to change radically its identity and potentialities.[85]

Thus, if by 'potential person' we mean an entity with *active* potential for personhood and not merely passive potential, then the moral difference between a fetus and sperm/ova becomes clear. Like the comatose adult, a fetus has active potential for personal traits like rationality and self-awareness, but gametes have merely passive potential for personhood. The same can be said of Dworkin's assemblage of body parts. While there is the probability of a person coming into existence, it would nonetheless take an external, *nature-changing event* for this to happen, and so the assemblage is not a potential person in the active and morally relevant sense. And if Tooley's 'personhood injection' is ever invented, kittens will still have only passive potential for personhood. That is, they are *possible* persons in the same way a tree is a possible table and an ovum is a possible person. Each would need an external, nature-changing event for the change to happen. A kitten being injected is akin to the ovum being fertilized or the tree being cut down and made into a table: the entity's original nature has been destroyed and become something else.

This distinction also responds to Charo's and Perrett's probability questions. Sure, a body cell may have a vanishingly low probability of becoming a person, but this is the wrong question to ask in determining whether or not the cell is a potential person in the morally relevant sense. It seems clear that, because a body cell will not of its own nature turn into person, we would impose an external nature-changing event to make it happen – thus making the original body cell a *possible* person and not a potential person.[86] And Perrett's 'Prince Charles' example meets the same fate. As Reichlin says, Prince Charles' becoming king "is in fact dependent on several external causes, such as social conventions and regulations, and in no way implies the kind of necessity shown by a natural

---

[85] *Ibid.*, 13.

[86] Charo's important point is that if one considered the zygote as a subject of stem cell research – outside the womb – it appears that it is only a possible person and not a potential person. She suggests this makes it reasonable to do research on human embryos, even given the AFP. I leave this claim unanswered for two reasons. First, it gets into complicated questions about the moral issues in creating IVF embryos that are beyond the scope of the chapter. Second, again, the focus of this argument is on the fetus.

development."[87] One's potential to become king has nothing to do with one's nature, and this is why it makes no sense to treat Charles as if he were the actual king. But if at 16 weeks a fetus has an 80% probability of actualizing personal traits because this kind of potential is due to her nature, it *does* make sense to treat her as a person.

Indeed, as Patrick Lee and Robert George nicely put it, an entity having full moral status (as opposed to having a right to perform a specific action in a given situation) follows from:

an entity's being the *type of thing* (or substantial entity) it is. And so, just as one's right to life does not come and go with one's location or situation, so it does not accrue to someone in virtue of an acquired (i.e., accidental) property, capacity, skill, or disposition. Rather, this right belongs to the human being at all times that he or she exists, not just during certain stages of his or her existence, or in certain circumstances, or in virtue of additional accidental features.[88]

Of course, much depends on accepting the metaphysical distinction that Aristotle and Reichlin make between active and passive potential – as well as the concept of a 'nature' in the first place. And not only does Singer seem to accept the concept of a human nature, but in this book's final chapter we see that he is considering changes to his moral theory which create space for these kinds of metaphysical concepts. Furthermore, for most people, the intuitive distinction between a tree becoming a table (passive potential) and a fertilized acorn becoming an oak tree (active potential) is convincing and would require significant work to rebut – let alone our intuitions about what the AFP means for those who have only temporarily lost actualized personal capacities.

But how are we to think about human beings who appear to have *no* potential to be rational and self-aware? We have already mentioned examples of these: those with advanced Alzheimer's disease, the permanently comatose, etc. If we accept a version of the AFP which claims that it is the future that matters and not the past, it appears that such individuals do not have moral status, for they will never again be rational or self-aware. And if we accept as a brute fact that mentally disabled or injured human beings do have full moral status, then it appears that the AFP fails.

Peter Singer, or any other ethicist who locates moral status in (either potential or actual) personal interests or preferences, must deal with this

[87] Reichlin, "The Argument from Potential: A Reappraisal," 6.

[88] Andrew I. Cohen and Christopher Heath Wellman, *Contemporary Debates in Applied Ethics*, Contemporary Debates in Philosophy, Vol. 3. (Malden, MA: Blackwell Publishing, 2005), 17. www.loc.gov/catdir/toc/ecip0420/2004016921.html.

same problem. If one wants to defend full moral worth in the above kinds of human beings (and, as we will see in the next chapter, Singer bites the bullet and claims that, in fact, they are not persons), they appear to be forced to make a move which distinguishes between having full moral *status* on the one hand and having some moral *value* on the other. The former would apply to persons and the latter to other beings and things that have a different kind of value. Perhaps, as several different thinkers have argued, those with advanced Alzheimer's disease or the permanently comatose are 'symbolic' of human life and that gives them some value? The weakness of this move, of course, is that without full moral status the lives of such human beings could easily be trumped by the interests of actual or potential persons – and thus open the door to ending their lives to serve those interests. Could we, for instance, aim at the death of those with Alzheimer's as a means to the ends of conserving resources or procuring organs? This is something that most of us would find morally repugnant, but perhaps we ought to follow our cue from Singer at this point, bite our lip, and just accept our repugnant conclusion. After all, if we truly require a Copernican revolution in ethics, we should not expect that our new conclusions will be comfortable.

But I believe that our moral intuitions about those with Alzheimer's and similar diseases need not be discarded. Consider that when one claims that such human beings have no potential to be rational or self-aware, the kind of potential used in making this judgment is passive, not active. We are talking about the *mere probability* that a human being will regain rationality and self-awareness. But consider a human being in a light coma who requires a heart transplant in order to live, but who unfortunately found himself in this situation before we had the medical expertise to transplant hearts. He has zero probability for rationality or self-awareness in that situation, but today, because of advances in medical expertise, he would have a fairly good probability of actualizing such traits. Both someone with advanced Alzheimer's, and the comatose person living before heart transplants, have the *nature* or active potential for personal traits. Though their intrinsic potential to express personal traits is being frustrated by some accidental factors (injury, availability of medical expertise, etc.), they remain the *kinds of things* that we call persons. Indeed, if we were suddenly to find a cure for their disease, it would be at best odd to claim that Alzheimer's patients would suddenly become persons and regain a moral status they had lost. It would be even more bizarre if, in a situation where a new cure existed only in New York City, someone with advanced Alzheimer's in remote sub-Saharan Africa did not count as a person, but someone in New Jersey (and thus within easy accessibility of the cure) with the very same disease *did* count as a person because of relative levels of probability. Accidental factors like the time in which one is born, or the relative technological sophistication of the area one inhabits, have nothing whatever to say about one's moral value. Each and every living human being, no matter how sick, damaged or immature, retains morally significant potential that is intrinsic to our nature. The very reason we extend personal dignity to those who have severe mental illness or injury is also the reason we must extend it to fetuses and infants. All living human beings have active potential for personal traits like rationality and self-awareness – traits which are essentially present in our natures as the kinds of things that we are.

CONCLUSION

Peter Singer supports the legal right not only to abortion, but also infanticide. The Church condemns not only the intentional killing of the fetus, but also of the early embryo. These views seem to be as far apart as they could possibly be. Yet in this chapter we have discovered that the disagreement between the two approaches with regard to abortion is actually quite narrow. We have seen in detail that both believe public policy cannot retreat into a privacy-centered moral neutrality with regard to both the moral status of the fetus and whether one can kill or refuse to sustain a fetus. Both agree that, assuming that a fetus is a person, any unintended negative effects of making abortion illegal would not justify allowing for the legal killing of fetuses. Both agree that the *Roe* v. *Wade* approach to abortion is a mistake.[89] Both agree that (again, assuming that a fetus is a person) not only would it be morally wrong to kill a fetus, but that one has a moral duty to support a fetus for nine months with one's body. Both also see a logical connection between one's view of abortion and one's view of infanticide.

Their narrow disagreement is about the moral status of the fetus. Both reject speciesism, but they disagree about what role potential should play in determining the moral status of the fetus. Both approaches agree that passive potential (or considerations of mere probability) cannot make one a person, but the Church's position is that any being of a rational *nature* – that is, a being with *active* potential for personhood – counts as a person.

[89] This includes not only fundamental matters of political philosophy, but also a specific rejection of viability as a morally significant dividing line.

Indeed, it is difficult to make sense of the claim that severely mentally disabled human beings are persons, to say nothing of the mildly comatose or even the asleep, without an appeal to the natural potential of such individuals – without an appeal to the *nature* of those individuals. If the argument of this chapter is correct, then Singer's claim that the overwhelming majority of abortions are justified because a woman's interests almost always outweigh the interests of a fetus is false. A fetus has the interests of a person and her fundamental interest in continued life will trump any less proportionately serious interests of her mother (or, as is often the case in a culture that privileges males, her father).[90] And indeed, Singer makes this kind of calculation when he claims that, if the fetus is a person, both the pregnant woman and the person attached to the violinist have a moral obligation to sustain the vulnerable person who depends on them.

Some might wonder whether the metaphysical concepts that undergird the Church's argument for the moral status of the fetus are ones which Singer, given other commitments, could ever accept. But as I show in some detail in the final chapter of this book, Singer has now realized that many of his claims about practical ethics cannot be justified without a fairly strong appeal to metaphysics – with the result that he is now rethinking fundamental aspects of his moral theory. This ongoing shift, coupled with his continuing suspicion of the kind of hyper-autonomy and consumerism which drives the broad support for abortion rights, provides an opening to rethink his approach to abortion.

---

[90] We of course skip a step or two in going from the claim that a fetus is a person to the claim that a fetus should get treatment equal to other persons. But though Singer and the Church address this topic in some detail in multiple places, the very complex discussion about equal treatment of persons (especially in a utilitarian context) goes well beyond my concerns in this chapter.

CHAPTER 2

Euthanasia and the end of life

[I]s it reasonable to hold that the doctor who gives the injection is a murderer who deserves to go to jail, whereas the doctor who decides not to administer antibiotics is practicing good and compassionate medicine?

Peter Singer, _Practical Ethics_

Euthanasia in the strict sense is understood to be an action or omission which of itself and by intention causes death.

Pope John Paul II, _Evangelium Vitae_

INTRODUCTION

If abortion is the first issue which jumps to mind when thinking about why a project like this one seems counter-intuitive, then end-of-life issues might come next. Peter Singer's championing of euthanasia seems hopelessly at odds with an ethic that understands such killing to be intrinsically evil.[1] Indeed, the Church claims that euthanasia is "hostile to life itself" and part of a violent culture of death. And Singer's support of euthanasia has been resisted, not only by Christians, but by secular groups as well. A recent example was the advocacy group Not Dead Yet sending a letter to the editor of the Sunday _New York Times Magazine_ claiming that Singer devalues the lives of those with special needs.[2] Nor has the blowback from such groups been limited to the United States. In an appendix to the second edition of _Practical Ethics_, which he entitled "On Being Silenced in Germany," Singer details several examples where his invitations to present his scholarship were withdrawn under pressure from these groups. Sometimes his speaking events were canceled, and on occasions

[1] Pope John Paul II, "_Veritatis Splendor_," 80.
[2] http://notdeadyetnewscommentary.blogspot.com/2009/08/peter-singer-in-ny-times-magazine.html (Accessed November 30, 2009).

41

where they were allowed to go ahead, Singer was often whistled at or shouted down. On one occasion, much of the crowd simply repeated the chant "Singer *raus*! Singer *raus*!" (Get out, Singer, get out!) The chant was so loud and sustained that he was forced to abandon his presentation.[3]

Despite a motivated coalition of both Christians and secularists against him, Singer maintains a very strong and consistent position on euthanasia and end-of-life issues. In *Rethinking Life and Death*, he suggests that his opponents are merely patching holes in an ethic that is on its way out. And he does so sometimes in quite disparaging and aggressive terms:

> The patching could go on, but it is hard to see a long and beneficial future for an ethic as paradoxical, incoherent and dependent on pretense as our conventional ethic of life and death has become. New medical techniques, decisions in landmark legal cases and shifts of public opinion are constantly threatening to bring the whole edifice crashing down.[4]

For Singer, his opponents' views on end-of-life issues are so obviously wrong that the question is not whether they will be replaced, but what the shape of the successor point of view will be.[5] Indeed, he sees himself as leading a revolution against the remnants of this view:

> It is time for another Copernican revolution. It will be, once again, a revolution against a set of ideas we have inherited from the period in which the intellectual world was dominated by a religious outlook. Because it will change our tendency to see human beings as the centre of the *ethical* universe, it will meet fierce resistance from those who do not want to accept such a blow to our human pride. At first, it will have its own problems, and will need to tread carefully over new ground . . . Yet eventually the change will come.[6]

This kind of rhetoric is both the result and the cause of much misunderstanding and confusion with regard to the debate over the issues under consideration in this chapter, and in the conflict between Singer's approach and Christian ethics in general. Singer's comparing his opponents to geocentrists and his describing their views as "incoherent" and "dependent on pretense" is little better than the rhetoric his opponents use when making their critiques.

---

[3] Jeffrey Schaler, *Peter Singer Under Fire: The Moral Iconoclast Faces His Critics* (Chicago, IL: Open Court, 2009), 420. Singer, who, as we saw in the Introduction is the grandson of three persons killed in Nazi concentration camps, claimed that he had "the overwhelming feeling that this was what it must have been like to attempt to reason against the rising tide of Nazism in the declining days of the Weimar Republic."

[4] Peter Singer, *Rethinking Life and Death: The Collapse of Our Traditional Ethics* (New York: St Martin's Griffin, 1996) 256, 189.

[5] *Ibid.*, 222.   [6] *Ibid.*, 189.

In this chapter, I will show that the two approaches have far more in common on these topics with each other than such rhetoric allows one to imagine. Indeed, much of the debate on euthanasia and end-of-life issues is directly connected to moral status and personhood, and we have just seen how narrow the disagreement is on that topic. Also, they share skepticism about whether we should use a brain-death criterion for determining when a human organism has died – a critical question in many bioethical situations, including when it comes to donating organs. Remarkably, they also share several conclusions about when one is morally justified in removing life-sustaining treatment, and even when one is justified in administering pain medication which will hasten a patient's death. I will also show that Singer is simply wrong in his view that the Church's distinction between forming the intention to kill and merely foreseeing death is somehow paradoxical or incoherent. In making an argument about what the genuine disagreement is, though obviously Singer and the Church disagree about theoretical arguments over aiming at the death of an innocent person at the end of life, I will focus instead on the more interesting disagreement over attempts to call euthanasia into question via a slippery-slope argument.

At various points in this chapter it will be helpful to refer to three cases that will be used to better illustrate various points. The reader may wish to bookmark this page in order to recall the three examples that follow here[7]:

Patient A: 'Brain Dead' but kept alive via artificial means. This individual has virtual whole brain failure; she is in a completely unresponsive coma and shows no drive to breathe. She needs a ventilator and feeding tube to continue to get oxygen, hydration and nutrition. There is no hope for recovery.

Patient B: Persistent Vegetative State. This individual has serious brain damage, and has symptoms similar to patient A. However, patient B has brain stem and even other kinds of brain activity; she opens her eyes, goes through sleep/wake cycles, breathes spontaneously, and even responds to pain. She requires a feeding tube. Although there is now evidence that some of these patients may be conscious, the prognosis is that there is no hope for recovery.[8]

---

[7] The first two are largely taken from The President's Council on Bioethics, *Controversies in the Determination of Death* (Washington, D.C.: The President's Council on Bioethics, 2008), 33, 42. www.thenewatlantis.com/docLib/20091130_determination_of_death.pdf (Accessed May 9, 2010).

[8] Indeed, 'Persistent Vegetative State' (PVS) is an ill-defined diagnostic category into which many patients get lumped if they don't fit into categories A or C. The *New England Journal of Medicine*, for instance, recently described research which found that some patients in PVS "showed traces of brain activity in response to commands from doctors." Indeed, according to a new report, some are able to communicate. "In response to simple questions, like 'Do you have any brothers?,' he showed distinct traces of activity on a brain imaging machine that represented either 'yes' or 'no.'"

Patient C: Terminal Pancreatic Cancer. This individual has been diagnosed with a painful, aggressive, and terminal cancer. Her physician guesses that she has less than six months to live. For now she is able to function as normal, but once again the prognosis is that there is no hope for recovery.

This chapter will build various details into each case as we get into the complexity of treatment and care at the end of life, but before this can happen we must once again begin with answering fundamental questions about moral status.

MORAL STATUS AT THE END OF LIFE

Recall that Peter Singer believes a person must have rationality and self-awareness. Patient C is therefore a person, but once one loses such capabilities permanently then personhood is lost. Therefore, with respect to patient A and others like her, we must say that they have no intrinsic value. These patients are alive biologically but not biographically.[9] But what about someone like patient B who is in a less certain category? Singer thinks that while those who are "merely conscious" have some value, it is only because they might have a few preferences which could be satisfied, and not because they are persons with a right to life.[10] In a now famous story (which was covered in a 1999 *New Yorker* article[11]), Singer even applied this definition to his own mother who had advanced Alzheimer's disease; indeed, he was willing to say that his spending significant resources on her care, despite her not being a person, revealed that consistently applying his view might be "more difficult than [he] thought."[12]

Is it no surprise that the Church has a different view of the moral status of patients A and B. Recall the Church claiming that any member of the species *Homo sapiens* is a person because of her natural and active

Benedict Carey, "Study Finds Activity in Brain That Seems to Be Shut Down," *The New York Times*, www.nytimes.com/2010/02/04/health/04brain.html (Accessed February 4, 2010).

[9] Singer, *Practical Ethics*, 168. For those who have expressed interests before falling into this state, however, Singer thinks that we should try to respect their past wishes whenever possible. Though more will be said about this in Chapter 6, it isn't clear why a preference utilitarian believes that we should respect preferences made in the past that (presumably) no longer exist in any meaningful sense.

[10] *Ibid.*, 85.

[11] Michael Specter. "The Dangerous Philosopher." *The New Yorker*. www.newyorker.com/archive/1999/09/06/1999_09_06_046_TNY_LIBRY_000018991 (Accessed December 3, 2009).

[12] Frustratingly, many Christians seem to think that Singer's lack of strength or will to consistently follow an ethical principle he believes to be binding somehow counts as evidence against that principle. Given our own sinfulness and having 'fallen short of the glory of God', I hope that my fellow Christians rethink the implications of this claim. Each of us has also lacked the strength or will to consistently follow the ethical principles we believe to be binding.

potential. Indeed, in an answer to a question posed by the US Bishops about persons like patient B above, the Vatican responded with the following answer:

In response to those who doubt the "human quality" of patients in a "permanent vegetative state," it is necessary to reaffirm that "the intrinsic value and personal dignity of every human being do not change, no matter what the concrete circumstances of his or her life. *A man, even if seriously ill or disabled in the exercise of his highest functions, is and always will be a man,* and he will never become a 'vegetable' or an 'animal.'"[13]

We know Singer thinks this is just speciesism, but there is little point in repeating in detail arguments from the previous chapter which responded to this mistake. Even patient A counts as a person for the Church because, though her potential is currently frustrated by injury or disease, she has all the active or natural potential to be rational and self-aware. Indeed, were we to inject neural stem cells into her brain and repair the damage, most of us would not claim that 'her life journey came to an end' and somehow the new journey of a new person began after the treatment.[14] We would instead claim that the same 'substance' or 'kind of thing' was there all along: she was injured and then healed.[15] But where Singer and the Church *agree* on moral status at the end of life is, in my opinion, far more interesting than where they disagree.

Peter Singer on brain death

It is popular in bioethics circles to use brain death as a criterion for determining when a human being has died. And especially because

[13] Congregation for the Doctrine of the Faith, "Commentary," Vatican: The Holy See www.vatican.va/roman_curia/congregations/cfaith/documents/rc_con_cfaith_doc_20070801_nota-commento_en.html (Accessed December 3, 2009).

[14] The latest research in neurobiology (led by Princeton researcher Elizabeth Gould) has shown that the old scientific dogma that neurons cannot be regenerated is simply false. In fact, 'neurogenesis' is one of the most dynamic and promising fields of scientific research today.

[15] Some might argue that, depending on how serious the brain damage was, what would actually be going on here is (to use the phrase from the last chapter) a 'nature-changing event': the original person died and a new person was created if the brain was repaired in this way. But this only follows if we identify persons with their brains rather than their bodies. The thorny philosophical questions about the relationship between minds, brains, and persons has a vast literature and cannot be addressed here. But it is worth mentioning that (1) most Christians would reject any dualistic understanding that would see the human person as, say, a 'brain living inside a body', and (2) there has been a major turn by some in consciousness studies away from simply identifying self-awareness with the brain. UC Berkeley philosopher Alva Noe's work is a good example: *Out of Our Heads: Why You Are Not Your Brain and Other Lessons from the Biology of Consciousness* (New York: Hill and Wang, 2010).

a 'dead donor' rule requires clinicians to determine that a patient has died before taking her organs for transplant, the question of whether brain death is actual death looms large for these matters of life and death – not only for the donor, but also for the individuals whose lives could be saved by her donation. Even President Bush's bioethics council (though there were important dissenters) seemed to favor this understanding of death.[16] But Singer rejects this approach:

> The idea that someone is dead when their brain is dead is, at best, rather odd. Human beings are not the only living things in the world. All living things eventually die, and we can generally tell when they are alive and when they are dead. Isn't the distinction between life and death so basic that what counts as dead for a human being also counts as dead for a dog, a parrot, a prawn, an oyster, an oak, or a cabbage? But what is the common element here? According to the classic account, death was "the permanent cessation of the flow of vital bodily fluids." Living things, this account assumed, have vital bodily fluids. They may be blood, sap or something else, but when they stop flowing forever, all living things die.[17]

And getting the definition of death right is of fundamental importance: for when "warm, breathing, pulsating human beings are declared to be dead, they lose their basic human rights. They are not given life support. If their relatives consent (or in some countries, as long as they have not registered a refusal of consent), their hearts and other organs can be cut out of their bodies and given to strangers."[18]

Singer gives a compelling history of how we got to this strange place. The late 1960s saw the beginning of the age of organ transplants, and with it an urgent impetus to answer the question of when someone had died so we could use their organs to save the lives of desperate patients on long waiting lists. But most vital organs must be taken from a body very close to death in order to be viable for transplant. And with the invention and wide use of the ventilator, which allowed many permanently or persistently unconscious patients to continue to breathe, it became tempting to take vital organs from such unconscious patients while they were still breathing and while their heart was still beating. But as Singer points out, there was a seemingly insuperable barrier to doing this: to remove a vital organ of a living patient would be murder.[19]

---

[16] www.bioethics.gov/reports/death/determination_of_death_report.pdf (Accessed December 6, 2009). Edmund Pellegrino – chairperson of the Council – was one important dissenter. His arguments will be explored below.

[17] Singer, *Rethinking Life and Death*, 20–21.   [18] *Ibid.*, 22.   [19] *Ibid.*, 24.

The process of getting around this problem in the United States would begin with Henry Beecher, chairperson of a Harvard University committee which oversaw the ethics of experimentation on human beings, writing to the dean of his medical school and suggesting that "the time has come for further consideration of the definition of death. Every major hospital has patients stacked up waiting for suitable donors."[20] The result was the now famous Ad Hoc Committee of the Harvard Medical School to Examine the Definition of Brain Death. Their report began with this remarkable paragraph:

Our primary purpose is to define irreversible coma as a new criterion for death. There are two reasons why there is a need for a definition: (1) Improvements in resuscitative and supportive measures have led to increased efforts to save those who are desperately injured. Sometimes these efforts have only a partial success so that the result is an individual whose heart continues to beat but whose brain is irreversibly damaged. The burden is great on patients who suffer permanent loss of intellect, on their families, on the hospitals, and on those in need of hospital beds already occupied by these comatose patients. (2) Obsolete criteria for the definition of death can lead to controversy in obtaining organs for transplantation.[21]

Singer's response is scathing, and understandably so. For

the Harvard committee does not even attempt to argue that there is a need for a new definition of death because hospitals have a lot of patients in their wards who are really dead, but are being kept attached to respirators because the law does not recognize them as dead. Instead, with unusual frankness, the committee said that a new definition was needed because irreversibly comatose patients were a great burden, not only on themselves (why to be in an irreversible coma is a burden on the patient, the committee did not say), but also on their families, hospitals, and patients waiting for beds.[22]

But as frank as this seems, Singer points out that an earlier draft of the report had even more direct language about what was really going on. It claimed that a "secondary" issue was that "there is a great need for tissues and organs of, among others, the patient whose cerebrum has been hopelessly destroyed, in order to restore those who are salvageable." Upon seeing this draft, the dean of the medical school insisted that Beecher change it because "it suggests that you wish to define death in order to make viable organs more readily available to persons requiring transplants."[23]

---

[20] *Ibid.*   [21] *Ibid.,* 25.   [22] *Ibid.*   [23] *Ibid.,* 25–26.

But a second remarkable aspect of the committee's report is its insistence that "irreversible coma" and "permanent loss of intellect" qualify as death. Such a definition not only applies to patient A, but also patient B in the persistent vegetative state. Even today, no legal system accepts this definition. It is true that the committee later claims that they are concerned only with those comatose individuals who have no discernable central nervous system activity, but Singer correctly wonders why this caveat is made. For "the reasons given by the committee for redefining death – the great burden on the patients, their families, the hospitals and the community, as well as the waste of organs needed for transplantation – apply in every respect to all those who are irreversibly comatose, not only those whose entire brain is dead."[24]

Despite this strange and disconcerting beginning, the brain-death criterion appears to have triumphed. By 1981, the President's Commission for the Study of Ethical Problems in Medicine wrote of the emergence of a medical consensus around what the Harvard committee proposed, and most of my colleagues in bioethics operate as if the question of brain death has been settled. But Singer highlights what this shift has done to our speech and suggests that it means we don't actually accept the brain-death criterion. Consider his citation from the *Detroit Free Press*:

A 17-year-old was pronounced brain dead after being accidently shot in the head . . . John Ziemnick of Hubbell was being kept alive on life-support system in Marquette General Hospital, nursing supervisor Pat Liana said. He was to be pronounced officially dead after doctors removed organs for donation to others, Liana said.[25]

Or consider these headlines surrounding pregnant and brain-dead women giving birth:

The *San Francisco Chronicle* headlined one of its stories 'Brain-Dead Woman Gives Birth, Then Dies' while the *Miami Herald* preferred 'Brain-Dead Woman Kept Alive in Hopes She'll Bear a Child.' The *Toronto Star* even found a love angle . . . 'Man Dreads Birth that Will Kill Lover.'[26]

This confusion exists in the medical profession as well. Case Western Reserve University did a study of physicians and nurses who worked with brain-dead patients and concluded that over half used a concept of death in an inconsistent way. When asked to justify their claim that someone was dead, "one third said either that the patient was 'irreversibly dying'

---

[24] *Ibid.*, 27.   [25] *Ibid.*, 33.   [26] *Ibid.*, 35.

or made reference to the patient's 'unacceptable quality of life.'" Another study at Michigan State University asked thirteen nurses and seven physicians (all of whom were neurologists or neurosurgeons with extensive experience with brain-dead patients) to describe what they would tell the family of a brain-dead patient. Here are some of the responses:

> "At this point in time, it doesn't look like the patient is going to survive."
> "The machine is the way he would have to live the rest of his life."
> "The machine is basically what's keeping him alive."
> "If kept on the respirator, the patient will die of sepsis."[27]

Why, if brain death is now the accepted standard, do people refuse to accept that brain death is really death? Singer's answer is that we are confusing two concepts: (1) being alive as a person and (2) being alive as a member of the species *Homo sapiens*. Because most of us still (wrongly) think of them as equivalent, we think that as long as there is a functioning human organism, the person is still there. But because we are in the process of a revolution in ethics that sees personhood as something different from merely being a living member of the species *Homo sapiens*, many of us also think that a 'person' can die while a human organism is still alive. We must at once acknowledge that a brain-dead individual is no longer a person (she is *biographically* dead) *and* that a functioning, living human organism remains.

Brain death: the Church's position

In response to the revolution in defining death, Singer is amazed that it occurred without much opposition from the speciesist sanctity-of-life crowd. Where was the pro-life movement? Where was the Roman Catholic Church? Perhaps understandably, the Church at first hesitated to get deeply involved with this issue because it has no particular expertise in complex matters of biology. Singer quotes Pope Pius XII claiming in 1957 that while the Church maintains that death is when the soul leaves the body, "It remains for the doctor, and especially the anesthesiologist, to give a clear and precise definition of 'death' and the 'moment of death' of a patient who passes away in a state of unconsciousness."[28] Pius apparently did not foresee what would happen in leaving the definition up to physicians, and had he known, he surely would have been

---

[27] *Ibid.*, 34.   [28] *Ibid.*, 29.

far less likely to make such a claim. But his basic point is still an important one: whether or not a living human organism is present is a question about which the Church (while a legitimate player in the public debate on these matters) has no special competence as a teacher of faith and morals.

Despite this, some Roman Catholic ethicists claim to be able to tell us what the Church teaches about brain death, and much attention is focused on Pope John Paul II's 2000 address to the 18th International Congress of the Transplantation Society. Although this address was in no way making doctrinal pronouncement, it does *refer* to something claimed in both an encyclical and the *Catechism of the Catholic Church*: namely, that donating organs is a wonderful way to contribute to a culture of life.[29] John Paul II, however, has an important warning:

Acknowledgement of the unique dignity of the human person has a further underlying consequence: *vital organs which occur singly in the body can be removed only after death*, that is from the body of someone who is certainly dead. This requirement is self-evident, since to act otherwise would mean intentionally to cause the death of the donor in disposing of his organs. This gives rise to one of the most debated issues in contemporary bioethics, as well as to serious concerns in the minds of ordinary people. I refer to the problem of *ascertaining the fact of death*. When can a person be considered dead with complete certainty?[30]

After noting that for some time certain scientific approaches to ascertaining death have shifted the emphasis from the cardio-respiratory signs to a neurological criterion, the Pope goes on to remind us that, "With regard to the parameters used today for ascertaining death – whether the 'encephalic' signs or the more traditional cardio-respiratory signs – the Church does not make technical decisions."[31] But he then seems to make a technical claim by stating that "the *complete* and *irreversible* cessation of all brain activity, if rigorously applied, does not seem to conflict with the essential elements of a sound anthropology."[32]

Some ethicists, like Fr Tad Pacholczyk, PhD, director of education for the National Catholic Bioethics Center (NCBC) in Philadelphia, claim that this means defining the death of the human person as

---

[29] See Pope John Paul II, "*Evangelium Vitae,*" 86 and the *Catechism of the Catholic Church*, paragraph 2296.

[30] Pope John Paul II, "Address of the Holy Father John Paul II to the 18th International Congress of the Transplantation Society," Vatican: The Holy See. www.vatican.va/holy_father/john_paul_ii/speeches/2000/jul-sep/documents/hf_jp-ii_spe_20000829_transplants_en.html (Accessed December 6, 2009), 4.

[31] *Ibid.*, 5.   [32] *Ibid.*

the death of the brain is compatible with the true nature of humanity. In an FAQ on the NCBC's website he even seems to indicate that the Church has accepted the neurological definition as definitive:[33]

Why Does the Church Accept this Definition of Death?

This is not a new definition of death but rather of the use of new signs to determine that death has occurred. The Christian understanding of death has always been that it is the separation of the soul from the body. The Catholic Church looks to the medical community to determine the biological signs that indicate with moral certainty that this event has already occurred. In recent years, medical research has indicated that the irreversible loss of brain function provides a firm indicator that death has already occurred.

Of course, it takes a biologically informed prudential judgment to determine whether or not it is in fact the case that medical evidence coheres with the Christian understanding of the human person.

But there are others who make quite a different judgment. James DuBois recently highlighted a front-page article in *L'Osservatore Romano* arguing that the Catholic Church must revisit the question of brain death because it rests on an understanding of human life that is contrary to Catholic teaching.[34] When the Vatican newspaper publishes a front-page article questioning the brain-death criterion, one can be fairly certain the Church doesn't have an official teaching on the matter. Indeed, the Italian press covering the article noted that the Church appears to be leaning toward skepticism of brain death:

But it is especially in the Church that critical voices [of the brain-death criterion] are gaining strength. Since 1989, when the Pontifical Academy of Sciences took up the question, Professor Josef Seifert, rector of the International Philosophical Academy of Liechtenstein, advanced strong objections to the definition of brain death. At that conference, Seifert's was the only dissenting voice. But years later, when from January 3–4, 2005, the Pontifical Academy of Sciences again met to discuss the question of the "signs of death," the positions had been reversed. The experts present – philosophers, jurists, neurologists from various countries – found themselves in agreement in maintaining that brain death is not the

---

[33] *Ibid.*, 4.
[34] James M. DuBois, "America Magazine – Brain Death and Organ Donation," *America Magazine* www.americamagazine.org/content/article.cfm?article_id=11369 (Accessed December 6, 2009).

death of a human being, and that the criterion of brain death, not being scientifically credible, should be abandoned.[35]

In looking around for a Roman Catholic intellectual authority on this matter, one could hardly find better credentials than those belonging to John Finnis – a professor of legal and ethical theory at both Oxford and Notre Dame who has served on the Catholic Bishops' Joint Committee on Bioethical Issues (1981–88), the International Theological Commission (1986–92), the Pontifical Council for Justice and Peace (1990–95), and (currently) the Pontifical Academy for Life. Finnis, in a response given to Peter Singer's paper 'Brain Death and the Sanctity of Life Ethic', said the following[36]:

Singer's second aim is "to show that there are serious problems with accepting brain death as a criterion of death." I think he succeeds in this aim.

Finnis notes that he, along with a fellow member of the Pontifical Academy for Life, the American clinical pediatric neurologist Alan Shewmon, no longer accepts the brain-death criterion. In particular, Finnis cites "Recovery from 'Brain Death': A Neurologist's Apologia"[37] in which Shewmon argues that the Church's *philosophical* definition of death is correct, but that the mounting empirical biological evidence leads us to reject brain death as a fundamental criterion.

While it seems clear there is no official teaching on the matter,[38] there is growing skepticism from some of the best thinkers the Church has to offer. The prudent course now, given the complexity of the biological

---

[35] Sandro Magister, "Transplants and Brain Death. 'L'Osservatore Romano' Has Broken the Taboo," *Chiesa: Notizie, analisi, documenti sulla Chiesa cattolica, a cura di Sandro Magister* http://chiesa. espresso.repubblica.it/articolo/206476?eng=y (Accessed December 6, 2009).

[36] John Finnis, Response to Singer's 'Brain Death and the Sanctity of Life Ethic', Response paper given at a meeting with the Philosophy Society, University of Oxford (May 14, 1998).

[37] D. Alan Shewmon, "Recovery from 'Brain Death': A Neurologist's Apologia," *Linacre* Q. 64 (1997), 30–96.

[38] And there may never be one. As Christian Brugger pointed out in an interview with ZENIT in which he argued against brain death, "The Church's (and hence the Pope's) authority to teach extends only to matters of faith and morals ... It is clear that the reliability of the scientific premise rests entirely upon the soundness of the scientific data and the interpretation of that data. Thus the papal affirmation that the neurological standard is a reliable indicator of death is not grounded in any truth of faith or morals." E. Christian Brugger, "Transplants From Murder Victims," ZENIT – The World Seen From Rome www.zenit.org/article-31647?l=english (Accessed June 29, 2011). Furthermore, in a 2008 address on organ donation, Pope Benedict refused to endorse the neurological standard, and instead notes that "where certainty has not been attained, the principle of precaution must prevail." Pope Benedict XVI, Address to participants at an International Congress organized by the Pontifical Academy for Life, Vatican: The Holy See, www.vatican.va/ holy_father/benedict_xvi/speeches/2008/november/documents/hf_ben-xvi_spe_20081107_acdlife_ en.html (Accessed June 29, 2011).

evidence, is to explore careful attempts to apply such evidence to ethical and moral/anthropological considerations.

Applying the science to the moral anthropology

One of the key confusions in the discussion of brain death is the concept of 'definition' in the first place. Edmund Pellegrino, in his personal statement concluding the President's Council on Bioethics report on determining death, reminds us that definitions of death fall into two categories: the philosophical and the empirical. The first seeks a conceptual understanding of the essential differences between life and death. The second seeks to determine clinical signs, tests or criteria which separate life and death more accurately.[39] A major problem with the current public discussion over the definition of death is that we are trying to find the second without determining the first. The Church has no such problem, for it has a clear conceptual definition: a person is dead if he has "irreversibly lost all capacity to integrate and coordinate the physical and mental functions of the body."[40] The next question, of course, is how best to determine this in the clinical world.

Bioethics Council member Alfonso Gomez-Lobo pointed out in his personal statement that the definition of death "is a definition of exclusion. It is a derivative account that is parasitic on the more primitive notion of life."[41] We therefore need to begin with *what counts as life* – that is, a human organism integrating and coordinating the physical and mental functions of her body – in order to determine death. In his view, if

a body is able to process nutrition, eliminate waste, and exhibit proportional growth, homeostasis, etc., and moreover, it engages in these functions in an integrated manner, we shall correctly deem it to be alive. If it fails to do this, and starts to decompose and disintegrate, we will rightly judge it to be dead.[42]

He then points out that the brain-death criterion seems to be unpersuasive because this form of 'death' often leaves behind not a cadaver, but an ostensibly living body which is currently integrating and coordinating its

---

[39] The President's Council on Bioethics, *Controversies in the Determination of Death*, 108.
[40] From the "Report on Prolonging Life and Determining Death" of the Pontifical Academy of Sciences (1985). Quoted in Kevin D. O'Rourke, OP and Philip Boyle, *Medical Ethics: Sources of Catholic Teaching* (Washington, D.C.: Georgetown University Press, 1999), 78.
[41] The President's Council on Bioethics, *Controversies in the Determination of Death*, 96.
[42] *Ibid.*

functions. Indeed, he agrees with Singer in claiming that the brain-death criterion "turns on the unpersuasive distinction between the death of plants and animals, and the death of a person."[43]

But David Albert Jones relates an important worry about this position.[44] Isn't it the case that "the brain has the function of organizing and integrating the body as whole" and that "the nervous and hormonal systems are entirely coordinated by the brain, and via these systems, the general activity and biochemistry of the body"? A body that is brain dead, therefore, is not self-integrating and organizing: rather, the life-support machines are giving the misleading appearance of life to a body that lives no longer. What *appears* to be life is really just the artificial animation of a corpse. But Jones is quick to respond with biological and medical data which suggest otherwise. Consider that in some cases, when first being cut open to harvest their organs "the patients were discovered to react strongly to the incision. The heart rate increased rapidly and blood pressure rose dramatically until general anesthetic was given, whereupon the blood pressure and heart beat returned to normal." Jones also points out that residual pituitary function appears to be intact after brain death, that brain-dead individuals can live for many months, and that brain-dead mothers have even gestated children.

But perhaps the physiological evidence for coordinated functioning can be explained by something other than the brain. Jones points out that some have tried to locate the source of these functions, which appear to be evidence of coordination and integration, in the spinal cord in order to uphold the claim that the brain has, in fact, died. But even if this is true (and there does seem to be some evidence to suggest that it is), Jones rightly responds by claiming it immediately raises the question of what is supposed to be at stake when it is claimed that a particular pathway is spinal rather than brainstem. Is it the anatomical position of the nerve which gives it its significance? If integrative brainstem functions can be performed by the spinal cord then the functioning of the spinal cord has the same significance as that of the brainstem.

After all, the question is not whether *the brain* is coordinating and integrating the body's functions (unless one has begged the question), but whether there is coordination and integration *at all.*

---

[43] *Ibid.*, 97.
[44] David Albert Jones, "Nagging Doubts About Brain-Death." *Catholic Medical Quarterly*, Feb. 1995. Available online at: www.catholicdoctors.org.uk/CMQ/Feb_1995/nagging_doubts_about_brain_death.htm (Accessed December 7, 2009).

In a fascinating observation, Gomez-Lobo gives us good reason to think that coordination and integration in the human body cannot be linked to a single organ like the brain or spinal cord. He makes the powerful point that during "the early embryonic stages of an organism, there is certainly integrated functioning of subsystems, and this happens before the brain is formed."[45] If the human organism can self-integrate and coordinate without a brain at one stage of development, this at least opens up the possibility that it can at other stages as well.[46] This suggests that we should think of this process as a product of the dynamism of the organism holistically considered.

But Nicholas Tonti-Filippini argues that we need to be more specific about what we mean by self-integration before we can be sure that it can be done without a functioning brain. While human persons are not reducible to our brain function, he believes that

some brain function is essential to integration of the entire human body because the neural and endocrine systems, the two systems of the body that communicate between the parts of the body, both rely on the brain to mediate between them. Without at least some brain function, not all the parts of the body are in communication with each other, and their functions cease to interrelate as a single-unified organism ... It does seem important that 'integration' at least means 'intercommunicative' and has the function of achieving the unity of the body.[47]

This seems correct as far as it goes, but we are given no reason why we should accept that neural/endocrinal interaction is necessary for there to be a self-integrating human organism. Indeed, human embryos are human organisms whose integration has no neural component at all. Furthermore, why should this be the only kind of interaction that is required? What about human beings who have had their *corpus callosum* severed such that the two halves of their brains are not communicating with each other and integrating the body, as in healthy human organisms? Surely this would be a case where "not all the parts of the body are in communication with each other," but it would hardly be an example of a body that had lost self-integration. Tonti-Filippini's choice about which parts of the body must be in communication is an arbitrary one.

---

[45] The President's Council on Bioethics, *Controversies in Determination of Death*, 99.
[46] It appears that what, precisely, is responsible for the integration of the human organism (referred to in traditional Christianity as 'the soul') – at whatever stage – is a mysterious thing that requires more careful study.
[47] Nicholas Tonti-Filippini, "Religious and Secular Death: A Parting of the Ways," *Bioethics* (forthcoming), 5.

But another member of former President Bush's bioethics council, Protestant Christian ethicist Gilbert Meilaender, raises another challenge. Why should we accept the Church's view that the fundamental philosophical issue is integration and coordination in the first place? This, he says, does not get to the heart of what makes someone living. If any organism is to remain alive it must carry out "the fundamental work of self-preservation" – which he thinks includes things like openness to the surrounding environment, ability to act upon that environment, and inner experience of need. For instance, Patient B above (in a persistent vegetative state) is not dead for Meilaender because, despite being permanently unconscious, a "human being who breathes spontaneously manifests openness to the surrounding environment in its need for oxygen, acts upon the environment by breathing to take in the oxygen it needs, and manifests an inner drive to breathe. Such a person is surely severely disabled, but is not dead."[48] This is not true, his position implies, of Patient A, the brain-dead individual who is being artificially fed, hydrated, and ventilated. There is no evidence of this kind of patient attempting to engage the world.

Aside from questioning why 'engaging the world' is more fundamental for determining death than 'self-organization and integration,' can the brain-death skeptic make an effective response to Meilaender? Perhaps one could ask for more information on what it means to "engage the world." Apparently he thinks that merely breathing on one's own is enough to demonstrate this, but this is quite a low standard. In fact, it is difficult to see why breathing on one's own should count as attempting to engage the world, but increased heart rate and blood pressure in response to being cut open should not. And what about a brain-dead body which gestates a fetus for multiple months? Surely this counts as engaging the world, given the breathing standard. Meilaender's approach actually turns out to call the neurological criterion into serious question, given how many brain-dead human organisms do in fact engage the world in some way.

And even scientists and medical professionals are beginning to realize that the current brain-death criterion just doesn't fit the science – or their current practices – and many wish to push the definition of death even further. For instance, a recent *Nature* editorial called for revisiting the criteria yet again using reasoning very similar to that of Beecher and the Harvard committee. Prompted by huge waiting lists for organs, and the fact that brain death is not a "clear, unambiguous boundary,"

---

[48] The President's Council on Bioethics, *Controversies in Determination of Death*, 104.

the editorial says "the law should be changed to describe more accurately and honestly the way death is determined in clinical practice." The current law requires that brain death be established, but "what if, as is sometimes the case, blood chemistry suggests that the pituitary gland at the base of the brain is still functioning? That activity has nothing to do with the person being alive in any meaningful sense." But it does seem to undermine the claim that all functions of the entire brain have ceased. And how long must a physician wait to determine whole brain death? Physicians have "occasionally observed a brainstem-mediated reflex – a cough for example – up to 36 hours after they would have been declared dead" had the person been being used for organ transplant. The lack of any clear boundary means that we should once again change "laws that push doctors towards a form of deceit" and that make them seem like "greedy harvesters eager to strip living patients of their organs." The editorial concludes that though death is a "sensitive" issue, concerns about "declaring death in someone who will never again be the person he or she was should be weighed against the value of giving a full and healthy life to someone who will die without a transplant."[49] That this kind of claim can appear in a major scientific journal is strong evidence that the supposed death of the Harvard committee's shoddy and dangerous methodology has been just as exaggerated as that of the living human beings from which they wish to harvest organs.

Both Singer and the Church resist this approach and instead insist that the definition of the death of a human person must be about who or what she is (or was) and why she is no longer there. This is determined by evidence that is independent of the interests of scientists, physicians or of those waiting for organ transplants. Singer and the Church, of course, part company with regard to ultimate conclusions about the moral status of patients A and B above, but we once again find that the disagreement is much more narrow than one might suppose and that there is broad agreement about several points in the argument.

MEDICAL TREATMENT AND CARE OF PERSONS AT THE END OF LIFE

Despite this interesting overlap on the question about moral status, isn't it the case that Peter Singer and the Church differ dramatically about

[49] "Delimiting Death," Editorial, *Nature* 461: 570 (October 1, 2009), www.nature.com/nature/journal/v461/n7264/full/461570a.html (Accessed July 31, 2011).

what counts as ethical medical treatment of persons at the end of life? Isn't it the case that Christians have "long argued that life should be preserved at all costs,"[50] while Singer often argues that living human persons may licitly have medical treatment rejected or removed, which results in the death of those persons? No, it is simply a mistake (and it is one that even many Christians themselves make) to claim that the Church insists on preserving life at all costs. Indeed, there is a centuries-old Christian tradition of precisely the opposite, and the *Catechism* is very clear about this:

Discontinuing medical procedures that are burdensome, dangerous, extraordinary, or disproportionate to the expected outcome can be legitimate; it is the refusal of "over-zealous" treatment. Here one does not will to cause death; one's inability to impede it is merely accepted.[51]

Pope John Paul II, in his encyclical on the Gospel of Life, allows for

the decision to forego so-called "aggressive medical treatment," in other words, medical procedures which no longer correspond to the real situation of the patient, either because they are by now disproportionate to any expected results or because they impose an excessive burden on the patient and his family ... Certainly there is a moral obligation to care for oneself and to allow oneself to be cared for, but this duty must take account of concrete circumstances. It needs to be determined whether the means of treatment available are objectively proportionate to the prospects for improvement. To forego extraordinary or disproportionate means is not the equivalent of suicide or euthanasia; it rather expresses acceptance of the human condition in the face of death.[52]

Indeed, the Christian tradition even has a name for the kind of sin involved in 'preserving life at all costs': idolatry. The source of one's ultimate concern should always be love of God and neighbor, and the Christian tradition is full of holy people who refused to put preservation of life ahead of such love.[53] But the Pope, in the very same paragraph cited above, claims that while euthanasia can obviously be an act (say, giving someone an overdose of pain medication), it can also be an *omission*. How, then, can we distinguish between an omission of life-sustaining medical treatment that is euthanasia and one that is not? To do so, we

---

[50] Nick Goodway, "Mobile Rivals Set for India Battle," *Daily Mail* Online www.dailymail.co.uk/money/markets/article-1605698/Mobile-rivals-set-for-India-battle.html (Accessed December 10, 2009).

[51] Catholic Church, *Catechism of the Catholic Church*, paragraphs 904, 2278.

[52] Pope John Paul II, "*Evangelium Vitae*," 443–453, 65.

[53] John Paul II was one of these people, having foregone some life-extending measures in advance of his own death.

must first understand the Church's tradition of distinguishing between ordinary and extraordinary means of treatment.

The Roman Catholic tradition on ordinary
and extraordinary means[54]

The distinction between a medical treatment that is 'ordinary' and there-fore morally required (in a possibly life-saving or life-prolonging situ-ation) and one that is 'extraordinary' and may be refused or withdrawn, while going back at least to medieval Roman Catholic thinkers, has been adopted (at least in some form) and invoked in the wider secular debate of these issues. However, it is important and appropriate to get perspective on this tradition by taking a quick look at its historical development.[55]

Many locate the beginning of this tradition's trajectory with Thomas Aquinas' thirteenth-century attempts to balance one's abiding respect for human life with some acknowledgement that the duty to sustain such life, a temporal good, is not absolute. God has dominion over human life and responsible stewardship of God's gifts may mean choosing other goods over those of human biological life. Three centuries later, Francisco de Vitoria started reasoning in a way that was similar to the current ordinary/ extraordinary means tradition. In dealing with the question of a very sick person's refusal of food, he claimed that if the patient is so depressed that taking food becomes "a kind of impossibility" then the patient is not guilty of the mortal sin of suicide – especially if there is little hope for life. Interestingly, Vitoria adds that even if it would be more nutritious (and thus more likely to yield a healthier state), the sick person is not required to eat the best or most expensive food. And he broadens out this point in claiming that one is not obliged to sacrifice one's whole means of subsistence, nor one's general lifestyle, nor one's homeland in order to acquire a cure or maintain optimum health.

Prior to the development of modern anesthetics, surgical procedures not only involved mutilation and disfigurement of the body, but also almost always involved virtually unimaginable pain. Also in the sixteenth century, Domingo Soto, OP claimed that such surgeries, and especially amputations, were necessarily optional because of their torturous nature. Even if necessary

[54] This section also appears in my previous work; Charles C. Camosy, *Too Expensive to Treat? – Finitude, Tragedy, and the Neonatal ICU* (Grand Rapids, MI: William B. Eerdmans Publishing Co., 2010).
[55] Most of the narrative here is owed to Richard Sparks, *To Treat or Not to Treat: Bioethics and the Handicapped Newborn* (Mahwah, NJ: Paulist Press, 1988), 94–100.

to preserve life, they could be foregone because the pain was beyond what the 'common man' could possibly be forced to bear. Though it appears that another sixteenth-century thinker, Dominican Domingo Banez, was the first to use the terms 'ordinary' and 'extraordinary' in this medical context, it was the Jesuit Gerald Kelly who explored, summarized and gave synthetic expression to the distinction in the mid-twentieth century. For Kelly, an ordinary treatment was one obtained without very great difficulty, whilst an extraordinary one was one obtained with excessive difficulty with respect to pain, repugnance, cost, "and so forth." Of course, such judgments depend on one's social circumstances, and a particular treatment could be considered ordinary in one era or culture but extraordinary in another.

A few years after Kelly's work came out, Pope Pius XII delivered an address which, despite it having appeared in the Roman Catholic moral manuals for centuries, gave the ordinary/extraordinary distinction clear papal confirmation:

Natural reason and Christian morals say that man (and whosoever is entrusted with the task of taking care of his fellow man) has the right and duty in the case of serious illness to take the necessary treatment for the preservation of life and health ... But normally one is held to use only ordinary means – according to circumstances of persons, places, times and culture – that is to say means that do not involve any grave burden for oneself or another. A more strict obligation would be too burdensome for most men and would render the attainment of the higher, more important good too difficult. Life, health, all temporal activities are in fact subordinated to spiritual ends.[56]

According to the Pope, we cannot make treatment decisions based simply on the medical indications of what will bring about health to the body. Indeed, before anything else, a physician should consider the whole, unified person – that is to say, not merely his physical condition but his psychological state as well as his spiritual and moral ideals and his place in society.[57]

Based on this tradition, we may describe some general principles that characterize the distinction between ordinary and extraordinary means of treatment:

1. Physical life is a basic precious value that one has an obligation to protect and preserve. However, physical life is a limited value subordinated to the pursuit of spiritual ends.

[56] Pope Pius XII, *The Prolongation of Life: Allocution to the International Congress of Anesthesiologists* (November 24, 1957), in "The Pope Speaks," 4 (1958), 395–396.
[57] Pope Pius XII, "Cancer, a Medical and Social Problem," as quoted in Sparks, *To Treat Or Not to Treat: Bioethics and the Handicapped Newborn*, 92.

2. One's moral obligation to prolong life through medical means is evaluated in light of one's overall medical condition and one's ability to pursue the spiritual ends of life.

3. One is morally obliged to prolong life with medical means when it offers a reasonable hope of benefit in helping one to pursue the spiritual ends of life without imposing an excessive burden.

4. One is not morally obliged to prolong life with medical means when death is imminent and medical treatment will only prolong the dying process; when medical treatment offers no reasonable hope of benefit in terms of helping one pursue the spiritual ends of life; or when medical treatment imposes an excessive burden on one and profoundly frustrates one's pursuit of the spiritual ends of life.

5. Benefit and burden are understood broadly in the Catholic tradition to refer not just to the physiological dimension of life, but the psychological, social and spiritual dimensions as well.[58]

6. Cost to the individual and family are social factors which may be considered when determining whether or not a treatment imposes an excessive burden.[59]

And when one combines the above principles with the classic Roman Catholic principle of double effect, one is able to see where the conversation with Singer can begin on this topic. As we saw above, one is never permitted to aim at the death of another. But according to the principle of double effect, one may forego treatment with an aim at something other than death, while foreseeing *but not intending* that death will likely be the result – as long as one has a proportionate reason for so doing.[60] Take the following case presented by Panicola, *et al.*:

Janice ... was diagnosed with ovarian cancer after months of nonspecific symptoms. When the cancer was finally discovered, it had spread to other parts of her body. The doctors were not optimistic about her prospects but told her that with investigational doses of chemotherapy they may be able to buy her some time, perhaps as much as a year. If sustaining life were the sole benefit

[58] The preceding principles are taken from Michael R. Panicola, "Quality of Life and the Critically Ill Newborn: Life and Death Decision Making in the Neonatal Context" (Ph.D., Saint Louis University, 2000), 218–219.

[59] This aspect of the tradition is somewhat controversial, but I have argued elsewhere that it is rather firmly grounded in said tradition. Camosy, *Too Expensive to Treat*.

[60] The Principle of Double Effect, among other things, attempts to hold together the views that (1) all human lives are of equal value and one may never directly aim against the good of another's life and (2) the good of *sustaining* that life can be trumped by higher spiritual goods – but only for a proportionate reason. Much more will be said about the principle of double effect in the chapters on duties to the poor and ethical method.

Janice was considering, she would have jumped at the chance. However, as it was, she debated whether to undergo chemotherapy at all. In talking with the doctors about treatment, she wanted to know how much pain she would experience, whether her insurance would cover the costs, how her relationships with her only child and other loved ones would be affected, how much time she would have to spend in the hospital, and whether she would be physically capable of working and pursing her life's passion of painting.[61]

Janice could licitly refuse the life-sustaining chemotherapy as long as she *was making a choice about how to live* rather than intending her own death. If she evaluated the burden that the treatment would cause (the pain, expense, making her unable to paint or see important people in her life, etc.), and came to the conclusion that it outweighed the benefit (added months of life), she would be perfectly justified in refusing the treatment. But suppose a different scenario: Janice needs a life-saving injection of medicine, but refuses because she doesn't like needles. Though this omission of life-sustaining treatment is not euthanasia because she doesn't intend or aim at her own death, it is nevertheless prohibited (and also gravely sinful[62]) under the principle of double effect because she does not give the kind of proportionate reason that was present in the case of the chemotherapy.

From what we have just seen, it is clear that the Christian tradition simply does not accept that life must be preserved at all costs. In fact, we can now see how there might be significant areas of overlap with Singer's point of view on this topic. Let us return to the three cases above and compare what Singer and the Church would say about each one.

Patient A: 'brain dead' but kept alive via artificial means

Both Singer and the Church would likely agree that this is a living member of the species *Homo sapiens*.[63] And though they would disagree about the moral status of this human person, both would agree that the ventilator may be licitly removed. Singer's reasons are obvious: we

---

[61] Michael R. Panicola, David M. Belde, John Paul Slosar, and Mark F. Repenshak, *An Introduction to Healthcare Ethics: Theological Foundations, Contemporary Issues, and Controversial Cases* (Winona, MN: Saint Mary's Press, 2007), 140–141.

[62] An important distinction in the Church's moral theology is that between the 'intrinsic' evil in an action and the 'gravity' of evil in an action. An action might be intrinsically evil, and actually be *less* grave or serious than an action which is not intrinsically evil, but nevertheless produces bad consequences such that its gravity is extremely high.

[63] As we saw above, the Church's current position appears to be that, in the face of uncertainty, we should take this position.

shouldn't spend these kinds of resources on non-persons. The Church would say that as long as one does not intend the death of the patient, but instead reasonably concludes that the burdens of treatment are disproportionate with any prospective benefits, then one may remove the ventilator foreseeing, but not intending, that death will result. *What by ANH?*

Patient B: persistent vegetative state

Once again, both Singer and the Church would agree that the patient is a living member of the species *Homo sapiens* while disagreeing about her moral status. Singer argues that one might licitly remove a feeding tube from patients diagnosed to be in a persistent vegetative state. Could the Church make a similar argument? Especially in light of the previous case, one might think the answer is yes, but the nature of giving someone food and water might make this different from keeping her on a ventilator. Perhaps it is closer to 'care' for a patient, and not medical 'treatment,' and therefore morally required. After all, one should almost never (perhaps disaster situations would be exceptional) abandon a patient by refusing to give very basic care.

The famous Terri Schiavo case in the United States very publicly raised these questions to a whole new level – one which prompted the US Catholic Bishops to ask Rome for clarification on the implication of the Church's teaching on ordinary and extraordinary means for tube-feeding and hydrating patients in a persistent vegetative state. Here is the question and the response of the Vatican:

Is the administration of food and water (whether by natural or artificial means) to a patient in a "vegetative state" morally obligatory except when they cannot be assimilated by the patient's body or cannot be administered to the patient without causing significant physical discomfort?

Response: Yes. The administration of food and water even by artificial means is, in principle, an ordinary and proportionate means of preserving life. It is therefore obligatory to the extent to which, and for as long as, it is shown to accomplish its proper finality, which is the hydration and nourishment of the patient. In this way suffering and death by starvation and dehydration are prevented.[64]

---

[64] Congregation for the Doctrine of the Faith, "Responses to Certain Questions Concerning Artificial Nutrition and Hydration" (Vatican: The Holy See), www.vatican.va/roman_curia/congregations/cfaith/documents/rc_con_cfaith_doc_20070801_risposte-usa_en.html (Accessed December 10, 2009).

Some who were pushing for Terri to remain sustained took this as a validation of their position. The Church appeared to have said that artificial nutrition and hydration for those in a persistent vegetative state was morally required.[65]

The problem with this position is that it fails to address the accompanying commentary to the short answer given in the above document. The following excerpt complexifies Rome's response:

When stating that the administration of food and water is morally obligatory *in principle*, the Congregation for the Doctrine of the Faith does not exclude the possibility that, in very remote places or in situations of extreme poverty, the artificial provision of food and water may be physically impossible, and then *ad impossibilia nemo tenetur*. However, the obligation to offer the minimal treatments that are available remains in place, as well as that of obtaining, if possible, the means necessary for an adequate support of life. Nor is the possibility excluded that, due to emerging complications, a patient may be unable to assimilate food and liquids, so that their provision becomes altogether useless. Finally, the possibility is not absolutely excluded that, in some rare cases, artificial nourishment and hydration may be excessively burdensome for the patient or may cause significant physical discomfort, for example resulting from complications in the use of the means employed.[66]

Upon further review, it is not clear what Rome said that is significantly new or different from the tradition of ordinary and extraordinary means. Except in rare cases, nutrition and hydration always benefits a human person. Especially in light of some very public claims that Terri was no longer a person who could benefit from tube-feeding and hydration, Church leaders wanted to drive home their argument about moral status and personhood in the wake of her tragic case. But the Church also claims that the real benefit of this treatment – which may be more substantial than previously thought, given that such patients may indeed be conscious – must be weighed against possible burdens: scarce resources (when the money or equipment isn't available), situations of significant physical discomfort, or other unnamed

[65] The social reality of what was going on here was far more complex, however. Terri Schiavo's case became a battleground for a proxy war over abortion policy. These pro-lifers saw themselves as fighting the culture of death here and thus furiously fought for Terri to be sustained. While it is admirable and important to defend her status as a person, whether or not she should have remained tube-fed and hydrated invokes a different set of complex questions which should be distinguished from the abortion debate.

[66] Congregation for the Doctrine of the Faith, "Commentary" (Vatican: The Holy See) www.vatican.va/roman_curia/congregations/cfaith/documents/rc_con_cfaith_doc_20070801_nota-commento_en.html (Accessed December 3, 2009).

burdens.[67] So let us be absolutely clear: the Church claims, along with Singer, that it may be licit to remove patient B's feeding tube.

Patient C: terminal pancreatic cancer

As it stands right now, there is no 'treatment' to forego which would lead us to reason in ways similar to the first two cases. For Singer, this is no problem at all. If a person "wants to die, and death would come more swiftly and with less suffering if brought about by an act (for example, giving a lethal injection) than by an omission," then it is morally acceptable to kill her.[68] Singer, therefore, would want to justify the euthanasia of patient C, perhaps by giving her a lethal dose of morphine or other pain medication.

Obviously, the Church would not permit this. Intending or aiming to kill an innocent person, even at their own request, is always going to be wrong. But notice what the Church could and does permit. One could give patient C a very high dose of pain medication to control her incredible pain, while foreseeing but not intending that this will speed her death. Pope John Paul II claims that this may be acceptable as long as "death is not willed or sought" and the goal "is simply a desire to ease pain effectively by using the analgesics which medicine provides."[69] Remarkably, even here both Singer and the Church permit what is practically (if not intentionally) the same act: giving patient C a high dose of pain medication which will hasten the patient's death. Singer permits the intention to kill patient C, while the Church would insist that one intends *to kill the pain* while foreseeing but not intending that patient C will die.

---

[67] The Vatican allows for other burdens, implicit in the treatment, which go beyond physical discomfort – though it is difficult to think of examples. Joseph Boyle points out that "pain, suffering and interference with the pursuit of valued activities which often provide reasons for discontinuing treatment are not possible for a patient in PVS." Joseph Boyle, "A Case for Sometimes Tube-Feeding Patients in Persistent Vegetative State," in John Keown (ed.), *Euthanasia Examined* (Cambridge University Press, 1995). Nor is it very expensive to provide a feeding tube in most developed societies. Though it goes beyond the scope of this chapter to make a full argument in this regard, let me suggest that the 'repugnance' of a treatment is a burden that can be licitly factored into the Roman Catholic ordinary/extraordinary distinction; if this were mentioned in the patient's advanced directive, or if it were communicated to a family member or other person, it might lead one to the conclusion that the feeding tube is, in fact, extraordinary treatment and should be withdrawn.

[68] Singer, *Rethinking Life and Death*, 196.

[69] Pope John Paul II, "*Evangelium Vitae*," 65. Some think that double effect is just something like Singer's utilitarianism masquerading as something else. And, indeed, there does appear to be a consequentialist judgment being made here. Look for an in-depth discussion of this issue in Chapter 5.

Acts and omissions

But we are not finished with the Singer/Church overlap even now. For what looks like a criticism of the Church's position actually focuses attention on yet another area of overlap: the distinction between acts and omissions.[70] Singer asks us to consider a patient who will die if she does not receive a rather simple antibiotic along with the possibility of her being injected with a lethal overdose of pain medication. He then asks if it is

> reasonable to hold that the doctor who gives the injection is a murderer who deserves to go to jail, whereas the doctor who decides not to administer antibiotics is practicing good and compassionate medicine? That may be what the courts of law would say, but surely it is an untenable distinction. In both cases, the outcome is the death of the patient. In both cases, the doctor knows that this will be the result and decides what she will do on the basis of this knowledge, because she judges this result to be better than the alternative. In both cases, the doctor must take responsibility for her decision – it would not be correct for the doctor who decided not to provide antibiotics to say that she was not responsible for that patient's death because she did nothing. Doing nothing in this situation is itself a deliberate choice, and one cannot escape responsibility for its consequences.[71]

Singer thinks that most advocates of the distinction simply claim there is a "rule against killing innocent human beings and none against allowing them to die." But as a utilitarian he will, of course, argue that "there is no *intrinsic* moral difference between killing and allowing to die."[72]

While Singer is no doubt correct that some people will reason this way, the Church argues that one is morally responsible for *both* actions and omissions. Indeed, Pope John Paul II claims that euthanasia "*in the strict sense* is understood to be an action or omission which of itself and by intention causes death."[73] So while the Church would agree with Singer that one is morally responsible for one's omissions and also that there is no intrinsic difference between killing and allowing to die, there may be an *extrinsic* difference: the intention of the agent. Allowing to die is euthanasia (and therefore intrinsically evil) only if one intends to cause death. If the physician refuses to give antibiotics to the woman Singer mentions because he wanted to bring about her death, then this omission

---

[70] The overlap on acts and omissions can be seen perhaps even more clearly when we compare Singer and Catholic Social Teaching on duties to aid the poor. Both will claim, for instance, that one is guilty of something like 'reckless homicide' by greedily refusing to assist the desperately poor.

[71] Singer, *Practical Ethics*, 182.   [72] *Ibid.*, 183.

[73] Pope John Paul II, "*Evangelium Vitae*," 65.

would indeed be an intrinsically evil act of euthanasia, according to the Church. But if it were instead determined that the treatment was too burdensome, then the refusal to give the medicine would have the aim of refraining from giving burdensome treatment, while foreseeing *but not intending* the death of her patient. It would not be euthanasia.

But Singer is not satisfied with this explanation:

> But the distinction between directly intended effect and side effect is a contrived one . . . We cannot avoid responsibility simply by directing our intention to one effect rather than another. If we foresee both effects, we must take responsibility for the foreseen effects of what we do . . . For example, a chemical company might want to get rid of toxic waste in the most economical manner, by dumping it in the nearest river. Would we allow the executives of the company to say that all they directly intended was to improve the efficiency of the factory, thus promoting employment and keeping down the cost of living? Would we regard the pollution as excusable because it is merely an unwanted side effect of the furthering of these worthy objectives?[74]

The answer, of course, is probably not. But the Church need not come to this conclusion – for the company appears to have failed to give a *proportionate reason* for allowing its foreseen but unintended consequence. Though the company has not formed the intention to pollute the water, they nevertheless have likely done something seriously wrong. Singer's response to this move is to claim that consequentialist reasoning lurks here, but this doesn't appear to be an important criticism of the Church's view. First, the reasoning doesn't "lurk" because the Church is quite clear that proportionate reasoning is going on once it is apparent that no rule is being violated.[75] Second, it just isn't the case that anyone who uses consequentialist reasoning at any time is therefore a consequentialist and logically forced to abandon rules like those that prohibit intentional euthanasia.[76] When applying proportionate reasoning back to the case of refusing to give antibiotics to the woman, he claims that the reason one might take the Church's position here "can only be because we have judged that the patient's prospects for a future life of acceptable quality are so poor that in this case relieving suffering can take precedence."[77]

---

[74] Singer, *Practical Ethics,* 184.

[75] However, one must grant Singer that the Church is less than clear about how central consequentialist reasoning is to its moral theory. This topic will be explored in considerable detail in Chapter 5.

[76] Indeed, Singer's use of rules in *his own* ethic doesn't force him to abandon his consequentialism. Most ethics (whether acknowledged or not) have a mixture of rule-centered and consequences-centered considerations.

[77] Singer, *Practical Ethics,* 184.

But this is simply false. Indeed, if one did determine that one's life was no longer worth living, then the Church's teaching is that one was in fact aiming at death by omission of the antibiotics. Such a person intended to kill by omission and engaged in an act of euthanasia. But, again, this need not be the intention behind the omission. Perhaps it was likely going to cause a painful allergic reaction, it was not likely to help the infection anyway, and it wouldn't have added that many weeks to her life even if it did work. If the woman makes a decision to forego such treatment, it could very well not be a choice to die. It might instead be a choice about how to live.

FROM MORALITY TO PUBLIC POLICY

But what about an act which both Singer and Church agree constitutes aiming at death? Leaving aside the *theoretical* argument to justify euthanasia (it is a difficult one to refute[78]), instituting it *as a public policy*, as we know from the previous chapter on abortion, is a very different kind of question. There are almost always unintended consequences that sometimes are even at odds with values behind the law itself. An ethic which attempts to develop virtues as a bulwark against the flawed, sinful nature of human beings, as a Christian ethic does, will be especially concerned about the unintended consequences of euthanasia's legalization. Even a cursory glance at history reveals that human beings push boundaries and hijack many different kinds of practices for their own self-centered and destructive purposes, and there is no reason to think that the case of euthanasia would be the exception to this rule. Furthermore, we live in a world dominated by the sinful social structures of consumerism and hyper-autonomy. Can we really add the gas of a public policy which permits and even promotes aiming at death (by providers of healthcare) onto that roaring fire?

---

[78] An example I often use with my medical ethics students when we begin to study euthanasia is from the movie *The Last of the Mohicans* starring Daniel Day Lewis. In the scene, Lewis' character is faced with a horrible situation: a man who had just courageously volunteered to be sacrificed in order to save his love interest is about to be burnt alive at the stake. He is standing a few dozen yards away in the forest, undetected, as his friend is being tied up. Having no chance of defeating the dozens of people witnessing the horrific execution, does he simply stand by and watch this man burn to death in excruciating pain, or does he take out his rifle and put him out of his misery? To the frustration of his friend's captors, Lewis' character shoots just as the screams of agony begin. For many, it is difficult to explain how this is intrinsically evil, but the Church would have to claim that any time one reduces the value of another's life and dignity to a mere object – as a mere means to an end – this is always going to be wrong. My focus in this chapter bypasses this theoretical question and instead focuses on practical questions of public policy.

In my attempt to show that we should not, I will lean heavily on Nigel Biggar, who, while not an ideological opponent of euthanasia, ends up challenging the policy via a slippery-slope argument. He begins by citing Peter Haas' claims about how the Nazis ended up where they did:

Instead of seeing the Holocaust as the result of the mysterious interruption of evil, Haas reads it as the fruit of a gradual change of ethical sensibility in Germany to the point where many people considered it morally *right* to exterminate certain groups of human beings, because they were deemed evil or worthless or socially burdensome.

He then goes on to quote the argument of Leo Alexander during the Nuremburg Trial:

Whatever proportion these [Nazi] crimes finally assumed, it became evident to all who investigated that they had started from small beginnings. The beginnings at first were merely a subtle shift in emphasis in the basic attitude of physicians. It started with the acceptance of the attitude, basic in the euthanasia movement, that there is such a thing as life not worthy to be lived.[79]

The dangers of the Nazi quest for racial health might have lessons for possible dangers in a quest for public health.

But hasn't the West already learned such lessons? Didn't the Nuremburg trials and the resulting code of ethics send us on a path toward respecting patient autonomy such that we are protected from such horrible things ever happening again? Indeed, Bruce Jennings claims that no single concept has been more important in the contemporary development of bioethics than the concept of autonomy, and none better reflects both the philosophical and political currents shaping the field.[80] Perhaps we have little to fear after all. Such radical respect for patient autonomy means we probably needn't worry about sliding down a slippery slope – to say nothing of alarmist invocations of Nazi Germany.

But this would be too quick. Jennings also shows that the West's energetic move toward autonomy is currently facing a backlash, and even when we do prioritize autonomy the practical and clinical reality often bears little resemblance to the abstract principle.[81] As Leon Kass soberly points out:

---

[79] Nigel Biggar, *Aiming to Kill: The Ethics of Suicide and Euthanasia* (Cleveland, OH: Pilgrim Press, 2004), 220, 158–159.

[80] Bonnie Steinbock, *The Oxford Handbook of Bioethics* (Oxford; New York: Oxford University Press, 2007), 747, 72.

[81] *Ibid.*, 76.

Truth to tell, the ideal of rational autonomy, so beloved of bioethicists and legal theorists, rarely obtains in actual medical practice. Illness invariably means dependence, and dependence means relying for advice on physician and family. This is especially true of those who are seriously or terminally ill, where there is frequently also depression or diminished mental capacity that clouds one's judgment or weakens one's resolve. With patients thus reduced – helpless in action and ambivalent about life – someone who might benefit from their death need not proceed by overt coercion.[82]

And often such dependence, even if it doesn't involve will-shattering depression or another similar malady, leads to a different kind of strain on autonomous choice. We have created a culture which worships youth, vigor, and production of capital; and rather than taking care of our aging family members in the mainstream of our communities, it is now simply expected that we will push older persons to the margins where we will not have to encounter them. The logical end of such a culture is that these older persons (often desperately lonely and depressed) will likely fail to see their own value and come to believe that they are a 'burden' on their family and community. In light of the values inherent to this culture, it is understandable why so many bioethicists believe that 'a right to die implies a duty to die.' John Hardwig, head of the department of philosophy at the University of Tennessee, makes the following remarkable claim:

The lives of our loved ones can be seriously compromised by caring for us. The burdens of providing care or even just supervision twenty-four hours a day, seven days a week are often overwhelming. When this kind of caregiving goes on for years, it leaves the caregiver exhausted, with no time for herself or life of her own. Ultimately, even her health is often destroyed. But it can also be emotionally devastating simply to live with a spouse who is increasingly distant, uncommunicative, unresponsive, foreign, and unreachable. Other family members' needs often go unmet as the caring capacity of the family is exceeded. Social life and friendships evaporate, as there is no opportunity to go out to see friends and the home is no longer a place suitable for having friends in.

We must also acknowledge that the lives of our loved ones can be devastated just by having to pay for healthcare for us. One part of the recent SUPPORT study documented the financial aspects of caring for a dying member of a family. Only those who had illnesses severe enough to give them less than a 50 percent chance to live six more months were included in this study. When these patients survived their initial hospitalization and were discharged, about 1/3 required considerable

---

[82] Kathleen M. Foley and Herbert Hendin, *The Case Against Assisted Suicide* (Baltimore, MD: Johns Hopkins University Press, 2002), 371, 24.

caregiving from their families, in 20 percent of cases a family member had to quit work or make some other major lifestyle change, almost 1/3 of these families lost all of their savings, and just under 30 percent lost a major source of income.[83]

For Hardwig, the duty to die becomes greater as we grow older, as our loved ones put more and more resources into our lives, and when "the part of you that is loved will soon be gone or seriously compromised."[84] That a respected philosopher can make such arguments and publish them in one of the most influential bioethics journals in the world means that we cannot dismiss them out of hand. Suppose that Hardwig's view was adopted by a patient nearing the end of her life – could we really say that her 'choice' to die would be truly autonomous and free? No, her choice would in fact be dramatically affected, if not coerced, by a number of underlying social factors including a perceived duty to die and get out of the way of her family and the broader society.

The test-case of the Netherlands

Euthanasia has been legal in the Netherlands since 1984, and though we would need many more generations to make anything approaching a final judgment, we at least have some data to use as a test-case for examining whether slippery-slope concerns are justified. Biggar, relying in part on the intense and well-respected study of the Dutch situation by John Keown, mentions that one of the fundamental problems with this or any other public policy on euthanasia is the elasticity of the concepts used in articulating it. For instance, as a safeguard against slippage down the slope, Dutch law prohibits euthanasia except in the case of 'unbearable suffering.' But

one leading Dutch practitioner – Dr Herbert Cohen – interviewed by Keown in 1989 seemed to think that [the unbearable suffering standard] could apply to a hypothetical case where an old man requests voluntary euthanasia because he feels a nuisance to relatives who want him dead so that they can get their hands on his estate. Further, in 1994 the Supreme Court ruled in the actual case of Dr. Chabot that [the unbearable suffering standard] applied to the persistent grief of a 50-year-old woman at the death of her two sons. And in 2000, a court in Haarlem implied in the case of Dr. Sutorius that a patient who wanted to die not because of any serious physical or mental illness, but because he felt his life to be "pointless and empty," could be considered subject to 'unbearable suffering.'

---

[83] John Hardwig, "Is there a Duty to Die?" *Hastings Center Report* 27:2 (1997), 36.
[84] *Ibid.*, 38–39.

Another important safeguard requires that there must be an explicit request of the patient, but Biggar cites a 1990 study which found that an astounding 30 percent of patient killings (1,000 times in 3,300 total cases) were done without such consent. Most of these patients killed were ruled non-competent (like those in a persistent vegetative state, for instance), and Keown notes that interviews with physicians established that 14 percent of the patients were totally competent and a further 11 percent partly competent. In addition, the reasons given for the killing involved

the absence of any prospect of improvement (60%); the futility of all medical therapy (39%); avoidance of 'needless prolongation' (33%); the relatives' inability to cope (32%) and 'low quality of life' (31%). Pain or suffering was mentioned by only 30%.[85]

These are striking figures. And they seem to indicate that the worry about a slippery slope sliding down to very bad things with the legalization of euthanasia is legitimate.

Defending legalized euthanasia as a public policy

In responding to those who disagree with him on euthanasia, Peter Singer acknowledges that the most powerful objection to his position is that "once we begin to allow some people to kill others, we will find ourselves sliding down a slippery slope that leads to killings of a kind that no one wants."[86] But after noting that the 1990 report gives no evidence of *involuntary* euthanasia (killing that is against the expressed will of the patient), and claiming that this "may soften our attitude to the fact that there were 1,000 cases in which doctors actively ended the patient's life without the patient's explicit consent," Singer challenges interpreters to find evidence that non-voluntary euthanasia was being practiced *to an increasing degree*. The Dutch figures cannot possibly show an 'increasing practice' of anything, because to show that we would need figures from two or more different years, preferably separated by a substantial gap.[87] Singer also points out that

critics invariably focus on the 1,000 cases in which doctors gave drugs with the intention of ending life without the patient's explicit consent. They do not mention the much larger number of cases in which doctors withdrew or withheld

---

[85] The survey reveals that a majority of doctors either had killed without request or were prepared to do so. Biggar, *Aiming to Kill*, 128–129.

[86] Singer, *Rethinking Life and Death*, 256, 150.   [87] *Ibid.*, 153.

treatment that could have prolonged life, again without the patient's explicit consent ... If we don't want doctors to hasten the deaths of their patients without an explicit request, why are we not as concerned about this when it happens as a result of withdrawing treatment as when it results from an injection?[88]

But while these arguments were perhaps convincing at the time he made them, they are now out of date.[89] Both Keown and Biggar, agreeing with Singer and the Church, understand that euthanasia can be an act or omission. And both point out that there were indeed "4,000 further cases [where] treatment was withdrawn or withheld, 'with the explicit purpose of shortening life.'" This means that "in more than 60 percent of the total of 9,050 cases where it was the doctor's primary purpose to hasten death by an act or omission, there was no explicit request made by the patient."[90] So Keown, Biggar and the Roman Catholic Church, at least, are all quite concerned with 'aiming at death' – perhaps especially in cases without the consent of the individual killed – whether it is by act or by omission.

Singer is on stronger ground when he says that one study on only one year's data cannot prove a slippery slope. A similar study done a few years later did not show a significant increase in non-voluntary euthanasia, but rather showed a decrease by 100 such cases. In addition, the reasons why physicians put their patients to death without consent, and the relative competency of such patients, had similar numbers.[91] And the most recent study shows an even sharper decrease: 'only' 550 patients were killed by their physicians without consent.[92] What we can conclude from these numbers, however, must be seen in light of the reliability of the data. In 2005, for instance, "80.2% of all cases of euthanasia or assisted suicide were reported. Physicians were most likely to report their end-of-life practices if they considered them to be an act of euthanasia or assisted suicide, which was rarely true when opioids were used."[93] Furthermore, based on the facts that were gathered, we learned that Dutch physicians do not do a very good job of following the guidelines against non-voluntary euthanasia:

---

[88] *Ibid.*, 155–156.

[89] It was 1996 when Singer wrote *Rethinking Life and Death*. See below for his latest thought on the slippery slope.

[90] Biggar, *Aiming to Kill*, 127–128.   [91] *Ibid.*, 131.

[92] Agnes van der Heide, *et al.*, "End-of-Life Practices in the Netherlands under the Euthanasia Act," *New England Journal of Medicine* 356:19 (May 10, 2007).

[93] *Ibid.*

With the publication of the first Van der Maas survey in 1991 it became clear that the so-called "strict safeguards" laid down in 1984 by the courts and the Royal Dutch Medical Association had largely failed. The survey cast doubt on central assurances which had been given by the advocates of voluntary euthanasia: that euthanasia would be performed only at the patient's explicit request and that doctors terminating life without request would be prosecuted for murder; that euthanasia would be used only in cases of "last resort" and not as an alternative to palliative care; and that cases would be openly reported and duly scrutinised. The Dutch reaction to the survey's findings was also revealing: the cases of nonvoluntary euthanasia it disclosed, far from being criticised, were largely condoned. In short, the survey indicated that, in less than a decade, the Dutch had slid down the slippery slope.[94]

While Biggar admits there is no reason in principle why regulations surrounding patient consent and what counts as unbearable suffering couldn't actually be enforced, the Dutch test-case, coupled with an honest acknowledgement about the reality of our culture and of human nature, gives him several good reasons for being skeptical that sufficiently tight restrictions could ever be imposed in practice in the Netherlands or anywhere in the West. After all, there is

the difficulty of ever achieving democratic consensus on where to draw the line with the consequence that it is drawn liberally; the predominant position of the value of individual autonomy in cultural common sense; and the influence of an expanded interpretation of the vocation of medicine that raises its sights beyond the mere promotion of physical health to the Promethean, utilitarian ambition of eliminating human unhappiness.

And Biggar points out that it would take "the taming and retraining of some of the most powerful cultural prejudices" to feel reasonably comfortable that such regulations could be formulated and enforced.[95]

Perhaps because so many who have the concerns above invoke Nazi Germany, Singer's most recent defense against slippery-slope arguments focuses on consent and non-voluntary euthanasia. In his updated version of *Practical Ethics*, after noting that the slippery-slope objection to euthanasia looms so large it merits a section to itself, for some reason he responds to claims that we will slide "all the way down into the abyss of state terror and mass murder."[96] But does the slippery slope need to be that dramatic in order to push against legalizing euthanasia? Consider this

[94] Henk Jochemsen and John Keown, "Voluntary Euthanasia Under Control? More Empirical Evidence from the Netherlands," *Journal of Medical Ethics* 1999; 25:16–21.
[95] Biggar, *Aiming to Kill*, 151.   [96] Singer, *Practical Ethics*, 186–190.

recent story coming out of the Netherlands, which supports Biggar's prediction about the role individual autonomy plays in a slippery slope:

A group of older Dutch academics and politicians have launched a petition in support of assisted suicide for the over-70s. They hope to attract over 40,000 signatures, enough to get the issue debated in parliament under citizens' initiative legislation. Under Dutch law, euthanasia can only be practised if the patient is suffering 'unbearable pain'. The doctor must be convinced the patient is making an informed choice and a second doctor must also give his or her opinion. But the new lobby group says people aged over 70 who are *tired of life* [emphasis added] should also have the right to professional help in ending it.[97]

It is something close to diabolical that, after creating a culture of which older persons do not feel a part and in which they do not feel welcome, a society would respond to the problem by creating a method by which older persons could kill themselves more easily. But the push for 'choice' in dying in the Netherlands is so strong that the Dutch Voluntary Euthanasia Society is planning to open an eight-person clinic in 2012 where people can go to end their lives free of even the modest regulations that the Dutch Medical Association requires. It estimates that about 1,000 people a year would take advantage of its facilities and it would cater to people whose doctors have refused to euthanize them.[98] Ironically, it is a hyper-focus on autonomy which is *facilitating* a slide down precisely the kind of slippery slope such a focus was supposed to avoid. It turns out that in a consumerist, youth-worshipping culture, giving older persons the choice to kill themselves makes them anything but free.

Nor are slippery-slope worries limited to this single country. Europe has grown increasingly divided about end-of-life practices, and an organization in Switzerland called *Dignitas* has stepped up to fill the void for those who live in countries where euthanasia is still unavailable. Indeed, *Dignitas* will accept travelers from all over the world who wish to come to Switzerland to have their lives ended. Another problem arises, however, when an organization like this makes a good deal of money on vulnerable, often depressed people who are convinced that their lives are no longer worth living:

[97] "Tired of life? Group calls for assisted suicide," Dutch News, www.dutchnews.nl/news/archives/2010/02/tired_of_life_group_calls_for.php (Accessed May 9, 2010).
[98] "Dutch activists planning euthanasia clinic," Free Republic, www.freerepublic.com/focus/f-news/2665426/posts (Accessed June 30, 2011).

First, you need to become a member of Dignitas; anyone can join if they pay an annual fee of 80 Swiss francs (£47). When you are ready to die, you need to send in copies of your medical records, a letter explaining why things have become intolerable and £1,860 ... Once they arrive in Zurich, the individual must pay £620 for two appointments with the doctor (to check their records and prescribe the drugs) and a further £1,860 to pay for two Dignitas staff members to organise and witness the death.[99]

One could also consider a disturbing trend in Belgium. Euthanasia was legalized there in 2002, and it took only six years for them to combine killing patients with procuring their organs for transplant. They have made efforts to separate the two requests, and are supposed to suggest organ donation only after the request for euthanasia has been made, but the practice is becoming widely and popularly known outside of the local context. Indeed, Belgian physicians are now going around Europe doing PowerPoint presentations demonstrating just how many quality organs they are procuring this way. But as Wesley Smith points out:

[C]oupling organ harvesting with mercy killing creates a strong emotional inducement to suicide, particularly for people who are culturally devalued and depressed and, indeed, who might worry that they are a burden on loved ones and society. People in such an anguished mental state could easily come to believe (or be persuaded) that asking for euthanasia and organ donation would give a meaning to their deaths that their lives could never have.[100]

Donating one's organs after euthanasia could be one last nod to a consumerist culture which demands we show production value in order to demonstrate our worth. What's more, Smith notes that this practice gives Belgian society an explicit stake in the deaths of people with seriously disabling or terminal conditions. And if we consider that these people are often the most expensive for whom to care, especially in light of the acute medical resource shortages we face, there is the potential for a perfect storm of considerations which, once again, show that the supposed 'free choice' to kill oneself is actually manipulated by a host of social factors operating beneath the surface of so-called patient autonomy.

99 Amelia Gentleman, "Inside the Dignitas House," *The Guardian*, www.guardian.co.uk/society/ 2009/nov/18/assisted-suicide-dignitas-house (Accessed June 28, 2011).
100 Wesley J. Smith, "At the Bottom of the Slippery Slope," *The Weekly Standard*, www.weeklystandard. com/articles/bottom-slippery-slope_575552.html (Accessed June 28, 2011).

Assisted suicide in Oregon

As Europeans try to figure out their end-of-life practices, some attention has come to the American state of Oregon and its legalization of assisted suicide. Though it does not have the Netherlands' history to examine, this state nevertheless gives us ample reason to continue to worry about a public policy that sanctions euthanasia. Although Oregon's law was billed as a "laboratory to the states" which could serve as our own test-case here in America, it has become anything but this. Sherwin Nuland, himself a proponent of euthanasia, has absolutely hammered Oregon for its lack of transparency:

Invoking patient confidentiality, the Oregon Health Department (OHD) does not ask doctors or families for much information about the cases of assisted suicide that are carried out under its jurisdiction. The information that it does possess, which is in the main epidemiological, is not available for inspection by the public, nor is there any provision for independent researchers to study it. Under present circumstances, the Oregon experience cannot be evaluated as would any other innovation in medical practice, with full disclosure and all participants and data made available for review by experts. In fact, a physician with cause to refuse a request for assisted suicide by a patient who later found a willing doctor is legally forbidden to talk about his or her reasons, in the misappropriated name of confidentiality.[101]

Furthermore, as N. Gregory Hamilton points out, the Oregon law actually forbids medical organizations and individual providers from censuring physicians for not following what few ethical safeguards exist. Here is how the law is worded:

No professional organization or association, or healthcare provider, may subject a person to censure, discipline, suspension, loss of license, loss of privileges, loss of membership or other penalty for participating or refusing to participate in good faith compliance with ORS 127.8000 to 127.8897.

Hamilton concludes that because "the profession of medicine itself would limit, control, and make practically nonexistent assisted suicide," this legally mandated silence "is the only basis on which legalized suicide and euthanasia continue." Kathleen Foley and Herbert Hendin also point out the unacceptable conflict of interest present when "those administering the law and those sanctioned by the government to analyze its operation have become its advocates and defenders."[102]

[101] Sherwin B. Nuland, "The Principle of Hope," *Human Life Review* (July 1, 2002).
[102] Foley, *et al.*, *The Case Against Assisted Suicide*, 173, 190–191.

But even what we manage to find out is going on in Oregon is disconcerting. Nuland points out several things that are missing from the legislation: a mandatory requirement for consultation by an expert in palliative care, a mandatory psychiatric consultation (the law requires it only when the attending physician thinks judgment is impaired), and a mandatory notification of next of kin. He then focuses on the second omission and the high numbers of persons seeking assisted suicide who are mentally ill:

Only 6 percent of those surveyed in Oregon felt very confident, absent a long-term relationship, that they could in a single visit determine whether a patient was competent to make a decision about suicide. And yet the law permits just that … This means that large numbers of people are being assisted to their deaths without anyone even attempting to find out whether the underlying reason for their suffering is a treatable depression.

And even if a patient is refused a deadly prescription by one physician, he may simply cycle through several physicians until he gets the answer he's looking for. And, remarkably, if other physicians wanted to call out a rogue colleague who gave him the drugs for not following the law in good faith, it is against the law for them to do so.

Given that the Netherlands struggles to get its legal mandates followed, it is prudent to see if Oregon is doing any better. According to a report by the International Task Force on Euthanasia and Assisted Suicide,

while patients are supposed to have just six months to live, a number of individuals who have been granted the prescriptions but who have subsequently decided not to end their lives go on to live longer. "The time between writing the assisted suicide prescription and death ranged from zero to 698 days," says the report. "Thus, some patients lived for almost two years after receiving the lethal drugs – well beyond the required six months' life expectancy."[103]

But even if one ignored the fact that it is virtually impossible to ensure these kinds of accurate predictions, given what we learned above, and given that the primary value in medicine (and in our broader culture) remains patient choice and autonomy, there is little reason to expect that even the formal limit will stay at six months. Indeed, if it is 'my body' and 'my choice,' how could Oregon limit the practice at all? Who is the government to tell me what I can or can't do with my body and

---

[103] Tom Rawstorne, "The chilling truth about the city where they pay people to die," *Daily Mail*, www.dailymail.co.uk/debate/article-1205138/The-chilling-truth-city-pay-people-die.html (Accessed January 24, 2010).

my life? Biggar's point about how autonomy functions in our Western culture once again looms large.

Assisted suicide has spread from Oregon to Washington and Montana. It is being considered in several other US states and countries like the UK, Canada, and Australia. But when euthanasia is legalized in cultures where the values of autonomy and consumerism rule the day, we have seen that (despite the practice only being around for at most a generation or two) we already end up with the kinds of deaths that almost no one wants. And in a related story, we are ending up with a *culture* that almost no one wants – one which pushes vulnerable older persons, not only to the margins of society, but *even to die* in order to make space for the young, vigorous, and productive. That trend, so long as autonomy and consumerism dominate the West, will do nothing but continue. In light of these considerations, I believe that Singer's attempts to defend against the slippery slope fail.[104]

Killing the pain, not the patient

Despite the fact that the unintended consequences of legalized euthanasia make its institution a bad idea, we should not forget that many who support its legalization do so out of an admirable compassion for those who are suffering. Is there any way to take this virtuous impulse and direct it down a better path? Happily, the answer is yes. We have seen above that the principle of double effect allows us to aim at killing the pain without aiming at the death of the patient. Countries that have forbidden euthanasia, while nevertheless feeling a deep, compassionate desire to reach out to suffering patients, have been forced to come up with solutions which focus on killing pain. And the things that have been and are being done with hospice and palliative care in these countries are absolutely astounding. As Nuland points out, in all but "a very few cases" the modern wonders of palliative care will eliminate the reasons for which pain-centered euthanasia requests are made.

But what of places like the Netherlands where they are not forced to come up with such alternatives? According to Zbigniew Zylicz, a fellow of palliative care in the Netherlands and the University of Nijmegen,

---

[104] It might be worth pointing out that Singer's mentor at Oxford, the Christian utilitarian R.M. Hare, appears to have accepted the slippery-slope argument. While he took the position that euthanasia might be morally defensible in theory, he claimed that "it should not be legalized." R.M. Hare, "A Philosophical Autobiography," *Utilitas* 14(3) (November 2002), 295.

"Palliative and hospice care in the Netherlands were neglected for many decades ... [and] discussion about the need for hospices and specialized units for palliative care emerged only recently." Those that are in existence usually have "a religious affiliation and did not accept euthanasia or assisted suicide as a normal medical practice."[105] In striking contrast to many countries where palliative medicine has developed rapidly, in the Netherlands "the benefits of this knowledge are not available." And this is not just because the Dutch have not been doing the requisite research,[106] but the problem is also institutional:

The caseload in general practice and in nursing home medicine is very high. Instead of the anticipatory, proactive, and preventive medicine that is the key to palliative care, [young physicians] are forced to react to critical situations that could have been avoided. This means that, at the end of the day, knowledge that should be available is not and problems that are soluble appear not to be so. If you add to this patients' freedom of choice and the easy option of euthanasia, the choice is often quick and inevitable.[107]

And this is starting to happen in the United States as well. Foley and Hendin point out that the physicians who can prescribe deadly drugs in Oregon are not required to be knowledgeable about pain management, and "without such knowledge the physician cannot present feasible alternatives." In this kind of situation, "offering a patient palliative care becomes a legal regulation to be met, rather than an integral effort to relieve the patient's suffering so that a hastened death does not seem like the only alternative."[108] Not surprisingly, this has produced problematic results. For "eighteen of the twenty-nine patients who by that time had been given prescriptions for lethal medications and nine of the seventeen who had died from taking the prescribed medication, there was no palliative care intervention of any kind."[109]

In thinking about the public policy concerns presented in this section of the chapter, we would do well to heed the words of Nigel Biggar:

Therefore our ordinary duty – the duty that respect for the exceptional value of individual human life entails – is to help each other endure. Such a duty will involve precisely *not* taking at face value 'autonomous' requests to be killed or

---

[105] Foley, *et al., The Case Against Assisted Suicide,* 124
[106] Indeed, Dutch medicine is otherwise at the top of the line. In researching their neonatal intensive care units for another project, I found their technological progress to be excellent –with the notable exception of palliative care. That there exists a protocol for euthanasia of newborns in the Netherlands cannot be an unrelated fact.
[107] *Ibid.,* 142–143.   [108] *Ibid.,* 145–146.   [109] *Ibid.,* 154.

aided in suicide, and yielding to them. In most cases, what the patient really wants is not death at all, but rather that excessively burdensome life-prolonging treatment ceases, that pain or other discomfort be controlled through palliative care, and that those around him affirm his continuing value.[110]

To a very serious extent, instituting legalized euthanasia (especially given the availability of viable alternatives like palliative care and hospice) does not send the message that a patient's life has value. It is not true *compassion*, which literally means 'suffering with.' Indeed, it is difficult, if not impossible, to suffer with someone without affirming the goodness of their existence.

CONCLUSION

As we will see with the primary topic of every chapter in this book, the overlap between Singer and the Church with regard to euthanasia and decision-making at the end of life is considerable. Much of the debate surrounds moral status questions, and we have already seen how much they have in common on this topic in Chapter 1. But we also find that the Church and Singer share skepticism about using brain death as a criterion to determine whether or not a human organism has died. We find that both refuse to make a hard and fast distinction between acts and omissions in many aspects of end-of-life care and treatment, with both acknowledging that one may be held morally responsible for others' deaths whether he actively kills them or refuses to act to benefit them. Singer and the Church also agree that one may be morally justified at various times in removing life-sustaining treatment and that 'consequence-centered' or proportionate reasoning can be used to determine whether such removal is justified. Finally, we learned that both Singer and the Church, despite disagreeing on the moral reasoning behind doing so, are at times willing to accept giving a patient a large dose of pain medication that will dramatically speed her death.

There are important disagreements as well. Singer pushes the Church to think more about the 'intrinsic evil' of aiming at the death of an innocent person, but the Church pushes back in highlighting the serious practical problems with putting in place a euthanasia public policy that prevents slides into various abuses. Especially in light of the vicious habits that are reinforced when one allows anyone, and especially physicians, to

---

[110] Biggar, *Aiming to Kill*, 147.

aim at the death of the vulnerable and needy, one has a legitimate worry that relying on slippery concepts such as 'unbearable suffering' and 'autonomous choice' are not winning strategies for keeping euthanasia policy from degenerating into something most would consider morally repugnant.

But despite these differences, it does seem as if proponents of Singer's position and those who support the Church could come together and support certain important public policies. And not only on the important question of brain death and organ donation, or in pushing for more consistency and precision about acts and omissions which aim at death, but also on end-of-life care which refuses to abandon patients by aiming at their deaths. Singer, as we will see in the next two chapters, is quite suspicious of autonomy and consumerism leading to bad things.[III] Perhaps Singer could also push back against these two values with regard to end-of-life issues and euthanasia by affirming the good of the lives of older and dying patients, by focusing on palliative care and hospice programs, and by hesitating to promote the so-called autonomous choice to die.

[III] Recall that Singer was also suspicious of autonomy in the previous chapter when discussing the right to abortion as coming from a right to privacy.

CHAPTER 3

Non-human animals

The wolf will live with the lamb,
the leopard will lie down with the goat,
the calf and the lion and the yearling together;
and a little child will lead them.

The cow will feed with the bear,
their young will lie down together,
and the lion will eat straw like the ox.

The infant will play near the hole of the cobra,
and the young child put his hand into the viper's nest.

They will neither harm nor destroy
on all my holy mountain,
for the earth will be full of the knowledge of the LORD
as the waters cover the sea.

Isaiah 11:6–9

INTRODUCTION

Peter Singer is perhaps best known for championing the moral status and ethical treatment of non-human animals. Indeed, he might be the person most responsible for bringing such issues to the Western world's attention. Of Singer's contribution, the Christian philosopher Robert Wennberg says:

In 1975, with the publication of Peter Singer's *Animal Liberation*, the cause of animal advocacy took a dramatic turn, as the book, in conjunction with forces already at work, served to radically change the entire arena of moral concern for animals. Here we have the beginnings of the animal rights or animal liberation movement as a pervasive presence on the contemporary scene. Indeed, things have not been the same since.[1]

[1] Robert N. Wennberg, *God, Humans, and Animals: An Invitation to Enlarge Our Moral Universe* (Grand Rapids, MI: William B. Eerdmans Publishing Co., 2003), 358, 6.

As it has gone through its multiple editions, *Animal Liberation* has generally become accepted as the seminal work in the field.[2] And Singer has gone on to write even more in recent years on this topic with *The Way We Eat: Why Our Food Choices Matter*[3] and *In Defense of Animals.*[4] That one person could have this kind of impact on how we think about other animals is simply extraordinary.

As we will see in some detail below, Christianity is Singer's favorite scapegoat for how we got so off-track with animal ethics. In particular he calls out the pro-life community for being a blatantly hypocritical part of the problem. When these people claim that life is sacred, according to Singer, they "almost never mean what they say." Indeed:

> They do not mean, as their words seem to imply, that life itself is sacred. If they did, killing a pig or pulling up a cabbage would be as abhorrent to them as the murder of a human being. When people say that life is sacred, it is human life they have in mind.[5]

Singer thinks that the Christian tradition is radically 'speciesist' in its assertion that members of *Homo sapiens* should have some special moral consideration in virtue of being uniquely created in the image of God. And though they claim to be 'pro-life,' this speciesist attitude ends up being the justification for how terribly or carelessly many of us treat the lives of other animals.

But in this chapter I will build on an argument made in Chapter 1 that the Christian tradition is not speciesist in the way Singer understands the concept and, indeed, is in the process of rediscovering important resources in its tradition on the value of other animals.[6] Furthermore, Wennberg points out that many different Christians have been broadly pro-life with regard to both human and non-human animals. William Wilberforce, evangelical Christian and perhaps the single most powerful force for the abolition of the British slave trade, led the fight to outlaw bull baiting and was a founding member of the Royal Society for the Prevention of Cruelty to Animals (RSPCA). Another evangelical, Anthony Ashley Cooper, the seventh Earl of Shaftesbury, was a tireless campaigner on

---

[2] Peter Singer, *Animal Liberation,* New rev. edn. (New York: Avon Books, 1990), 320.

[3] Peter Singer and Jim Mason, *The Way We Eat: Why Our Food Choices Matter* (Emmaus, PA; New York: Rodale; Distributed to the trade by Holtzbrinck Publishers, 2006), 328.

[4] Peter Singer, *In Defense of Animals: The Second Wave* (Malden, MA: Blackwell Publishing, 2006), 248.

[5] Peter Singer, *Practical Ethics,* 3rd edn. (New York: Cambridge University Press, 2011), 395, 83.

[6] This is not to say, of course, that all or even most Christians avoid speciesism, but simply that it doesn't necessarily follow from the Christian tradition. Quite the contrary, in fact.

behalf of the child factory workers while also serving as vice-president of the RSPCA. Frances Power Cobbe, the 'grande dame of English anti-vivisection,' also spent much of her life educating poor children. Samuel Gridely Howe, Head of the Perkins School for the Blind, was a strong advocate of prison reform, improved treatment and care for the mentally disabled, and promoted the abolition of slavery, as well as serving as director of the Massachusetts Society for the Prevention of Cruelty to Animals. Harriet Beecher Stowe was a leader both in the slavery abolitionist movement, and in sensitizing people to cruelty to other animals.[7] Even the current Pope,[8] known by Singer and many others primarily as a defender of human rights, has been outspoken on the dignity of non-human animals – even to the point where People for the Ethical Treatment of Animals (PETA) is using his likeness and quotes in their advertisements.[9] St. Francis of Assisi had an overwhelming concern for human poverty, but his valorization of all creation and a special love and concern for animals has made him arguably the most beloved saint in the Christian tradition.

The first part of this chapter will focus on Singer's approach to other animals by detailing his critique of factory farming practices, what he thinks undergirds these practices, and his argument for why Christianity is largely to blame. The second part of the chapter will show that not only is Singer mistaken about a Christian ethic being the major problem, but that because of the significant amount of overlap between the two approaches, it is part of the solution. I will continue to show that an authentic Christian ethic is far from speciesist and actually supports many of the conclusions about non-human animals for which Singer argues. Finally, I will explore whether Christians could accept Singer's claim that some non-human animals are persons with a right to life. Despite finding that each approach can helpfully push the other in various ways, the chapter will conclude by showing that adherents of both approaches can and should work together toward changing our relationship with other animals.

SINGER ON HOW WE TREAT NON-HUMAN ANIMALS

Singer begins with the point that for most of us living in developed urban and suburban areas today, the most direct form of contact we have with

---

[7] Wennberg, *God, Humans, and Animals*, 8.
[8] He made most of his comments as Cardinal Ratzinger before he became Pope Benedict XVI.
[9] "Pope Benedict XVI: Save the Earth," People for the Ethical Treatment of Animals (PETA), www.peta.org/b/thepetafiles/archive/2007/09/04/pope-benedict-xvi-save-the-earth.aspx (Accessed February 12, 2010).

other animals is when we eat them. Indeed, we are so disconnected from
the process by which our food gets to our dinner plate that most of the
time we are largely unaware that what we are eating is the flesh of an
animal, not to mention what kind of life that animal was forced to live.
Often the very words we use lead us away from this kind of thinking: we
eat beef, not bull, steer, or cow – and pork, ham, or bacon, but not pig.[10]
And it is likely that many of us would not want to know the story behind
our food. Far from the traditional image of a family-run farm with
animals roaming free, almost all meat production in the developed
world is controlled by large corporations designed to produce animal
flesh for human consumption in the most profitable way possible. They
use 'factory farms' in which non-human animals "are treated like
machines that convert low-priced fodder into high-priced flesh, and
any innovation will be used if it results in a cheaper 'conversion ratio.'"[11]
Though as a former meat-eater myself I found it difficult not to feel
guilty when I first read these words, Singer insists that his goal is not to
condemn factory farmers or those who materially support them. These
practices are just a logical outgrowth of largely unexamined speciesist
and consumerist attitudes that will be detailed later in this chapter. In
the accounts of the practices that follow, Singer uses mainly his own
research into factory farming via sources expected to be most favorable
to the industry: the magazines and trade journals of the factory farmers
themselves.

Treatment of chickens and turkeys

Just sixty years ago, having a bird at the dinner table was relatively rare,
but today over 100 million chickens are slaughtered *each week* in the
United States alone. A particular factory farm will get a load of several
thousand-day-old chicks and simply dump them into a long windowless
shed where they will live the rest of their lives and in which every aspect of
their environment is controlled to "make them grow faster on less feed."[12]
Each bird spends virtually their entire lives in half a square foot of living
space, which, because no attempt is made to remove their feces, is full of
"rotting, dirty, ammonia-charged litter." As a result, these birds often
suffer from ulcerated feet, breast blisters, and hock burns.[13] And in the
interests of economic productivity, chickens and turkeys are now bred to
produce the maximum amount of meat in the minimum amount of time.

[10] Singer, *Animal Liberation*, 95.   [11] *Ibid.*, 97.   [12] *Ibid.*, 99.   [13] *Ibid.*, 105.

Not surprisingly, the rapid growth of fat and muscle is too much for their bone structure to handle and 26 percent have chronic pain as a result of bone disease.[14] Indeed, there are even times where the birds' vertebrae simply snap under the immense pressure. Obviously such birds cannot get to food and water, and because the growers don't bother or have time to check on individual birds, they die of thirst or starvation.[15] Turkeys in particular are bred with breasts so big that they cannot mate naturally and therefore must be artificially inseminated. In a practice that can only be described as disgusting, the males are manually stimulated by a factory farm worker to procure semen while hens are 'broken' so that insemi-nators can insert "a straw of semen connected to the end of a tube from an air compressor" into their bodies.[16]

Though these birds are not naturally attacking or aggressive, their stress level from having to live in such wretched conditions brings out 'vices' like feather-pecking and even cannibalism. Factory farms cannot improve their living conditions without driving up costs (and in turn losing market share and profitability), so they try other solutions to these behavioral problems. One technique used is to keep them in almost total darkness, but a more certain step – simply cutting off their beaks – is the one now being widely used in the industry. When the practice first started in the 1940s it was done with a blowtorch, but we are slightly more humane today when we use

specially designed guillotine-like devices with hot blades [as] the preferred instrument. The infant chick's beak is inserted into the instrument, and the hot blade cuts off the end of it. The procedure is carried out very quickly, about fifteen birds a minute. Such haste means that the temperature and sharpness of the blade can vary widely, resulting in sloppy cutting and serious injury to the bird . . . Even when the operation is done correctly, it is a mistake to think of it as a painless procedure, like cutting toenails.[17]

Indeed, the damage done to this very sensitive tissue is thought to cause such pain that recently debeaked birds eat and weigh significantly less than other birds for several weeks.

Apologists for factory farming "often argue that if the birds or other animals were not happy, they would not thrive and hence would not be profitable."[18] But this is simply not what the industry itself claims in its own publications. Even if the horrible conditions cause up to 6.4 percent of the birds to die, most factory farms can still operate at the optimum

[14] Singer and Mason, *The Way We Eat*, 26.   [15] *Ibid.*, 26.   [16] *Ibid.*, 28.
[17] *Ibid.*, 101.   [18] *Ibid.*, 106.

level of profitability without getting diminishing returns. After all, what is important for the corporation's bottom line is not 'mean monetary returns per bird,' but rather returns 'per unit of floor area.' These birds are treated as nothing more than things or products to be used as profit-making machines in light of their flesh's value as inexpensive food.

Treatment of pigs

Despite having an intelligence and social life very similar to that of dogs, pigs are also raised in factory farms where they have nothing to do but eat, sleep, stand up and lie down. Indeed, their lives are so boring that British researchers have found that "if they are given both food and an earth-filled trough, they will root around in the earth before eating," simply glad to have something less monotonous to do for a few minutes.[19] Like the birds just mentioned, pigs are also prone to 'vices' which usually consist of biting each other's tails. This leads to fighting, which leads to weight loss, which in turn leads to reduced profit margins. In response, factory farmers simply cut off their tails. Indeed, the US Department of Agriculture recommends that one cut tails from a quarter to half an inch from the body with side-cutting pliers or another blunt instrument. The crushing action helps stop the bleeding.[20] And one candid pig producer is at least honest about both what the pigs think of this practice and why factory farmers do it:

They hate it! The pigs just hate it! And I suppose we could probably do without tail-docking if we gave them more room, because they don't go crazy and mean when they have more space. With enough room, they're actually quite nice animals. But we can't afford it. These buildings cost a lot.[21]

Pigs also die and are otherwise damaged at rates similar to those of factory-farmed chickens, but, again, this is of little concern to the industry as long as profits are maximized.

The reproductive practices forced onto factory-farmed pigs are worth noting as well. Piglets are now reared in cages away from their mothers. This is done not only to make sure the pigs get as little exercise as possible (to maximize the possibility that their flesh will be tender when eaten) but also because this increases efficiency in breeding. Either by weaning the piglets early (which causes them significant distress), or by having them totally suckled by a machine, "a sow can produce an average of 2.6 litters a

---

[19] *Ibid.*, 120–121.   [20] *Ibid.*, 121.   [21] *Ibid.*

year, instead of the maximum of 2.0 that can be produced if the pigs are allowed to suckle for three months as they would naturally do."[22] Of course, this technique turns the mother into nothing more than a repro-duction machine, forced to lead a life dominated by confinement and pumping out piglets. When a sow is ready to give birth, she is moved to a 'farrowing pen' in which an iron frame restricts almost all movement of the normally active sows. Singer quotes sow researcher G. Cronin on the reactions of these animals being so confined:

The sows threw themselves violently backwards, straining against the tether. Sows thrashed their heads about as they twisted and turned in their struggle to free themselves. Often loud screams were emitted and occasionally individuals crashed bodily against the side boards of the stalls. This sometimes results in sows collapsing to the floor.[23]

These hours-long tirades generally end with frustrated groans and whining noises. Sometimes, as they lay there exhausted, they will haplessly even try to chew their way through the iron bars.

As with birds, the reasons for this kind of treatment almost always come back to profit maximization – and the reasoning can be utterly callous. Singer recalls the story of a veterinarian working with a large swine operation who noticed that one of the sows in the gestation crates had a hind leg sticking out at an odd angle. Upon learning that it was broken, the vet offered to splint the leg at only the cost of the materials, but was told that the operation could not afford the manpower involved in separating and caring for the sow. Indeed, their plan was to let her farrow one last time and then shoot her and foster off her pigs.[24]

Slaughter of chickens and pigs

The way these animals are killed is also driven largely by the logic of profit and consumerism. Workers grab the legs of four or five chickens in each hand and thrust them into crates, often dislocating and breaking their hips and wings in the process, and then truck them to the slaughterhouse. When their turn to be slaughtered comes, the chicken's "feet are snapped into metal shackles hanging from a conveyor belt that moves toward the killing room" at the remarkable speed of more than 100 birds a minute.[25] Though not required by US law to be rendered unconscious, most chickens do have their heads dipped into an electrified bath which,

---

[22] *Ibid.*, 125.   [23] *Ibid.*, 127.   [24] *Ibid.*, 55.   [25] *Ibid.*, 25.

though it stuns them, is not adequate to make the birds immediately unconscious. Indeed, the level of electricity required for that would risk harming the quality of the meat. The next step is systematized throat-cutting, but because of the speed of the line many throats are inevitably missed, and thus millions of birds "go alive and conscious into the next stage of the process, a tank of scalding water."[26]

What is in store for the billions of pigs slaughtered each year is not much better. Singer cites a *Washington Post* article detailing their fate:

The process begins when the squealing hogs are corralled from their pens up a wooden plank where a worker stuns their heads with an electric shock. As they fall from the shock, a worker quickly hangs the pigs upside-down on a conveyer belt, placing their rear legs in a metal clamp. Sometimes the stunned hogs fall off the conveyer belt and regain consciousness, and workers have to scramble to hoist the hogs' legs back into the metal clamps before they begin running wildly through the confined area. The hogs are actually killed by a worker who stabs the stunned and often still squirming animals with a knife in the jugular vein and lets most of the blood drain out.[27]

Of course, there are other kinds of factory-farmed animals, but this should suffice for getting a sense of the kinds of practices involved.[28] That our culture is willing to cruelly treat such sophisticated animals (again, pigs have mental capacities very similar to dogs) as mere 'things' or 'objects' should deeply disturb us. But beyond consumerism and a disconnected mechaniza-tion of our culture,[29] what has paved the way for such grotesque practices in the first place?

The root cause: speciesism

Recall our discussion in Chapter 1 of Singer's criticisms of a speciesist approach which gives "greater weight to the interests of members of their own species when there is a clash between their interests and the interests of those of other species. Human speciesists do not accept that pain is as bad when it is felt by pigs or mice as when it is felt by humans."[30] Singer argues discrimination on this basis is as unjustified as sexism or racism. Many aspects of our Western culture (especially in

---

[26] *Ibid.*, 26.   [27] Singer, *Animal Liberation*, 150–151.
[28] Space does not permit detailing the awful ways in which, for instance, cows or other kinds of birds are treated and slaughtered in factory farms.
[29] Which has replaced a rich 'cosmic vitalism' that existed before the arrival of the secular enlightenment.
[30] Singer, *Practical Ethics*, 50–51.

the United States) operate with an implicit assumption that non-human animals exist merely as tools or objects to serve human beings. We think little about making them suffer and die to fulfill our needs and even our very superficial wants. But as the public outrage over National Football League quarterback (and former dog-fighting ring owner) Michael Vick's torturing and drowning of dogs shows us, the American public isn't speciesist 100 percent of the time. In that case, most understood that these dogs had a dignity which went beyond being a mere tool for the entertainment of Vick and his companions. They knew that the interest the dogs had in not being tortured and drowned superseded any interests the spectators had in gaining the pleasure of being entertained or making money. To say that the dogs' interests didn't count simply because they were not human beings is a kind of speciesism that the American public largely rejected.

Interestingly, however, a few dog-fighting defenders made the point that most of those who criticized Vick were hopelessly hypocritical. Consider this blog entry as a representative example of the argument:

The way Vick has been crucified is one of the most ridiculous and hypocritical things I've ever seen in my life. What is it with people and their holier-than-thou defense of dogs? For God's sake, far worse things are done in far greater numbers every single day to all sorts of animals and very few people say anything. How about people who shoot moose, deer, and other wildlife for pure entertainment or competition? We call that "sport." What about the thousands of pigs, chickens, ducks, cows, and other animals that are killed in the cruelest and most inhumane ways every single day? Most of these indignant idiots are eating those same animals every day and have no idea what process is involved to get them that food.[31]

Singer would agree with the logic here, but push it in the other direction. Because we admit that the interests of the dog-fighting spectators in getting pleasure from watching the fights is outweighed by the interests of the dogs not to be tortured and killed, we should also admit that, for most people in the developed world, our interest in getting pleasure from eating the flesh of animals at a cheap price is outweighed by their interest in not being tortured and killed. Simply because chickens, turkeys, and pigs belong to species which are not traditionally human companions does not give us a good reason to value their interests any less.

---

[31] "Vick Suffers the Wrath of the Hypocrites," Experience Project, www.experienceproject.com/ stories/Hate-Michael-Vick/50226 (Accessed February 13, 2010).

The moral status of non-human animals

Animals that can feel pain and prefer certain states of affairs to others have a certain level of moral value that we are bound to respect. But some criticize the animal rights movement for equating non-human animals with human beings. Singer is very clear, however, that a rejection of speciesism does not imply that all lives are of equal worth.[32] While similar interests in, say, not feeling pain should be given the same moral weight across various sentient species, certain animals have morally important interests that others do not have. For instance, it is not speciesist "to hold that life as a self-aware being, capable of abstract thought, of planning for the future, of complex acts of communication, and so on, is more valuable than the life of a being without these qualities."[33] Human beings who have these qualities, therefore, would be more valuable than other animals that do not have them. So while one may not kill a pig because one likes the taste of its flesh, one may kill a pig if one is starving in the forest. Unlike the former case, the latter suggests a situation where it is 'life vs. life', and for Singer the life of the rational and self-aware creature matters more.

But Singer famously argues there are non-human animals who seem to be rational and self-aware:

The chimpanzee, whom they called 'Washoe,' learnt to understand about 350 different signs and to use about 250 of them correctly. She put signs together to form simple sentences and, in doing so, provided strong evidence of a sense of self. When shown her own image in a mirror and asked 'Who is that?' she replied: 'Me, Washoe.' Later ... she adopted an infant chimpanzee and soon began not only signing to him but even deliberately teaching him signs, for example, by moulding his hands into the sign for 'food' in an appropriate context.[34]

And Koko the gorilla outdid Washoe with a vocabulary of over 500 signs. In a funny and telling story, when someone remarked of Koko, "She's a goofball!" Koko (perhaps not understanding the term) signed: "No, gorilla."[35] These primates not only demonstrate self-awareness, but a sense that they exist in time as well. Koko understands and remembers that she will get ice cream on her birthday, for instance. In response to the first snowfall of the year, and referring to last year's Christmas tree and thus

---

[32] Singer, *Animal Liberation*, 20.

[33] *Ibid.* As we will see in Chapter 5, however, Singer's preference utilitarianism struggles to justify such a ranking.

[34] Singer, *Practical Ethics*, 95.   [35] *Ibid., Practical Ethics* (1993), 112.

displaying clear evidence that she knew the Christmas season was coming, a chimpanzee named Tatu signed "Candy Tree?"[36]

But these might not be the only kinds of non-human animals that are rational and self-aware persons. Dolphins are arguably more intelligent than great apes, and the researchers themselves claimed that dolphins should be considered "non-human persons":

> Dolphins have long been recognised as among the most intelligent of animals but many researchers had placed them below chimps, which some studies have found can reach the intelligence levels of three-year-old children ... The studies show how dolphins have distinct personalities, a strong sense of self and can think about the future. It has also become clear that they are "cultural" animals, meaning that new types of behaviour can quickly be picked up by one dolphin from another.[37]

And what about elephants? Along with great apes and dolphins, they can recognize themselves in a mirror, but they also appear to understand the concept of death and will visit the grave sites and handle the bones of their deceased companions. At any rate, it is clear that if rationality and self-awareness (as Singer describes it[38]) is the threshold to meet, then if one is to avoid wrongfully discriminating on the basis of species, the set of beings with the moral status of 'person' must be expanded to include some non-human animals.

SINGER ON REFORMING OUR PRACTICES AND ATTITUDES

If we wish to form social practices which show concern for the dignity of non-human animals, Singer suggests we begin with taking responsibility for our own lives and make them as free of cruelty as we can. Not surprisingly, the first step in doing this is that we cease to eat animals.[39] For Singer, this is not merely a symbolic gesture or an attempt to keep oneself 'pure' in isolation from the ugly reality of the world. Instead, he considers this a highly practical and effective step one can take toward ending many of the unethical practices mentioned above. After all, the people who profit by exploiting large numbers of animals do not need our

---

[36] *Ibid.*, 95.

[37] Jonathan Leake, "Scientists say dolphins should be treated as 'non-human persons,'" *The Sunday Times*–Times Online, www.timesonline.co.uk/tol/news/science/article6973994.ece (Accessed February 13, 2010).

[38] Later in this chapter we will examine a traditional Christian understanding of rationality and self-awareness that, while sharing some of what Singer is after here, is significantly different.

[39] Singer, *Animal Liberation*, 159.

approval, but they do need our money.[40] We could do more than this, but Singer says that refusing to buy or eat the flesh or other products of animals that have been reared in modern factory farm conditions is "the absolute minimum that anyone with the capacity to look beyond considerations of narrow self-interest should be able to accept."[41]

The Singer narrative: how did we get here?

The attempts to change our speciesist attitudes detailed above are what Singer calls a "frontal assault" on the "tyranny" of human beings over non-human animals, but he also attempts "to undermine the prevailing attitude by revealing its historical origins."[42] His basic narrative is rather simple:

> Western attitudes to animals have roots in two traditions: Judaism and Greek antiquity. These roots unite in Christianity, and it is through Christianity that they came to prevail in Europe. A more enlightened view of our relations with animals emerges only gradually, as thinkers begin to take positions that are relatively independent of the Church; and in fundamental respects we still have not broken free of the attitudes that were unquestionably accepted in Europe until the eighteenth century.[43]

This fits very well with the 'Copernican revolution' Singer wants to facilitate which would replace a Christian sanctity-of-life ethic with a more serious and defensible ethic. But let's see how he lays out his narrative in more detail.

Appropriately, Singer starts with the biblical creation story in Genesis. God gives humanity "dominion" over every living creature. And after Noah and his family get off the Ark we are told the following in Genesis 9:1–3:

> Then God blessed Noah and his sons, saying to them, "Be fruitful and increase in number and fill the earth. The fear and dread of you will fall upon all the beasts of the earth and all the birds of the air, upon every creature that moves along the ground, and upon all the fish of the sea; they are given into your hands. Everything that lives and moves will be food for you. Just as I gave you the green plants, I now give you everything."

Singer admits that the Hebrew Bible can be more complex on these issues than is generally known, but he nevertheless says that there is "no serious challenge to the overall view, laid down in Genesis, that the human species is the pinnacle of creation and has God's permission to kill and eat other animals."[44] Singer also claims that Christianity brings into the

---

[40] *Ibid.*, 161–162.   [41] *Ibid.*, 170.   [42] *Ibid.*, 185.   [43] *Ibid.*, 186.   [44] *Ibid.*, 188.

Roman world the idea of the uniqueness of the human species. The idea is based in part on the above biblical considerations, but it also comes from an emphasis on the human immortal soul. With this came the distinctively Christian idea of the sanctity of all human life. Other religions taught that all life is sacred, and others taught that killing members of one's social group was wrong, "but Christianity spread the idea that every human life – and only human life – is sacred."[45]

And what about the value of non-human animal life? Singer pulls no punches in detailing his critical narrative:

The New Testament is completely lacking in any injunction against cruelty to animals, or any recommendation to consider their interests. Jesus himself is described as showing apparent indifference to the fate of non-humans when he induced two thousand swine to hurl themselves into the sea – an act which was apparently quite unnecessary, since Jesus was well able to cast out devils without inflicting them upon any other creature. Saint Paul insisted on reinterpreting the Old Mosaic law that forbade muzzling the ox that trod out the corn: "Doth God care for oxen?" Paul asks scornfully. No, he answered, the law was intended "altogether for our sakes."[46]

This attitude, Singer maintains, can be seen clearly when we examine what happened to the Roman games when Christianity came to power. Because of its emphasis on the dignity of the human person, the Church was "implacably opposed" to gladiatorial combat. The gladiator who survived by killing his opponent was regarded as a murderer. Even attendance at gladiatorial games was punishable by excommunication. And by the end of the fourth century such combat had ceased altogether. But combats with wild animals continued into the Christian era, and "apparently declined only because the declining wealth and extent of the empire made wild animals more difficult to obtain."[47]

Singer claims that this example illustrates a more general trend. Not only did Christianity fail to temper the worst of Roman attitudes toward non-human animals, but "it unfortunately succeeded in extinguishing for a long, long time the spark of wider compassion that had been kept alight by a tiny number of more gentle people."[48] Ovid, Seneca, Porphyry, and Plutarch all wrote with some compassion for animals, but "we have to wait nearly sixteen hundred years, however, before any Christian writer

---

[45] *Ibid.*, 191. Many, and perhaps especially students of classical history, will find Singer's view expressed here to be terribly frustrating. Several non-Christian cultures believe human life to be sacred and, as we will see below, the Christian tradition is far more complex than Singer believes when it comes to the sacred value of non-human animals.
[46] *Ibid.*   [47] *Ibid.*, 192.   [48] *Ibid.*

attacks cruelty to animals with similar emphasis and detail and ground other than that it may encourage a tendency toward cruelty to humans."[49]

But surely this is rhetorical overstatement. Can Singer really mean that for *sixteen centuries* no Christian thinker had this as a serious emphasis? He does admit that "a few Christians" had concern for non-human animals, but because "it is a tedious process" he decides not to explore or detail Christian thought from the early Church fathers through the medieval scholastics. Instead, he skips right to Thomas Aquinas, who he notes is "singularly representative of Christian philosophy prior to the Reformation."[50] When asking whether the prohibition on killing applies to creatures other than humans, Aquinas answers by saying the following in II:II 64:1 of the *Summa Theologica*:[51]

> There is no sin in using a thing for the purpose for which it is. Now the order of things is such that the imperfect are for the perfect, even as in the process of generation nature proceeds from imperfection to perfection. Hence it is that just as in the generation of a man there is first a living thing, then an animal, and lastly a man, so too things, like the plants, which merely have life, are all alike for animals, and all animals are for man. Wherefore it is not unlawful if man use plants for the good of animals, and animals for the good of man, as the Philosopher states (Polit. i, 3). Now the most necessary use would seem to consist in the fact that animals use plants, and men use animals, for food, and this cannot be done unless these be deprived of life: wherefore it is lawful both to take life from plants for the use of animals, and from animals for the use of men. In fact this is in keeping with the commandment of God Himself: for it is written (Genesis 1:29–30): "Behold I have given you every herb ... and all trees ... to be your meat"; and again (Genesis 9:3): "Everything that moveth and liveth shall be meat to you."

In response to Thomas' claim that eating animals is justified based on our rational capacity to conform to the order of justice described above, rather than savagery and brutality, Singer responds with dismissive incredulity: "Human beings, of course, would not kill for food unless they had first considered the justice of so doing!"[52]

But perhaps, though eating animals is permitted, the *suffering* of such creatures is an evil. Thomas cannot say this, according to Singer, because he has no room for wrongs of this kind in his moral schema, which are divided

---

[49] *Ibid.*, 193. [50] *Ibid.*
[51] It should be noted that this article of the *Summa* was specifically asking the question about whether killing animals involved a particular kind of injustice, which violates the commandment against murder. Whether non-human animals have any moral claim on us at all is a different question.
[52] *Ibid.*, 194.

into sins against God, self, and neighbor.[53] But perhaps, Singer asks, it is at least charitable (as the *Catechism* seems to imply) *to be kind* to them? Aquinas, at least as Singer understands him, answers in the negative:

Charity, he says, does not extend to irrational creatures for three reasons: they are "not competent, properly speaking, to possess good, this being proper to rational creatures"; we have no fellow feeling with them; and, finally "charity is based on the fellowship of everlasting happiness, to which the irrational creatures cannot attain." It is only possible to love these creatures, we are told, "if we regard them as the good things that we desire for others," that is "to God's honor and man's use."[54]

Singer playfully tries to get Thomas off the hook by wondering if perhaps he, like some other philosophers, held the "absurd" view that non-human animals didn't suffer. For this "would at least excuse him on the charge of indifference to suffering."[55] But Singer says that this possible escape route is closed off by Thomas' own words when, in attempting to explain why our pity is aroused by non-human animals, he says that even irrational animals are sensible to pain. And such pity, according to Aquinas, is not good for the sake of its object – the animal – but rather because it helps create a similar concern for human beings. "No argument," says Singer, "could reveal the essence of speciesism more clearly."[56]

Though he is willing to admit the Christian tradition is becoming more complex, Singer's narrative nevertheless insists that his interpretation of Thomas Aquinas' approach with regard to non-human animals is still the dominant one for Christianity and for Roman Catholicism. But I argue that Singer is missing an important part of the Christian tradition on non-human animals. Not only is this tradition not the enemy, but Singer should see a Christian understanding of non-human animals as an *ally* in his noble struggle for animal liberation.[57]

THE CHURCH ON NON-HUMAN ANIMALS:
CURRENT TEACHING

That my attempts in this section to give both the current teaching of the Church, and to survey the rich tradition which serves as its foundation,

[53] *Ibid.*   [54] *Ibid.*, 194–195.   [55] *Ibid.*, 195.   [56] *Ibid.*, 196.
[57] Some may find this phrase problematic, but (as this chapter will make clear) I think 'liberation' – in a sense that is analogous with other liberation movements – is precisely what is needed in light of the grave bondage under which billions and billions of non-human animals are suffering.

will fail to even do a barely adequate job is strong evidence that Peter Singer's thin narrative is ultimately inadequate.[58] But let's begin with the teaching of the Church today. Singer's critique sounds plausible if one starts with paragraph 2417 of the *Catechism*:

> God entrusted animals to the stewardship of those whom he created in his own image. Hence it is legitimate to use animals for food and clothing. They may be domesticated to help man in his work and leisure.

But it sounds much less plausible if one reads the surrounding paragraphs for context:

> [Humanity's] dominion over inanimate and other living beings granted by the Creator is not absolute; it is limited by concern for the quality of life of his neighbor, including generations to come; it requires a religious respect for the integrity of creation. Animals are God's creatures. He surrounds them with his providential care. By their mere existence they bless him and give him glory. Thus men owe them kindness. We should recall the gentleness with which saints like St. Francis of Assisi or St. Philip Neri treated animals ... It is contrary to human dignity to cause animals to suffer or die needlessly.[59]

Though I think Singer helps Christians think more carefully and consistently about what it means for us to have dominion over non-human animals, his suggestion that it can be reduced to treating animals as mere tools – and that the only specifically theological reasons Christians have for treating animals well can be reduced to a moral claim about human beings – is in need of serious nuance. Let us be absolutely clear about one matter, at least: the official teaching of the Roman Catholic Church is that we owe non-human animals kindness and that it is morally wrong to cause animals to suffer and die needlessly.

The last two Popes have views consistent with this teaching. Benedict XVI is well known for being an animal lover; apparently he has to be reminded that he cannot take in stray cats from the surrounding Roman streets, and throughout his life he has often been given pets as Christmas presents. As mentioned above, PETA has latched onto this fact and heralded his words in their advertisements. One that got a significant amount of public attention focused on his answer to the following question asked

---

[58] Many books have been written – and there is a particular explosion of interest in them at the moment – just on the moral value of non-humans in the Christian tradition. In what follows I will attempt to highlight what I can from these texts, but I would strongly recommend following the footnotes to further reading.

[59] *Catechism of the Roman Catholic Church*, paras. 2415, 2416, and 2418.

by German journalist Peter Seewald not long before he became Pope, and during which time he was the doctrinal watchdog for the entire Church: "Are we allowed to make use of animals, and even to eat them?" Here is his response:

That is a very serious question. At any rate, we can see that they are given into our care, that we cannot just do whatever we want with them. Animals, too, are God's creatures. Certainly, a sort of industrial use of creatures, so that geese are fed in such a way as to produce as large a liver as possible, or hens live so packed together that they become just caricatures of birds, this degrading of living creatures to a commodity seems to me in fact to contradict the relationship of mutuality that comes across in the Bible.[60]

And in his recent encyclical *Caritas in Veritate*, the Pope writes about our need to be faithful to a "covenant" between humans and the rest of creation.[61] Indeed, Benedict's view of non-human animals appears to flow from a determined focus on ecological ethics more generally.[62] Now being called by many 'the Green Pope,' he has been something of an ecological hero in making explicit and public efforts to strongly connect moral imperatives toward creation with the Church's broader social teaching. Tellingly, this theme was part of Benedict's first homily as Pope:

The external deserts in the world are growing because the internal deserts have become so vast. The earth's treasures no longer serve to build God's garden for all to live in, but they have been made to serve the powers of exploitation and destruction.[63]

And this is not mere rhetoric. Under his watch, the Vatican has become the world's first carbon-neutral country by offsetting its carbon emissions though renewable energies and carbon credits. Benedict has personally

[60] Joseph Cardinal Ratzinger, *God and the World: A Conversation with Peter Seewald* (San Francisco, CA: Ignatius Press, 2002), 78–79.
[61] Pope Benedict XVI, *Caritas in Veritate* (Vatican: The Holy See), www.vatican.va/holy_father/benedict_xvi/encyclicals/documents/hf_ben-xvi_enc_20090629_caritas-in-veritate_en.html (Accessed February 14, 2010), 50.
[62] In addition to concern directly for the animals themselves, one might be skeptical of factory farming for purely ecological reasons. The methane gas and waste run-off produced by such farms contaminate the air and water supply at rates just as serious as the emissions of automobiles. Furthermore, one can get far more calories per acre by simply growing and eating vegetables, rather than growing vegetables, feeding them to an animal, and then eating part of the animal. And because there would no longer be a need for grazing, land is saved as well.
[63] Quoted in Woodeene Konenig-Bricker, *Ten Commandments for the Environment: Pope Benedict Speaks Out for Creation and Justice* (Notre Dame, IN: Ave Maria Press, 2009), 2.

led on the topic of renewable energy by instituting projects to put thousands of solar panels on various Vatican buildings – reducing carbon dioxide emissions "by about 225 tons" and saving "the equivalent of eighty tons of oil each year."[64] John Allen notes that "the project captured the 2008 Euro Solar Prize, awarded by the European Association for Renewable Energy, a secular body."[65] This already impressive project is part of an even more impressive commitment to have 20 percent of the Vatican's energy come from renewable resources by 2020.[66]

The social teaching of Pope John Paul II also had an important ecological focus. He took the teachings of his predecessors on "the dangers of consumerism" and of a "desire to have and to enjoy rather than to be and to grow" and applied it with a concern not just for human beings, but all of creation.[67] He says:

Once again it is evident that development, the planning which governs it, and the way in which resources are used must include respect for moral demands. One of the latter undoubtedly imposes limits on the use of the natural world. The dominion granted to man by the Creator is not an absolute power, nor can one speak of a freedom to "use and misuse," or to dispose of things as one pleases.[68]

In his important book *Dominion*, Matthew Scully (a former speech-writer for George W. Bush) recalls John Paul II's words in an address to European farmers in the fall of 2000 in which he asked them to resist the temptations of productivity and profit that work to the detriment of respect for nature. For when one forgets this principle, becoming tyrants and not custodians of the Earth, "sooner or later the Earth rebels."[69] And, as Scully notes, John Paul II applied this reasoning specifically to how we treat non-human animals:

Many would be surprised to hear [John Paul's] call to follow the example of St. Francis, who "looked upon creation with the eyes of one who could recognize in the marvelous work the hand of God. His solicitous care, not only toward

[64] *Ibid.*, 8–9.
[65] John L. Allen, *The Future Church: How Ten Trends are Revolutionizing the Catholic Church* (New York: Doubleday, 2009), 298.
[66] www.reuters.com/article/idUSTRE4AO8C820081125 (Accessed August 8, 2010).
[67] Catholic Church, Pope John Paul II, *Centesimus Annus* (Washington, D.C.: Office for Publishing and Promotion Services, United States Catholic Conference, 1991), 113, 37.
[68] Catholic Church, Pope John Paul II, *Sollicitudo Rei Socialis* (Washington, D.C.: Office of Publishing and Promotion Services, United States Catholic Conference, 1988), 102, 34.
[69] Matthew Scully, *Dominion: The Power of Man, the Suffering of Animals, and the Call to Mercy*, 1st edn. (New York: St. Martin's Press, 2002), 434, 388.

men, but also toward animals is a faithful echo of the love with which God in the beginning pronounced his 'fiat' which brought them into existence. We are too called to a similar attitude."

"It is necessary and urgent," said the Pope in marking the eight-hundredth anniversary of the saint's passing, "that with the example of the little poor man from Assisi, one decides to abandon unadvisable forms of domination, the locking up of all creatures."[70]

Though the English-speaking press apparently failed to pick up on it, during a papal audience in 1990 John Paul II made his most striking claims about the dignity of non-human animals. Drawing on the biblical theology of what it means to have the 'breath of life,' the Pope claimed that "animals possess a soul" and that we "must love and feel solidarity with our smaller brethren."[71]

And in a book chapter entitled 'The Redemption of Animals in an Incarnational Theology,' the Roman Catholic priest Denis Edwards combines the Pope's point above with an insight that taps deep into an often forgotten Christian understanding of the value of all creation. He says, remarkably, that non-human animals "can be thought of as participating, at least in part, in the redemptive way of life revealed in Christ."[72] Edwards believes Christians have a tradition which commits us to a spirituality in which other animals have their place as fellow sentient creatures before God. To participate in the life of God is to seek to participate in God's feeling for individual creatures. It involves remembering that every sparrow that falls to the ground is loved and held in the living memory of God.[73]

But Singer could accept what has been said so far and still claim that Christianity is merely grafting a concern for non-human animals onto a tradition which has no such resource.[74] Perhaps the Church is borrowing

---

[70] *Ibid.*, 24.

[71] "Pope Benedict XVI Continues Tradition of Papal Concern for Animals," People for the Ethical Treatment of Animals (PETA), www.peta.org/features/pope-benedict-xvi.aspx (Accessed February 14, 2010).

[72] David Clough and Celia Deane-Drummond (eds.), *Creaturely Theology* (Norwich: SCM Press, 2009), 96–97.

[73] *Ibid.*, 99.

[74] Indeed, some Christians on the 'right' might dismiss the above as a phenomenon of modern-day leftist ideology infiltrating an authentically Christian message. But in addition to the 'conservative' presidential speech-writer, Matthew Scully, mentioned above, later in the chapter we shall see in some detail that right-leaning Christian intellectuals like Germain Grisez and Mary Eberstadt are also allies for Singer when it comes to animal liberation. No, even within the Church, concern for the dignity of non-human animals is something that transcends simplistic and unhelpful 'liberal/conservative' binary distinctions.

from a modern, post-Christian understanding that has developed since the Enlightenment. But this point of view would involve a fundamental misunderstanding of the Church's tradition on these matters.

THE CHURCH ON NON-HUMAN ANIMALS: SCRIPTURE AND TRADITION

Having a two-millennia-long tradition, and especially one influenced by so many different cultures from all over the world, brings with it a significant amount of complexity and even tension. While many are no doubt familiar with the Church failing to see much value in non-human animals and the practice of vegetarianism, there is also an important counter-tradition that is less well known. Many Christians throughout the centuries have refused to eat meat, and Holly Roberts has helpfully shown that many dozens of these persons, beyond the obligatory mention of Francis of Assisi, have been canonized saints.[75] It also turns out that one of the central marks of holiness in the Judeo-Christian tradition is kindness to animals.[76] Indeed, as we will see below, the fact that someone could interact with fierce animals as friendly companions, rather than adversaries, was thought to be proof of being close to God.

One might be tempted to stop here and claim that Singer's narrative has already been refuted, but this would be too quick. Though many of the above saints were vegetarian for reasons connected to animal dignity, many had complex, and even non-Christian, reasons for refusing to eat meat.[77] Furthermore, I want show that not only is Singer wrong about Christianity being the scapegoat, but that the Church should be an ally for the cause of animal liberation. I therefore have a much higher threshold to meet. So, toward that end, let us explore the tradition in more detail: we will start with scripture, move to the early Church, focus some serious attention on Thomas Aquinas (especially in light of Singer's critique), and finish with the views of some modern Christian thinkers.

---

[75] Holly R. Roberts, *Vegetarian Christian Saints* (Anjeli Press, 2004).

[76] This was true of several biblical figures. Jacob and David, for instance, were considered holy based in part on how they cared for other animals. Also, Rebekah was thought to be an appropriate wife for Isaac because of her kindness to animals, and the Talmud specifically states that Moses was chosen for his leadership role because of his skill in caring for animals.

[77] In particular, some of the early Christian saints had the influence of Manichaean philosophy which prohibited meat-eating. But such Manichaean-influenced Christians apparently saw no contradiction between their vegetarianism and their Christianity.

Scripture

Day six of creation in Genesis is very important for our discussion and therefore it is worth quoting the relevant passage in its entirety:

And God said, "Let the land produce living creatures according to their kinds: livestock, creatures that move along the ground, and wild animals, each according to its kind." And it was so. God made the wild animals according to their kinds, the livestock according to their kinds, and all the creatures that move along the ground according to their kinds. And God saw that it was good.

Then God said, "Let us make man in our image, in our likeness, and let them rule over the fish of the sea and the birds of the air, over the livestock, over all the earth, and over all the creatures that move along the ground."

So God created man in his own image,
in the image of God he created him;
male and female he created them.

God blessed them and said to them, "Be fruitful and increase in number; fill the earth and subdue it. Rule over the fish of the sea and the birds of the air and over every living creature that moves on the ground."

Then God said, "I give you every seed-bearing plant on the face of the whole earth and every tree that has fruit with seed in it. They will be yours for food. And to all the beasts of the earth and all the birds of the air and all the creatures that move on the ground – everything that has the breath of life in it – I give every green plant for food." And it was so. God saw all that he had made, and it was very good. And there was evening, and there was morning – the sixth day.

First, it is worth noting that human and non-human (terrestrial) animals are created on the same day, implying a kind of special relationship or kinship. Recall Pope John Paul's mentioning above that both humans and non-human animals have 'the breath of life.' This understanding is also backed up by the Hebrew Bible in Ecclesiastes 3:18–20:

I said in my heart with regard to human beings that God is testing them to show that they are but animals. For the fate of human beings and the fate of animals is the same; as one dies, so dies the other. They all have the same breath, and humans have no advantage over the animals; for all is vanity.

The Christian feminist theologian Rosemary Radford Ruether agrees that the Hebrews saw themselves "as kin of the animals" and contrasts this with classical Greek culture which

shifts to a hierarchical worldview in which women, slaves and animals are lined up in descending order of inferiority under the ruling Greek male.

The rational soul is seen as both the principle of rule over these inferiors and as the ultimate escape from mortality of the body.

Non-human animals, says Ruether, are lumped into a totally different category – along with women and slaves – because they lack "by nature the capacity for reason and self-rule."[78]

Second, it is worth noting once again the essential point that non-human animals are pronounced "good" by God without reference to human beings; indeed, God proclaims this even before human beings are created. Singer and others have pressed the point that human beings have dominion over the rest of creation; but given that God has given plants for both humans and non-humans to eat, such dominion doesn't appear to involve eating other animals. And whatever dominion humanity has over non-human animals, it is to be in the spirit of the "relationship of mutuality" which Pope Benedict XVI explicitly mentions and that runs through much of what John Paul II had to say. Indeed, in the second story of creation this special, mutual relationship is confirmed. For why are animals created in that story? Not because Adam is hungry or needs help with manual labor, but because "it is not good that man should be alone." Animals are brought to Adam *to be his companions* (Genesis 2:18–19).

But then what is the explanation for Genesis 9:1–5 where the "fear and dread of you will fall upon all the beasts of the earth and all the birds of the air, upon every creature that moves along the ground, and upon all the fish of the sea; they are given into your hands. Everything that lives and moves will be food for you?" Whatever God may have intended at first, clearly the dominion that God has instituted here is one that predicts and even produces "fear and dread" in non-human animals in reaction to human beings. And how true, how tragically true, this prediction turned out to be after all: the fear and dread experienced in the suffering of the tens of billions of non-human animals tortured and killed in our factory farms is on a scale that Noah and company couldn't even imagine. What more does Singer need to show that we need a Copernican revolution in our ethics more generally, and with regard to our relationship with non-human animals in particular?

Andrew Linzey, an Anglican priest and for many years a voice crying in the virtual Christian wilderness on these issues, reminds us that the above permission is granted to Noah only after God has brought a flood to destroy the world. Genesis 6:11–13 is striking:

---

[78] Charles Pinches and Jay B. McDaniel (eds.), *Good News for Animals? Christian Approaches to Animal Well-Being* (New York: Orbis, 1993), 16–17.

Now the earth was corrupt in God's sight and was full of violence. God saw how corrupt the earth had become, for all the people on earth had corrupted their ways. So God said to Noah, "I am going to put an end to all people, for the earth is filled with violence because of them . . ."

God was apparently angered by the violence that had permeated the earth. And God's "ambiguous permission" to eat animals therefore needs to be seen, according to Linzey, in the context of accommodation to human sinfulness and in particular, human *violence*.[79] But that accommodation is not as total as one might think, and certainly not consistent with how many Christians have treated non-human animals. There are imposed limits on when and how we can kill non-human animals for food. Linzey says that God's prohibition against eating an animal still containing its "life blood" is to be understood as a reminder that we may kill only on the understanding that the life we kill is not our own, it belongs to God. Indeed, "properly speaking there is no *right* to kill. God allows it only under the conditions of necessity."[80]

And most importantly, the Bible is clear that our current relationship with other animals is not the moral ideal and, indeed, only a temporary state of affairs.[81] The prophets Isaiah, Ezekiel, and Hosea all predict a return to the non-violence of Eden. And the way Isaiah describes the "Peaceable Kingdom" in chapter 11:6–9 is, in my opinion, the most beautiful part of the Bible:

> The wolf will live with the lamb,
> the leopard will lie down with the goat,
> the calf and the lion and the yearling together;
> and a little child will lead them.
>
> The cow will feed with the bear,
> their young will lie down together,
> and the lion will eat straw like the ox.
>
> The infant will play near the hole of the cobra,
> and the young child put his hand into the viper's nest.

[79] Kerry S. Walters and Lisa Portmess, *Religious Vegetarianism: From Hesiod to the Dalai Lama* (Albany, NY: State University of New York Press, 2001), 203, 128.

[80] *Ibid.*, 129. Interestingly, this language mirrors that of the *Catechism*, which also invokes "need" as the only circumstance that would justify killing a non-human animal.

[81] And even in this fallen and sinful world the Bible has restrictions, which nevertheless uphold the dignity of non-human animals. Consider that animals rest on the Sabbath, along with human beings. A human being is enjoined to help free not only one's own animals, but also those of one's enemy, from a crushing burden. There are even specifications for the sharpness of the slaughtering knife to ensure the animal gets a quick death. Proverbs 12:10 says that, "[t]he righteous care for the needs of their animals, but the kindest acts of the wicked are cruel."

> They will neither harm nor destroy
> on all my holy mountain,
> for the earth will be full of the knowledge of the LORD
> as the waters cover the sea.

God's will from the beginning, and even now going forward, is non-violence and peace for all creation.

Wennberg asks us to consider, if we are serious when asking in the Lord's Prayer for God's will to be done on earth as it is in heaven, how killing and eating animals could be a matter of indifference for Christians. Furthermore, though the Church knows that the reign of God is both already and not yet here, aren't we nevertheless an eschatological community which "seeks to embody that future manifestation of God's will when God's kingdom comes in its fullness?"[82] Wennberg helpfully quotes Stanley Hauerwas and John Berkman on this question:

> Christian vegetarianism might be understood as a witness to the world that God's creation is not meant to be at war with itself. Such a witness does not entail romantic conceptions of nature or our fallen creation, but rather is an eschatological act, signifying that our lives are not captured by the old order.[83]

Part of what it means to be a human person, Wennberg reminds us, is that we are free to participate in God's redemptive work and reclaim what has been lost through sin. One of those things, as scripture shows us, is non-violent companionship with other animals.

Particular problems for the New Testament?

But Singer seems to be willing to admit that perhaps the Hebrew Bible offers some positive resources, while nevertheless insisting the Christian tradition was and remains a serious problem for the fight for animal liberation. And, truth be told, three particularly difficult New Testament passages do require an explanation. First, Jesus, though never described as eating meat himself,[84] apparently shows little regard for the value of pigs in this episode:

---

[82] Wennberg, *God, Humans, and Animals*, 358, 294.

[83] *Ibid.*, 294. We will read more from both Hauerwas and Berkman below.

[84] Some claim that because Jesus 'was a good Jew' he would have eaten meat at least at Passover. But it is not clear that a man who violated all sorts of other Jewish laws and rules (including scandalous violations of the Sabbath) would have necessarily followed this one. Indeed, Jesus even appears to be changing certain laws (those related to divorce, for example) while citing his authority as the Son of God. It is an argument from silence, and certainly not persuasive on its own, but in the context of other evidence it is worth noting that Jesus is never described as eating meat. Furthermore, if one assumes (despite lack of direct evidence) that Jesus did eat meat, his doing so in the ancient Middle

Catching sight of Jesus from a distance, he ran up and prostrated himself before him, crying out in a loud voice, "What have you to do with me, Jesus, Son of the Most High God? I adjure you by God, do not torment me!" (He had been saying to him, "Unclean spirit, come out of the man!")

He asked him, "What is your name?" He replied, "Legion is my name. There are many of us." And he pleaded earnestly with him not to drive them away from that territory. Now a large herd of swine was feeding there on the hillside. And they pleaded with him, "Send us into the swine. Let us enter them."

And he let them, and the unclean spirits came out and entered the swine. The herd of about two thousand rushed down a steep bank into the sea, where they were drowned. (Mark 5:6–13)

And though there are multiple ways of interpreting this story, many scriptural scholars see it as a fairly obvious parable of resistance against Rome rather than a historical account of something Jesus actually said or did. The demon's name, Legion, seems to be a dead giveaway here – as is the fact that the placeholder for the Roman soldiers is thrown into what was considered an unclean animal. The theological point of the story does not seem to be about the value of non-human animals, but rather about the relationship between Jesus, Christians and the Roman occupiers.[85]

Second, what about the following dream of Saint Peter's? Isn't this a very clear problem for the vegetarian Christian?

The next day, while they were on their way and nearing the city, Peter went up to the roof terrace to pray at about noontime. He was hungry and wished to eat, and while they were making preparations he fell into a trance. He saw heaven opened and something resembling a large sheet coming down, lowered to the ground by its four corners. In it were all the earth's four-legged animals and reptiles and the birds of the sky. A voice said to him, "Get up, Peter. Slaughter and eat." But Peter said, "Certainly not, sir. For never have I eaten anything profane and unclean." The voice spoke to him again, a second time, "What God has made clean, you are not to call profane." (Acts 10:9–15)

Here it looks like God is explicitly condoning the slaughter and eating of non-human animals.[86] But the central theological point is made clear later in the chapter when Peter says, "I now realize how true it is that God does

East (where protein was more difficult to obtain and factory farming didn't exist) doesn't shed much light on our own context.

[85] One of the things which makes Singer, along with many speciesist Christians, poor interpreters of scripture is that they have virtually no background in scholarly scriptural interpretation.

[86] It should be noted that getting protein from sources other than meat (and fish) in the ancient world would have been a much more difficult task than it is today. So even if one rejects this line of scriptural interpretation, it should have little impact for our current context in which other sources

not show favoritism but accepts men from every nation who fear him and do what is right."[87] Indeed in the next chapter when he is asked to explain why he is hanging out and eating with the unclean Gentiles, Peter cites this vision as his reason.[88] The point of the story and vision, once again, seems to have nothing to do with the moral value of animals, but about the proper relationship between Christians and non-Christians.[89]

But this third passage from Saint Paul's letter to the Corinthians might present a more difficult problem:

> It is written in the law of Moses, "You shall not muzzle an ox while it is treading out the grain." Is God concerned about oxen, or is he not really speaking for our sake? It was written for our sake, because the plowman should plow in hope, and the thresher in hope of receiving a share.[90]

Here St. Paul appears to be telling us that the proper way to interpret any divine rules or commands which seem to imply the independent value of non-human animals is to ultimately reduce the reason for the rule or command to the value and good of human beings. Though some people attempt to make a defense of Paul here by claiming that he never denies that oxen have intrinsic value – and that he merely points out the broader meaning of the command – I agree with F.F. Bruce who claims that Paul "must be allowed to mean what he says."[91]

But Paul was a man of classical Greek culture who had problematic views not only about non-human animals but also about women.[92] Whatever Paul tells us about animals (and women, for that matter[93]) must be looked at in the context of what Jesus, the very Word of God, tells us. And what Jesus tells us seems difficult to misunderstand:

> Therefore I tell you, do not worry about your life, what you will eat (or drink), or about your body, what you will wear. Is not life more than food and the body more than clothing? Look at the birds in the sky; they do not sow or reap, they gather nothing into barns, yet your heavenly Father feeds them. Are not you more important than they? Can any of you by worrying add a single moment to your life-span?[94]

---

of protein and nutrition are far more accessible. It also says nothing about our participation in factory farming, a practice totally foreign to the ancient world.

[87] Acts 10:34–35.   [88] *Ibid.*, 11:4–14.

[89] I owe this important insight to David Clough.   [90] 1 Corinthians 9:9–10.

[91] Robert N. Wennberg, *God, Humans, and Animals: An Invitation to Enlarge Our Moral Universe* (Grand Rapids, MI: William B. Eerdmans Publishing Co., 2003). 298.

[92] Paul infamously tells women to be, among other things, submissive to their husbands. (Colossians 3:18)

[93] Jesus is depicted, especially in the Gospel of Luke, as uncommonly valuing the moral status of women.

[94] Matthew 6:25–27.

And there is more:

Are not five sparrows sold for two small coins? Yet not one of them has escaped the notice of God. Even the hairs of your head have all been counted. Do not be afraid. You are worth more than many sparrows.[95]

Does God care for oxen? Though Paul implies that the answer is 'no,' the Gospel of Luke depicts a Jesus who would deny Paul's claim. Though human persons are worth more than non-human animals, Jesus invokes the fact that God has concern and care for non-human animals[96] as reassurance for human beings that God is concerned and cares about each of us.

The early Church

The tradition of the early Church on non-human animals, like that of Christianity more broadly, was complex. And there is apparently a real danger of Christian ethicists who are interested in animal ethics seeing things that aren't there.[97] But let us begin by examining the early Church's fascinating belief that other animals could at least sense, and perhaps even understand, goodness and holiness. Maureen Tilley explains that this was especially true in the stories of the martyrs:

In two separate incidents in *The Acts of Paul* lions recognized the goodness of Paul and Thecla and refused to harm them ... Animals were also on the side of the martyrs in the story of Perpetua and Felicitas. A bear brought to torture the martyrs refused to come out of its cage, and a boar refused to attack the martyrs, turning against the Romans instead. When animals could not prevent the martyrdom, they could at least reverence the bodies of the holy ones as they did in the case of Anahid and the wasps, and that of the Carthaginian martyrs whose bodies dolphins brought back to land for proper burial and veneration.[98]

Many more stories involve the relationship between non-human animals and the holy ascetics of the desert. Tilley recalls that animals and humans engaged in relationships of mutual aid:

---

[95] Luke 12:6–7.   [96] Which, interestingly, is presented as non-controversial in the text.
[97] There are some animal-friendly references to the Church fathers in current Christian animal ethics literature (about St. Basil in particular) which appear to have been fabricated.
[98] Michael Horace Barnes and College Theology Society. Meeting, *An Ecology of the Spirit: Religious Reflection and Environmental Consciousness*, Vol. 1990, v. 36 (Lanham, MD: University Press of America: College Theology Society, 1994), 242, 105.

A hyena prevailed on the monk Macarius to heal one of her cubs which had been born blind. She recognized his spiritual power and realized it could benefit her brood. In return for his care she brought him [a] ram's skin to use as a bed covering. In their turn, the animals may come to the aid of the monk in the wilderness ... The Abba Amoun called on snakes to guard his cell. The Abba Helle was ferried across the river by a crocodile.

Furthermore, and many centuries before Francis of Assisi was described as doing something similar, "Abba Bes in Egypt preached to both hippos and crocodiles. Inspired by his words, they ceased ravaging the country-side."[99] Tilley admits that, especially in its Stoic strains, the early Church emphasized the qualitative differences between human and non-human animals, but "Christian folklore came down squarely on the neo-Platonic side with a sense that the animals knew what they were doing and with whom they were dealing. Thus they acted appropriately around the saints, martyrs and ascetics."[100]

And the early Church of the East seems to have done an even better job acknowledging the biblically supported moral value of non-human animals than did the Western Church. John Chrysostom and Basil the Great, for example, appear to be much more friendly to other animals (and to creation more broadly) than their counterparts in the West.[101] Though one could point to many other similar examples from the Orthodox Christian churches, the third-century Orthodox martyr, St. Mamas of Paphlagonia, is worth mentioning in particular – especially because he is still invoked today by various Orthodox Christians when *praying for* non-human animals.[102] Western Christianity, however, was to be dramatically influenced by St. Augustine on these issues (along with countless other matters), and thus pushed in Stoic, anti-Manichean directions which were far less friendly.[103]

But contrary to what Singer claims, many important leaders of the early Church criticized the cruelty to non-human animals in the Roman games. The classical historian Thomas Wiedermann notes that it was the effect

[99] *Ibid.*, 106. [100] *Ibid.*, 107.
[101] Wennberg, *God, Humans, and Animals*, 303.
[102] Joanne Stefanatos, *Animals and Man: A State of Blessedness* (Minneapolis, MN: Light and Life Publishing Company, 1992), 236. The prayer is especially common when such animals are sick. And dozens of other Orthodox Christian saints are recounted in this book insofar as they have a connection to concern for non-human animals.
[103] Gnostics generally believed that, because meat is derived from the devil and consuming it strengthens the body's sensual lusts, it was not to be eaten. Against this kind of vegetarianism, Augustine moves both himself and, subsequently, the Western world in the direction of a Stoic's understanding of other animals.

on the onlooker that was the primary concern of these Christian mora-lists.[104] But unlike, say, hacking a tree to death, it was *the moral status of the non-human animal* which caused those who witnessed the vicious deaths of these animals to become, in the view of the Christian father Tertullian, "savages." And the savagery Tertullian deprecates is not of the kind inflicted on each other by the gladiators, but the emotion experi-enced by the onlooker while watching an animal get slaughtered this way.[105] Nor was Tertullian alone in this kind of criticism. Gregory of Nazianzen puts both "men killing one another" and "the slaughter of wild beasts" on the same list of problems with the games themselves, and Basil criticizes the "wealthy men" who for "secular honor" make men fight wild beasts.[106]

Thomas Aquinas

As mentioned above, I am unable to do even a survey of the Christian tradition on other animals. But especially because Singer invests so much energy in criticizing him, let us now turn to Thomas Aquinas, a man who put his work in intellectual solidarity with the pagan Greek philosopher Aristotle and who (perhaps relatedly) accepted the ancient Greek under-standing that other animals lack rational souls. Later in this chapter we will explore whether Thomas and some other thinkers might have some resources Christians could use to challenge the claim that non-human animals are not rational, but for now let us explore Thomas simply on the moral value of non-human animals, broadly speaking.

John Berkman claims that "if one is willing to dig and piece together his references, Thomas in fact presents a rather sophisticated – even if arguably inadequate and incomplete – view of non-human animals, one worthy of extended review." It should be noted at the outset (perhaps with some surprise[107]) that Thomas never takes up the nature of various

---

[104] Thomas E.J. Wiedemann, *Emperors and Gladiators* (London; New York: Routledge, 1992), 198, 148.
[105] *Ibid.*, 147. Again, the appeal to virtue ethics here doesn't take away from the understanding of animals implicit in the condemnation. If, as the early Church thought, one's virtue is affected differently by watching another animal get hacked to death vs. watching a tree get hacked to death, then the reason is because the animal has a *greater moral value* than does the tree.
[106] *Ibid.*, 158–159.
[107] Especially given the massive amount of material that Thomas Aquinas covered in his enormous corpus, and that his teacher, Albert the Great, was arguably the greatest zoologist of the medieval period, it seems odd that he doesn't deal with these issues in more detail.

non-human animals in any sustained fashion.[108] However, one can put non-human animals in the context of Thomas' larger picture of:

> the entire physical universe (for example plants, birds, non-human and human animals) ordered toward 'ultimate perfection,' which is in turn ordered to God, and by its perfection gives glory to the goodness of God. Each creature manifests the goodness of God by living according to its own *telos* … In other words, Aquinas' view is that '[t]he perfection of the universe is marked essentially by the diversity of natures, by which the diverse grades of goodness are filled up.' Thus, for Aquinas, God's plan in creation, while hierarchical, is by no means anthropocentric.[109]

For Thomas, the highest good after God

> among the created things, is the good of the order of the whole universe, since every particular good of this or that thing is ordered to it as to an end … and so, each part is found to be for the sake of its whole. Thus, among created things, what God cares for most is the order of the universe.[110]

William French notes that while there is obvious diversity between human and non-human animals for Thomas, the distance is not as great as one might imagine for humans are of the "same *genus* as other animals, but differ in species."[111] And when looking at creation as a whole, this difference becomes even less stark because, for Thomas, human beings do not have a particularly high 'slot' in the order of creation, actually being ranked *the lowest* of creatures with intellectual natures. Thus, when human and non-human animals are seen within the grand scheme of God's creation, their differences – however significant in their own right – seem not so great.[112]

One important thing that non-human animals share with human animals, for Thomas Aquinas, is a spiritual reality or soul. While human animals have a 'rational' soul, non-human animals have a 'sensitive' soul. Leaving aside for now whether certain non-human animals in fact do have a rational capacity in the sense that Thomas meant, it is remarkable how much sophisticated behavior is left for those non-human animals who nevertheless lack rationality. Thomas believes that the sensitive soul can feel emotions, for instance, and thus he would have "no difficulty thinking of a fearful zebra, a sheep that hates, an angry monkey, or

---

[108] Clough and Deane-Drummond, *Creaturely Theology*, 22.   [109] *Ibid.*, 24.
[110] Saint Thomas Aquinas, *Summa Contra Gentiles*, translated by Anton C. Pegis (Notre Dame, IN: University of Notre Dame Press, 2005), Book III, 1, 64, paragraph 10.
[111] Pinches and McDaniel (eds.), *Good News For Animals?* 58.
[112] Clough and Deane-Drummond, *Creaturely Theology*, 22.

a joyful dog." But there are a host of activities that we normally associate with human beings that are also done 'without reason' as Thomas understands it: a child learning to walk or ride a bicycle, to hit a baseball or learn to play the piano, a student learning to regurgitate information for a test or memorize the Bill of Rights, or an adult knitting or making a sandwich.[113] Berkman (along with Alasdair MacIntyre and Marie George[114]) also interprets Thomas as understanding that both human beings and some non-human animals have practical reason: that is, the capacity to *have a reason* why one acts in a certain way.

On Thomas' own terms, then, non-human animals can engage in fairly sophisticated behavior that might indicate a high moral status. Why, then, in the quote Singer gives us from the *Summa* on killing other animals cited above, does Thomas appear to locate the moral value of non-human animals as entirely dependent on the moral value of human beings? There are two question to raise here. First, does Thomas fully articulate the Christian stance (even on his own terms) on the purpose of non-human animals? Second, does it follow from what is said in the article that non-human animals have no claim on human beings?

Keeping in mind Berkman's point that Thomas Aquinas does not treat the question of non-human animals in any sustained fashion, and that his focus in this particular article is quite narrow,[115] it is hardly surprising that what we have here is an incomplete attempt at expressing the value of non-human animals. While it may be true that the purpose of such animals is connected to that of human beings, from scripture we know that the pre-fall relationship between human and non-human animals was one of kinship and companionship. Thomas selectively cites Genesis 9:3 which, as has already been pointed out above, does not tell the whole story about our relationship with non-human animals. Furthermore, on Thomas' own terms, non-human animals (and the whole created order) have a much larger purpose beyond simply relating to human beings in various ways: their existence and flourishing not only glorifies God, it also moves them toward an independent *telos* in which they have their own unique being. And there are many, many ways in which human beings violate and frustrate these other purposes: with gratuitous violence which undermines God's peaceable kingdom, and factory farming which keeps non-human animals from expressing their particular *telos* serving as obvious examples.

---

[113] *Ibid.*, 29.   [114] *Ibid.*, 38–40.
[115] Thomas Aquinas is focusing on the specific question of whether killing other animals violates the commandment against murder.

With regard to the second question, regardless of what Thomas says about the purpose and moral status of non-human animals, it does not follow that a 'more perfect' being has no moral duties to the 'less perfect' one. Indeed, Wennberg points out that even if one accepts that non-human animals are available for human use, "we still do not want to say that animals can be used in any way we please without any consideration of the animal; we do not want to say that the well-being of the animal can be sacrificed on a whim, that the interests of the animal, no matter how weighty, can be sacrificed for the interests of human beings, no matter how trivial."[116]

In answering these questions it looks as if one is suggesting that Thomas Aquinas could envision a moral standing for animals such that Christians should show them something like charitable or loving concern. But didn't we see that Thomas thought this was impossible? As we will see below with the concept of 'reason,' we must be careful about using a modern concept of 'charity' (as Singer does) when reading Aquinas. Wennberg points out that Thomas means a kind of charity which presupposes friendship, and specifically a friendship of 'everlasting happiness':

Aquinas may be correct in this; *in that sense* perhaps we cannot love animals. Further, many Christians may understandably be sympathetic to the claim that there is a circle of love reserved exclusively for what is personal and to which animals cannot gain admittance. Nevertheless, there is no reason – and Aquinas certainly provides us with no such reason – why we cannot legitimately feel affection for animals, have compassion for them, and make them the object of our concern when they suffer.[117]

THE CHURCH ON NON-HUMAN ANIMALS: SOME MODERN APPROACHES

Given what we have just encountered in the Church's tradition, it is perhaps less surprising to learn of important modern Christian expressions of concern for other animals. We have already seen that the current teaching of the Roman Catholic Church is explicit in making such expressions – with even established authorities claiming that factory farming does not cohere with biblical values. But the Christian tradition has had several more prominent figures who have led public lives with the value of non-human animals as central concern. Though we will explore

---

[116] Wennberg, *God, Humans, and Animals*, 128.   [117] *Ibid.*, 129–130.

the concept of personhood and rights in non-human animals later in the chapter, let us now focus on thinkers who do not locate their concern for such animals within this framework.[118]

C.S. Lewis

Anyone familiar with his *The Chronicles of Narnia* series might be able to guess that Clive Staples Lewis had a deep love for non-human animals. Though he rejected his Christian upbringing as a teenager in favor of atheism, Lewis returned to the faith of his youth in no small part due to conversations and arguments with his devout Roman Catholic friend, Oxford colleague and fellow animal lover, J.R.R. Tolkien. An orthodox Anglican, and one interested in providing a public, rational defense of his faith, Lewis was particularly focused on exploring the problem of the vast amount of suffering in a world created by a loving God and the attention he gave to the particular problem of the suffering of non-human animals was quite thorough. He wrote an essay called "On the Pains of Animals," devoted an entire chapter to animal suffering in his classic work *The Problem of Pain*, and even wrote a book which he simply entitled *Vivisection*.[119]

Interestingly, and like Singer,[120] Lewis makes the sentience of non-human animals a central concern. He flatly says that life "in the biological sense has nothing to do with good and evil until sentience appears."[121] And the pain which such sentience brings with it for non-human animals, according to Linzey, caused Lewis himself to suffer:

Note the unmistakable sense of personal distress in the way in which he approaches this issue: 'I know there are moments when the incessant continuity and desperate helplessness of what seems at least to be animal suffering makes every argument for Theism sound hollow' … Lewis 'turn(s) with distaste from "the easy speeches that comfort cruel men," from theologians who do not seem to

---

[118] I will delimit this section by avoiding important authors that we have already engaged above: David Clough, Robert Wennberg, Denis Edwards, Andrew Linzey, etc. Instead, I will focus on those lesser-known voices in the animal rights and welfare discourse.

[119] See C.S. Lewis, *The Problem of Pain*. Also see, C.S. Lewis, "The Pains of Animals: A Problem in Theology," in *God in the Dock: Essays on Theology and Ethics* (Grand Rapids, MI: William B. Eerdmans Publishing, Co., 1994) and C.S. Lewis, *Vivisection*, New England Anti-Vivisection Society, 1947.

[120] Another way Lewis mirrors Singer is his concern for the problem of evil, particularly manifested in the apparent unnecessary suffering of human and non-human animals. See in particular Dallas Willard (ed.), *A Place for Truth: Leading Thinkers Explore Life's Hardest Questions* (Downers Grove, IL: InterVarsity Press, 2010), 170–171.

[121] C.S. Lewis, *The Problem of Pain*, 144, 133.

see that there is a real problem, who are content to say that animals are, after all, only animals.' And why should animals present this difficulty? Chiefly because 'pain without guilt or moral fruit, however low and contemptible the sufferer may be, is a very serious matter.'[122]

Lewis spills most of his theological ink on this issue attempting to explain such suffering in light of a belief in the Christian God, but he also has much to offer the Christian about how one is to relate to animal suffering:

The only rational line for the Christian vivisectionist to take is to say that the superiority of man over beast is a real objective fact, guaranteed by Revelation, and that the propriety of sacrificing beast to man is a logical consequence . . . yet that very superiority ought partly to consist in not behaving like a vivisector: that we ought to prove ourselves better than the beasts precisely by the fact of acknowledging duties to them which they do not acknowledge to us.[123]

Lewis makes the claim that a friend of Thomas Aquinas' position could also make: the theologically revealed superiority of human animals over non-human animals does not negate the moral duties we have toward them. Quite the contrary: for Lewis, it is precisely because animals are so often unprotected, undefended, vulnerable, and morally innocent that their misery should be deserving of special moral solicitude.[124]

Stanley Hauerwas

Hauerwas, it is often mentioned, has been proclaimed American's best theologian by *Time* magazine. Well known for attempting to separate Christian theology and practice from the influence of the Enlightenment, he is at pains to show that Christians should not be governed by allegiance to either the political 'right' or 'left' or even to the interests of the nation-state in which one lives. Instead, we should focus on our ancient Christian narrative which cannot authentically be made to fit into any of these modern political categories. What does such a narrative reveal about the value of non-human animals? According to Hauerwas,

the only significant theological difference between humans and animals lies in a unique *purpose* (original emphasis) given to humans by God. Herein lies what it means for God to create humans in God's image. This *unique purpose* which God gives humans with regard to animals lies in our job of telling animals who they are. [Here he references the Genesis narrative where Adam names the animals.]

---

122 Andrew Linzey, "C.S. Lewis's Theology of Animals," Anglican Theological Review (Winter 1998), 62.
123 C.S. Lewis, *Vivisection*, quoted in Linzey, 66–67.
124 Linzey, "C.S. Lewis's Theology of Animals," 74.

We do this by the very way we relate to other animals. We think there is an analogous relation between the fact that animals need humans to tell them their story and the fact that we who are Gentiles need Jews to tell us our story.[125]

Aghast at the practices our secular society has adopted in its treatment of non-human animals, Hauerwas refuses to accept the secular, Enlightenment framework of 'rights' to argue for different practices. The language of rights (at least in the Enlightenment context) is freighted with the very kind of consumerism, anthropocentrism and hyper-autonomy that got us into the problem in the first place. He claims that "Christians have far richer resources by which to address the question of how we should relate to other animals. Any appeal to rights pales in relation to the peace and love of Christ to which the Christian is called."[126] Indeed, we need to realize that our understanding of how we are to rule over animals is directly connected with how we understand God to be ruling over us. It is from "the vision of a peaceable creation, both between human and animal and between animal and animal" that we can "throw off the view that dominion means domination over the animals."[127]

Hauerwas is a pacifist who argues that this is what an authentically lived life looks like when modeled on the teaching and example of Jesus in the Gospels. He also thinks that

there is a significant similarity between the issues of pacifism and vegetarianism. Just as we believe that Christians are not called to be nonviolent because nonviolence is a strategy to free the world from war, but because as Christians we cannot conceive of living other than nonviolently in a world of war, so it may also be true that Christians in a world of meat eaters are called to live nonviolently.

Such a choice to be vegetarian, says Hauerwas, "might be understood as a witness to the world that God's creation is not meant to be at war with itself." Indeed, he continues the war analogy by claiming that, just as those Christians who argue for killing in war have the burden of proof in Just War theory, those who eat meat should have a similar burden of proof:

This is because Christian Just-War theory is most appropriately understood as a theory of exceptions, exceptions for allowing Christians to engage in limited forms of violence in order to protect the neighbor. Analogously,

[125] Stanley Hauerwas and John Berkman, "The Chief End of All Flesh," *Theology Today* vol. 49: No. 2 (July 1992), 199.
[126] *Ibid.*, 201.   [127] *Ibid.*, 70.

we believe that Christians need to develop similar criteria of just meat
eating, if it is not to be forbidden entirely.[128]

Even for Stanley Hauerwas, this is a remarkable claim. If we are to push
the analogy through, Christians should only be able to kill and eat animals
when there is a grave reason to do so. In a footnote he hints that such
situations might be limited to human starvation, and for most of us in the
developed world this requires something like vegetarianism.

Mary Eberstadt

A research fellow at the conservative Hoover Institute, and committed
Roman Catholic, Mary Eberstadt has been a regular writer for conservative publications like *First Things*, *The Weekly Standard*, and *The
Wall Street Journal*. She must have perplexed much of her readership in
an article she wrote for *First Things* titled, "Pro-Animal, Pro-Life."[129]
Much like Hauerwas' attempt to link violence toward non-human animals
and violence in war, Eberstadt attempts to link ethical vegetarianism with
moral suspicion of abortion:

The sheer decibel level of unreason surrounding the issue of abortion in academic
writing about animal rights tells us something interesting. It suggests that,
contrary to what the utilitarians and feminists working this terrain wish, the dots
between sympathy for animals and sympathy for unborn humans are in fact quite
easy to connect – so easy, you might say, that a child could do it.

Despite the fact that "traditionalists" have relished in bashing vegetarianism for decades, she claims that it "is not easily dismissed morally or
intellectually." Ethical vegetarianism as a practice "appears commonly
rooted in an *a priori* aversion to violence against living creatures" and is
often triggered by a 'Damascus moment'[130] which is shared by those who
oppose cruelty to non-human animals and abortion alike:

A sudden insight, igniting empathy on a scale that did not exist before and
perhaps even a life-transforming realization – this reaction should indeed be
thought through with care. It is not only the most commonly cited feature of the
decision to become a vegetarian. It is also the most commonly cited denominator
of what brings people to their convictions about the desperate need to protect
unborn, innocent human life.

---

[128] *Ibid.*, 72.
[129] Mary Eberstadt, "Pro-Animal, Pro-Life," *First Things*, www.firstthings.com/article/2009/05/
pro-animal-pro-life-1243228870 (Accessed April 2, 2010).
[130] This is a reference to St. Paul's life-changing vision and conversion while on the road to Damascus.

Often, says Eberstadt, this moment occurs in the young – or at least those young enough at heart to question a widely accepted and habitual practice. She highlights the instinctive repulsion many children feel at the prospect of "eating the animals they just petted on the farm" as something which should give the rest of us moral pause as well. Indeed, pro-life Christians and vegetarians, she says, are strangers to one another for reasons of accident rather than essence.

Matthew Scully

Nor is public and serious Christian concern for non-human animals limited to the ivory tower of the scholar or prelate.[131] As mentioned briefly above, while a special assistant and senior speech writer for then President George W. Bush, Matthew Scully wrote the important and accessible book *Dominion* which attempts to bring the issues away from the margins of our culture and to turn the average person's gaze toward the suffering animal.[132] Though admittedly not a particularly pious Christian, his book refuses to shy away from religious imagery and principle. Indeed, as the title implies, much of the book is an exploration of the power the Bible describes as having been given to human animals over non-human animals. Of this he says:

Animals are more than ever a test of our character, of mankind's capacity for empathy and for decent, honorable conduct and faithful stewardship. We are called to treat them with kindness, not because they have rights or power or some claim to equality, but in a sense because they don't; because they all stand unequal and powerless before us.[133]

He is certainly worried about the anti-humanism that he (and many others in the 'animal welfare' crowd) believes comes with claiming non-human animals have 'rights.' But he rejects as prideful and pedantic the lengths to which some in his camp will go to in claiming that, when treating other animals poorly, the real wrong is to ourselves or the moral

---

[131] Many popular Christian vegetarian websites, for instance, have been around for the better part of a decade. One particularly good example is www.catholic-animals.org (Accessed February 5, 2011).

[132] As his friend and fellow political commentator, Joseph Sobran, said on hearing of Scully's dietary preferences: "A conservative, with a Catholic upbringing, and a vegetarian? Boy, talk about aggrieved minorities!" Natalie Angier, "The Most Compassionate Conservative," *The New York Times*, www.nytimes.com/2002/10/27/books/the-most-compassionate-conservative.html?pagewanted=1 (Accessed April 2, 2010).

[133] Matthew Scully, *Dominion: The Power of Man, the Suffering of Animals, and the Call to Mercy*, 434, xi–xii.

law. While in the spiritual realm any Christian knows that sin always hurts the sinner more than any victim because that person is estranging himself from God, in the temporal realm

we can safely assume that [non-human animals] can be wronged, and that the victim of bear-baiting is really the bear. All that animals need, and what we owe them under our laws, are specific, clear, and above all consistent criminal sanctions declaring Thou Shalt Not subject them to human cruelty, as a matter of simple decency and an obligation of justice.[134]

ARE SOME NON-HUMAN ANIMALS PERSONS?

Many in the animal liberation movement, including Singer, claim that certain non-human animals are *persons*. We have already seen how the Church could get behind the animal liberation movement for other reasons, but could Christians agree with Singer and others on this dramatic and (for many) counter-intuitive claim? At first blush, and especially for those like Singer who wish to disparage the Church as speciesist, the answer would appear to be no. Isn't it the case that human beings are the pinnacle of creation and therefore the only ones who can rightly claim the moral status of a person? Indeed, the Church's supposed speciesism would seem to have produced two important claims about the relationship between human beings and personhood:

1. All humans are persons.
2. All persons are humans.

The first claim was largely answered in the opening chapter which demonstrated the reasoning behind the Church's position that all humans, regardless of age or level of impairment, are persons. Recall that this was an argument not grounded in some kind of arbitrary designation based on biological species, but rather on the claim that being *Homo sapiens* is an indicator of what really constitutes personhood: namely, being a substance of a rational nature. There have been sad times in the Church's history where Christians (again, following Aristotle that some human beings are not fit by nature for self-rule) made a case for the non-personhood of some *Homo sapiens*. But the second claim points us in the direction of some interesting arguments we have yet to consider.

---

[134] Scully, *Dominion*, 349.

Late 5th uth (480 524)

Are all persons human beings?

This question was also raised briefly in Chapter 1, but let us now get into the kind of detail necessary to consider whether some non-human animals could be considered persons in the Christian tradition. Recall that perhaps the most influential definition of person was proposed by Boethius who claimed that a person was simply an individual substance of a rational nature. Human beings fit into this category, but do any other creatures have a rational nature? The influential theologian Pseudo-Dionysius (likely a contemporary of Boethius) certainly thought so and makes his case in his influential *The Celestial Hierarchy*.[135] His view is that within creation there is a hierarchy based on the extent to which various creatures participate in the life of God:

All inanimate things participate in It through their being; for the 'to be' of all things is the Divinity above Being Itself, the true Life. Living things participate in Its life-giving Power above all life; rational things participate in Its self-perfect and pre-eminently perfect Wisdom above all reason and intellect.

But are there rational creatures that are not human beings? Not only is the answer yes, but human beings are *the least* of such creatures:

On this account the holy ranks of the Celestial Beings are present with and participate in the Divine Principle in a degree far surpassing all those things which merely exist, and irrational living creatures, and rational human beings.

He takes the rational natures of these Celestial Beings (read: angels) so seriously that much of this text is an extended accounting of the hierarchies that exist within this community of beings.

Thomas Aquinas, who as we saw in Chapter 1 accepts Boethius' definition of personhood, also agrees with Pseudo-Dionysius on this question. Not only are angels rational, but what makes them higher than human beings is that they are *intellectual*.[136] Merely rational creatures reason discursively in that they know one thing through another – such as a human person knowing something about God through sacred scripture or through the witness of the saints. But if human beings possessed the fullness of intellectual knowledge, like the angels, "then in the first aspect of principles they would at once comprehend their whole range, by

---

[135] "The Celestial Hierarchy-Dionysius the Areopagite," Esoterica, www.esoteric.msu.edu/VolumeII/CelestialHierarchy.html (Accessed April 23, 2010). All quotes from Chapter 4.
[136] Thomas and Dominicans. English Province, *Summa Theologica*, 3057, I, 93, 3.

perceiving whatever could be reasoned out from them."[137] So, for Aquinas, not only are there persons who are not human beings, but human beings are also *the most limited kind of persons.*

But a Christian understanding of personhood which extends beyond the species *Homo sapiens* is not limited to these well-known Christian thinkers; nor is it limited to celestial beings like angels. Indeed, many medieval Christian thinkers took seriously the idea from certain ancient authors that there are *homines* in unknown parts of the Earth who are biologically different from us, and saw no contradiction between this belief and their other theological commitments. Often citing St. Augustine as their source,[138] there was a particular focus on 'cynocephali': creatures, otherwise human, who had the heads of dogs. Many serious medieval theologians write about them specifically: the Benedictine monk Ratramnus of Corbie, for instance, wrote a work specifically titled *Epistola de Cynocephalis*. The medieval historian Karl Steel demonstrates Ratramnus' understanding of these creatures by acknowledging their bestial nature, but noting that there is obviously a rational aspect to their nature, given that they have formed a community with towns, agriculture, and the rule of law.[139] These creatures are found pictured in many places in various artistic contexts: including in the well-known tympanum at Vézélay Abbey in France. Remarkably, in the Theolodore Psalter (one of the most important texts surviving from Byzantine Christianity), Christ is shown *preaching* to Cynocephali. And according to some Christian legends, St. Christopher himself was thought to be Cynocephalus (one can find icons of him with the head of a dog) before he was rewarded with full human form for aiding the Christ-child.

And Tom O'Meara reminds us that Christian conceptions of non-human personhood were not even limited to the planet Earth:

The Franciscan School in the Middle Ages was open to the idea of several worlds, while the Dominicans opted for a single, tightly ordered world. However, in the Renaissance, two Dominicans, Tomasso Campanella (1568–1634) and Giordano Bruno (1548–1600), did hold for multiple worlds. Bruno concluded that there was an infinite universe and a plurality of worlds; he not only populated the planets and stars but endowed stars and meteors with souls. In his view, we see

[137] *Ibid.*, I, 58, 3.
[138] Henry Bettenson (trans.), *Concerning the City of God Against the Pagans*. 2003 edn. (New York: Penguin Books, 1972), Book 16, Chapter 8. I owe this insight to my colleague, Richard Viladesau.
[139] Karl Steel, "Cynocephali, Animal Savagery, and Terror," In the Middle, www.inthemedievalmiddle. com/2007/07/cynocephali-animal-savagery-and-terror.html (Accessed April 24, 2010). The last example is particularly important because it shows evidence of the 'self-rule' required for rationality.

from earth these complex worlds as single stars because they are so remote, but in fact a star includes planets and moons and comets and other bodies.[140]

He also quotes the remarkable view of Nicholas of Cusa (an important fifteenth century philosopher, jurist, mathematician, astronomer and Roman Catholic cardinal) on this question:

For if God is the center and circumference of all the regions of the stars and if from him natures of diverse nobility proceed, living in every region – many regions of heavens and stars are not empty – since intellectual nature living on this earth is what is most noble and perfect ... there would be other kinds of inhabitants of other stars.[141]

Indeed, the advances in astronomy in the early modern period led the Baroque Scholastics to speculate further on the possibility of rational biological life in worlds other than ours. The great philosopher and theologian Francisco Suárez, for instance, claimed that an incarnation of God could take place more than once[142] – an idea which opens up the possibility of other incarnations in other worlds, and therefore of other rational creatures capable of salvation. Suárez also taught that the object of Christian charity should be "every rational creature" or every creature that is capable of beatitude.[143]

Nor is the serious consideration of extraterrestrial rational life on the part of the Church limited to its history. The Vatican Observatory and the Pontifical Academy of Sciences recently hosted its second conference on astrobiology in five years. The director of the Observatory, Fr. Jose Funes, SJ, began his remarks by answering the question:

"Why is the Vatican involved in astrobiology?" Fr. Funes stated that despite the field's newness, "the questions of life's origins and of whether life exists elsewhere in the universe are very interesting and deserve serious consideration."[144]

---

[140] Thomas O'Meara, "Christian Theology and Extraterrestrial Intelligent Life," *Theological Studies* 60 (1999), 5–6. It is worth noting that Bruno's view, though perfectly acceptable today, was not accepted by the institutional Church of his day.

[141] P. Wilpert (ed.), *De docta ignorantia* 2.12, in *Nikolaus von Kues, Werke* (Berlin: de Gruyter, 1967), 1.65.

[142] Francisco Suárez and Jean Malou, *De incarnatione pars prima* in *Opera Omnia* (Venetiis: Balleoni, 1745), disp. 13, sect. 3. I also owe this insight to Richard Viladesau.

[143] Francisco Suárez and Jean Malou, *Tractatus Tertius de Caritate* in *Opera Omnia* (Venetiis: Balleoni, 1745), disp. 1, sect. 1, no. 3.

[144] "Vatican Observatory examines theological implications of finding alien life," Catholic News Agency, www.catholicnewsagency.com/news/vatican_observatory_examines_theological_implications_of_finding_alien_life/ (Accessed April 24, 2010).

One of the issues discussed was the possibility of rational creatures existing on other worlds not descended from Adam:

The possibility raises a difficult theological question concerning redemption from the original sin, which by Christian tradition occurred in the Garden of Eden when Adam and Eve ate the forbidden fruit of a particular tree. Funes told the Osservatore Romano: "If other intelligent beings exist, it's not certain that they need redemption."[145]

It should be clear from the preceding discussion that not only is a non-human person a theoretical possibility for the Christian tradition, but many influential thinkers, both past and present, have believed that they actually exist (especially in the case of angels). We now know that the Church *could* agree with Singer that some non-human animals are persons. But *should* they be considered persons?

The capacities of non-human animals

I already gestured at some of the capacities of non-human animals above when examining why Singer argued for non-human personhood, but in exploring the issue now before us, we must be more detailed and systematic. Indeed, both Singer and the Christian tradition have a focus on rationality, but it is not at all clear that they mean the same thing. In this section we will examine whether or not some non-human animals have several traits or capacities that one might think are conditions for personhood: consciousness, rationality, self-awareness, second (and third) order reflection, empathy, and morality.

Consciousness. It might seem perfectly obvious to us that some non-human animals are conscious, but many brilliant people have argued for a very long time that non-human animals are mere automata. Wennberg, though he eventually gives us several good reasons to reject their point of view, warns us that this issue might not be as neat and clean as we imagine. Much of what we base our views upon, when pressed, ends up being simple appeals to common sense rather than a grounded, systematic argument. "*Of course* when a dog gets hit by a car they feel pain and suffering because that's what I would feel if *I* was hit by a car." Fortunately for those who cannot imagine anything else being true, there are

[145] American Foreign Press, "Vatican searches for extra-terrestrial life," Google, www.google.com/hostednews/afp/article/ALeqM5iXaUKFhkbVieQAqtllc-sCKsba9w (Accessed April 24, 2010).

two lines of argument that give us good reason to think that some non-human animals are in fact conscious. The first involves appeals to the physiological and anatomical similarities between humans and many animals. If we accept that human subjective experiences arise as a result of certain processes in our brains and central nervous systems, then where there are certain physiological and anatomical similarities between humans and animals, there we may reasonably conclude there are also similar subjective experiences.[146]

In determining whether or not a chicken feels pain as we do when she is debeaked, for example, we would simply point out that the soft tissue that is cut is replete with many nerve fibers and that a chicken brain has pain receptors similar to those of human beings. The second line of argument is one that appeals to explanatory adequacy. Why, if the chicken is not feeling pain, does she struggle and squawk? Why would an abusive and cruel pet owner beat his dog if she didn't feel it? While it is true that we cannot directly access the inner life of other animals, the combination of similar physiology with the lack of any better explanation for various behaviors leads one to reasonably conclude that some non-human animals are conscious.

Rationality. For our purposes in this section, rationality will refer to the ability to think abstractly and symbolically and to solve problems systematically.[147] We have already seen primates use the abstractions of American Sign Language to signify various concepts – including those of future events. Oliver Putz cites evidence that apes can "make and use tools" and "use plants for self-medication." He also cites studies of chimps and bonobos which indicate "both cardinal and ordinal [number] skills, including, in the case of the female Ali, the concept of zero."[148] Some non-human animals, at least given the definition above, are clearly rational.

Self-awareness. This concept goes well beyond merely having experiences and the capacity to think abstractly and solve problems. If an entity is self-aware, it is able to identify itself as a distinct entity and display some evidence that it knows that distinct entity is oneself. Perhaps the best evidence for self-awareness is the aforementioned 'mirror test': if an entity can recognize oneself in the mirror, as opposed to thinking that it is an

---

[146] Wennberg, *God, Humans, and Animals*, 96.
[147] This is a more modern understanding of rationality, but we will explore other understandings of concept – including that of Thomas Aquinas – in more detail below.
[148] Oliver Putz, "Moral Apes, Human Uniqueness, and the Image of God," *Zygon* 44:3 (September 2009), 615 and 617.

image of another animal (or simply ignoring the image), then that is strong evidence that the entity is self-aware. Recall from the discussion above that great apes, dolphins, and elephants have all passed the mirror test. In addition, as we saw above, some great apes can use sign language to indicate self-awareness by referring to themselves as a distinct entity.

Third-order reflection. First-order reflection is, according to Putz, "simply having a representation of something." Second-order reflection consists in knowing that another individual has the same representation. But third-order reflection requires that an individual must know that another knows that the first individual knows.[149] Do we have evidence that some non-human animals exhibit this sophisticated capacity? Strong evidence would be other animals engaging in deceptive behavior. In order to attempt to deceive another, one must know that they can know something which one is trying to represent in a misleading way. Wennberg also notes the following example where the gorilla Koko engaged in deception:

On one occasion Koko broke a sink by sitting on it and when asked if it was she who had broken the sink she replied, seeking (it is claimed) to falsely accuse Francine Patterson's assistant, "Kate . . . there . . . bad."[150]

This capacity for third-order reflection is a necessary condition for the last two capacities to be considered: empathy and morality.

Empathy. Putz directly links the third-order reflection of the chimpanzee Washoe with his capacity to be empathetic (and ultimately altruistic):

Washoe, an adult female chimpanzee, saw three-year-old female Cindy jump the fence of their enclosure and fall into a moat. Washoe, who was unrelated to Cindy, likewise jumped the fence and, despite his innate fear of water, stepped into the moat and pulled the drowning infant to safety.[151]

Wennberg also cites a couple of examples of Koko's empathy. She was said

to show "touching sympathy" toward other animals and upon seeing a horse with a bit in its mouth signed "Horse . . . sad." When she was asked why the horse was sad she replied by signing "teeth." When she was shown a photograph of another gorilla struggling against taking a bath, Koko, who also hates baths, is reported by Patterson to have signed "Me Cry There" while pointing to the picture.[152]

---

[149] Putz, "Moral Apes, Human Uniqueness, and the Image of God," 616.
[150] Wennberg, *God, Humans, and Animals,* 105.
[151] Putz, "Moral Apes, Human Uniqueness, and the Image of God," 618.   [152] Wennberg, 105.

Celia Deane-Drummond claims that many other animals "also seem capable of showing care, even when there seems to be no advantage to them. Companionships between blind animals (including humans) and other animals abound, including some unusual liaisons such as that between a one-year-old hippopotamus and a century-old tortoise."[153] Or consider this stunning relationship between Bella the dog and Tarra the elephant:

"When it's time to eat they both eat together. They drink together. They sleep together. They play together," Buckley says.

Tarra and Bella have been close for years – but no one really knew how close they were until recently. A few months ago Bella suffered a spinal cord injury. She couldn't move her legs, couldn't even wag her tail. For three weeks the dog lay motionless up in the sanctuary office.

And for *three weeks* [emphasis added] the elephant held vigil: 2,700 acres to roam free, and Tarra just stood in the corner, beside a gate, right outside that sanctuary office.

"She just stood outside the balcony – just stood there and waited," says Buckley. "She was concerned about her friend."[154]

Deane-Drummond makes the important point that several "social animals show a degree of acceptance toward those in their social group that are injured or born with difficulties, as shown by examples of tolerance of, for example, a mentally retarded monkey in a group of rhesus macaques."[155] Recent studies of primates have also shown both a remarkable awareness of death and of empathy for their companions going through the grieving process.[156]

Morality. On this question, Deane-Drummond cites the fascinating research of Marc Bekoff, who

has observed play behaviour among canids. Dogs, coyotes, and wolves all learn quickly to play in a way that is fair according to the rules set up by the particular species. Those that fail to engage in fair play become more isolated and drift away

---

[153] Clough and Deane-Drummond, *Creaturely Theology*, 196.

[154] Steve Hartman, "On Elephant Sanctuary, Unlikely Friends," CBS News, www.cbsnews.com/stories/2009/01/02/assignment_america/main4696340.shtml?tag=currentVideoInfo;videoMetaInfo (Accessed April 25, 2010).

[155] Clough and Deane-Drummond, *Creaturely Theology*, 194.

[156] "Chimps may be aware of others' deaths," ScienceNews, www.sciencenews.org/view/generic/id/58652/title/Chimps_may_be_aware_of_others'_deaths (Accessed February 5, 2011) and Richard Alleyne, "Chimpanzees grieve for loved ones," *Telegraph* online, www.telegraph.co.uk/science/science-news/7634918/Chimpanzees-grieve-for-loved-ones.html (Accessed February 5, 2011).

from the group ... Particular 'rules' for fair play include invitation signals, variations in sequence of actions, self-handicapping, and role-reversing.[157]

Putz also cites Bekoff, but in a similar kind of study on great apes:

In the game juvenile bonobos cover their eyes with either an object or their hand and then stumble around the climbing frame some 15 feet in the air. This play requires individuals to agree to play by the rules – not look unless one loses one's balance – and also the understanding that others can see and judge whether or not one is truly covering one's eyes.

Putz claims that the presence of traits previously mentioned should lead one to conclude that the fairness and rule-following in the bonobo games "can result from moral decision making."[158] Deane-Drummond, though a bit more hesitant, nevertheless makes a similar interpretation. Especially because Bekoff cites examples of the game's rule-breakers feeling shame or embarrassment, something she thinks could be the evolutionary primordia of a moral conscience, Deane-Drummond claims that this is evidence of morality "of some sort." And while she doesn't equate it with the "universal reasoning" of which human persons are capable, the difference "seems to be one of degree, rather than absolute distinction."[159]

We have already seen that, given Singer's definition of a person as a rational and self-aware creature, many non-human animals are persons. But how might the Church approach and evaluate the evidence just presented? Christian discussions surrounding what traits are indicative of personhood (and whether personhood should be identified or described in terms of traits at all) are incredibly complex and go back to the earliest foundational debates of the tradition.[160] In what will no doubt be a disappointment for some readers, for the sake of argument and space, I will simply assume Boethius' and Thomas Aquinas' "substance of a rational nature" definition of personhood.[161] I do this not only because it is so influential in the Christian tradition, but also because it matches up well with Singer's definition which also invokes rationality. And at first blush, and in light of

---

[157] Clough and Deane-Drummond, *Creaturely Theology*, 195.
[158] Putz, "*Moral Apes, Human Uniqueness, and the Image of God,*" 619.
[159] Clough and Deane-Drummond, *Creaturely Theology*, 207.
[160] This is not surprising given that some of the earliest of the most important debates in the Christian tradition were about ways of understanding Jesus as one person with two natures and God as one being in three persons.
[161] In particular, more than a few will be worried that this definition does not sufficiently take into account the relational aspect of what it means to be a person. But as we will see below, a more traditional understanding of rationality is far more connected to relationality than is the one born of the Enlightenment.

the evidence just presented, it appears that several different kinds of non-human animals are persons, given that they are rational. But this reaction is supported only by an Enlightenment concept of rationality. Thomas Aquinas has a very different understanding.

A substance of a rational nature?

Thomas Aquinas has a lot to say about rationality, but to understand what he means when he claims that human beings are substances of a rational nature, we must first understand what he means when he claims that human beings are made in the image of God. He says, "While in all creatures there is some kind of likeness to God, in the rational creature alone we find a likeness of 'image' as we have explained above (1,2)."[162] And this image is to be found in the intellect:

Since man is said to be the image of God by reason of his intellectual nature, he is the most perfectly like God according to that in which he can best imitate God in his intellectual nature. Now the intellectual nature imitates God chiefly in this, that God understands and loves Himself. Wherefore we see that the image of God is in man in three ways. First, inasmuch as man possesses a natural aptitude for understanding and loving God; and this aptitude consists in the very nature of the mind, which is common to all men.[163]

But what is this reference to 'intellect'? Wasn't the key aspect 'reason'? But, for Thomas, they are the same thing:

Reason and intellect in [humanity] cannot be distinct powers. We shall understand this clearly if we consider their respective actions. For to understand is simply to apprehend intelligible truth: and to reason is to advance from one thing understood to another, so as to know an intelligible truth. And therefore angels, who according to their nature, possess perfect knowledge of intelligible truth, have no need to advance from one thing to another; but apprehend the truth simply and without mental discussion, as Dionysius says (Div. Nom. vii). But man arrives at the knowledge of intelligible truth by advancing from one thing to another; and therefore he is called rational. Reasoning, therefore, is compared to understanding, as movement is to rest, or acquisition to possession; of which one belongs to the perfect, the other to the imperfect. And since movement always proceeds from something immovable, and ends in something at rest; hence it is that human reasoning, by way of inquiry and discovery, advances from certain things simply understood – namely, the first principles; and, again, by way of judgment returns by analysis to first principles, in the light of which it examines what it has found.[164]

[162] Thomas and Dominicans. English Province. *Summa Theologica*, I, 93, 6.
[163] *Ibid.*, I, 93, 4.   [164] *Ibid.*, I, 79, 8.

And as we can tell from what has been cited of his view already, it is now clear how this kind of rational capacity is very different from the Enlightenment concept described in the previous section:

Thus the image of God is found in the soul according as the soul turns to God, or possesses a nature that enables it to turn to God ... The meritorious knowledge and love of God can be in us only by grace. Yet there is a certain natural knowledge and love as seen above (12, 12; 56, 3; 60, 5). This, too, is natural that the mind, in order to understand God, can make use of reason, in which sense we have already said that the image of God abides ever in the soul; "whether this image of God be so obsolete," as it were clouded, "as almost to amount to nothing," as in those who have not the use of reason; "or obscured and disfigured," as in sinners; or "clear and beautiful," as in the just; as Augustine says (De Trin. xiv, 6).[165]

Therefore, what Thomas Aquinas means when he claims that human beings are substances of a rational nature is that we are the kinds of things which have *the capacity to know and love God*. This, quite clearly, is an understanding which goes beyond a kind of thinking to engaging in a particular kind of relationship. Unfortunately for those who want to see clear evidence of personhood in the non-human animals described above, it must be admitted that we do not see evidence of a capacity to know and love God even in the most sophisticated species considered.[166]

This, however, is not the end of the discussion. Consider once again that, for Thomas, the whole ontological structure of creation is on a hierarchical scale with respect to the extent to which something or someone reflects the image and/or likeness of God. Human beings might be substances of a rational nature, but we know he thinks that human beings are very low on the hierarchy of such creatures. Could one appropriate this aspect of Thomas' thought to conceive of some non-human animals, while not substances of a rational nature, nevertheless *fairly close* to human persons in a hierarchy of being? Or is there some sort of dramatic ontological firewall between the two that would preclude this way of thinking?

The image and likeness of God

The key to answering the above question is to look carefully at what Thomas Aquinas means by the "image and likeness" of God, and especially

---

[165] *Ibid.*, I, 93, 8.
[166] This appears to be true even if we define God as something like "one's source of ultimate concern." None of the animals cited above appear to be able to order their lives with this level of sophistication.

in the context of I, 93, 2[167] where he asks, "Whether the image of God is to be found in irrational creatures?" As we just discovered, he ends up answering this question in the negative, but in good scholastic fashion he begins by considering the best arguments against his position. At first it seems as if the image of God *is* found in irrational creatures: for isn't the image of God to be found in *everything* God creates, rational and irrational creatures alike? Indeed, he considers the following very important objection:

Further, Boethius (De Consol. iii) says of God: "Holding the world in His mind, and forming it into His image." Therefore the whole world is to the image of God, and not only the rational creature.

After also citing the authorities of Dionysius and Genesis to further bolster the objection, Thomas' ultimate answer – that "things without intellect are not made to God's image" – looks difficult to sustain.

The key for Thomas here is to make a move we have already seen above: to distinguish between a creature that is made *merely in the likeness* of God and one that is in *both* the image and likeness of God. He is quite willing to admit that all creation bears the likeness of its creator. Indeed, he says that "some things are like to God first and most commonly because they exist; secondly, because they live; and thirdly because they know or understand." But even though non-human animals bear the *likeness* of God in some or all three of these ways, Thomas stops short of saying that this means they bear the *image* of God:

Not every likeness, not even what is copied from something else, is sufficient to make an image; for if the likeness be only generic, or existing by virtue of some common accident, this does not suffice for one thing to be the image of another. For instance, a worm, though from man it may originate, cannot be called man's image, merely because of the generic likeness. Nor, if anything is made white like something else, can we say that it is the image of that thing; for whiteness is an accident belonging to many species. But the nature of an image requires likeness in species; thus the image of the king exists in his son: or, at least, in some specific accident, and chiefly in the shape; thus, we speak of a man's image in copper.

So even though some non-human animals 'know and understand,' for Thomas, the knowing and understanding of which substances of a rational nature are capable (that which allows them to know and love God) so far surpasses those of non-human animals that it puts them in

---

[167] From which all the quotes of this section come.

a different ontological category. And consequently, Thomas thinks very differently about their moral status.

But need this ontological firewall exist? Could one accept Thomas' claim that no non-human animal can know and love God in the sense that a human person can, while also claiming that some non-human animals are in such proximity to human persons with regard to knowing and loving that they would nevertheless have a very, very high moral status? The answer seems to be yes, for Thomas himself admits that many animals know and understand. And we have seen above that for several kinds of non-human animals, such knowing and understanding are very high indeed and involve rationality, self-awareness, third-order reflection, empathy, and even a sense of fairness or morality. The last example is particularly important – and especially when one considers the Church's teaching on how agnostics or atheists might come to be saved. Consider this remarkable claim from the Dogmatic Constitution on the Church:

> Those also can attain to salvation who through no fault of their own do not know the Gospel of Christ or His Church, yet sincerely seek God and moved by grace strive by their deeds to do His will as it is known to them through the dictates of conscience.[168]

Could non-human animals, in some sense, strive by their deeds to do God's will by following their conscience? The answer, as we saw from the discussion of certain non-human animals' capacity for morality above, is not obviously in the negative.

At the very least, many kinds of non-human animals bear the likeness of God at a very high level. They are rational, self-aware, empathetic, and have a sense of fairness. Even if we refused to say that such creatures had the moral status of full persons, perhaps we should not take a binary approach in which personhood is an either/or proposition. Perhaps we should extend the hierarchy of persons down from angels and human persons to include several kinds of non-human animals. Indeed, I can find no reason to deny many of them a moral status similar to that of human persons. For if there is some evidence which suggests that *in some limited sense* non-human animals like primates and dolphins can know and love God, they should also be described as persons in some limited

---

[168] Pope Paul VI, "Dogmatic Constitution on the Church – *Lumen Gentium*" (Vatican: The Holy See), www.vatican.va/archive/hist_councils/ii_vatican_council/documents/vat-ii_const_19641121_lumen-gentium_en.html (Accessed July 31, 2011), 16.

sense. And this is no mere ivory-tower, abstract, intellectual argument: multiple countries (including Britain, New Zealand and, most recently, Spain) have moved toward legally supporting something like the Great Ape Project, "which argues that three essential human rights – life, liberty and freedom from physical and psychological torture – should be extended to our closest hominid relatives."[169] This is not only compatible with a Christian approach to non-human animals, but ought to be something toward which Christians – especially in light of what has been presented in this chapter – should be directing significant energies.

CONCLUSION

As we have seen with the topics of the first two chapters, there is significant and wide-ranging overlap between Singer and the Church on non-human animals. Such common ground opens the door for productive exchanges which can challenge both approaches in various ways. For instance, Singer's criticisms and arguments can help Christians to both (re)discover our own tradition and also push the growing edge of the tradition to develop new insights – especially in light of modern-day institutions like factory farms and laboratory testing. The Church can also push Singer in several ways, and we have already seen the historical and theological mistakes behind his view that the Christian tradition is simply 'the bad guy' when it comes to animal liberation. But also consider that, because he is a preference utilitarian, Singer finds it difficult to condemn the wanton slaughter of certain animals (for pleasure, sport, etc.) in a way that doesn't violate their preferences.[170] A Christian ethic – which can appeal to the intrinsic goodness of non-human animals apart

---

[169] Lisa Abend, "In Spain, Human Rights for Apes," TIME.com, www.time.com/time/world/article/0,8599,1824206,00.html (Accessed May 1, 2010). We have seen that Stanley Hauerwas criticizes the concept of animal rights because it doesn't give them the proper defense of their moral value (and instead absorbs consumerist categories foreign to a Christian ethic), but others like David Oderberg object precisely because they do not think that non-human animals have enough moral value. Indeed, Oderberg claims that the only kinds of entities that have rights are those who pursue goods freely and with the knowledge that one is pursuing a good – and no animal *knows* why it lives the way it does; no animal is *free* to live in one way or another. Animals, from the smallest single-celled organism to the most human-like ape, are governed purely by *instinct*. David S. Oderberg, "The Illusion of Animal Rights," *Human Life Review* (Spring/Summer 2000), 42. But as should be clear by now, in light of what we know about non-human animals like primates and dolphins, that claim is just too strong to be accepted.

[170] This could be done by painlessly killing a non-self-aware creature with no capacity to have an interest in continuing to live, for example.

from human beings, the *telos* of all members of the created order, the spiritual reality of non-human animals, and the morally problematic nature of the (often vicious and violent) act of snuffing out a non-human animal's life – has powerful resources to condemn practices that Singer's ethic does not.

The massive scale on which our culture inflicts overwhelmingly cruel practices on non-human animals cries out for a partnership between Singerites and Christians geared toward non-human animal liberation. For Singer, such common cause would involve refusing to see biological species as a morally significant category in and of itself, and dramatically changing our consumerist, self-obsessed practices toward non-human animals in sweeping ways. Obviously, he believes that we should cease to eat meat, refuse to buy animal products from factory farms and many products tested on non-human animals, make those in our community aware of the cruel practices used in factory farms and in (some) university and commercial laboratories, and push for legislation giving limited rights to certain non-human animals.

Could a Christian find common ground? I would argue that not only could Christians do so, but that we are actually seriously morally blame-worthy if we fail to act to undermine our culture's practices toward non-human animals. We have already seen that the Church's tradition is not speciesist, but the Church also currently teaches that we owe non-human animals kindness and we are prohibited from letting non-human animals suffer and die needlessly.[171] That there have been many dozens of vegeta-rian saints, and that their kindness to animals was considered to be a mark of holiness, is a telling and profound Christian witness in this regard. And far from being an idolatrous movement imported from the ideology and politics of the political left,[172] a push for the liberation of non-human animals has come from many influential Christian thinkers who could hardly be considered liberals: C.S. Lewis, Pope John Paul II, Stanley Hauerwas, Mary Eberstadt, Matthew Scully, and Pope Benedict XVI.[173]

---

[171] The Christian tradition claims that we are morally responsible not only for what we do, but what we fail to do. Much more on this to come in the next chapter.

[172] We also saw in Chapter 1 that the pro-life movement need not be seen as an idolatrous movement imported from ideology and politics of the political right.

[173] Especially in light of the forthcoming dissertation of Jacaranda Turvey, "Natural Law and the Environment: A Critical Engagement with Grisez School Ethics and Theology of Creation" (University of Chester), I think we should also add Germain Grisez to the list. Turvey convincingly argues that the moral norms he puts forth, especially with regard to factory farming, come close to advocating for a vegetarian diet.

If one believes that we have a duty to treat non-human animals with kindness, to refuse to let them suffer and die needlessly, and to be non-violent witnesses of the Kingdom of God, then let me be very direct: this means that almost all of us are morally required to stop eating meat grown in factory farms. Buying and eating the flesh of other animals produced and grown in such consumerism-obsessed farms is a classic example of participation in what Catholic Social Teaching calls "sinful social structures."[174] After all, what could be more cruel and unnecessary than the kind of treatment of non-human animals raised in such institutions? Eating factory-farmed meat simply because it gives one pleasure, or because it is cheaper, or because it is more difficult to get one's dietary requirements from other sources, does not rise to the level of need.[175] And for most of us, eating meat *of any kind* fails to reach this level – and also violates the relationship between humans and other animals envisioned by the authors of Genesis 1 and 2 and the prophet Isaiah. The institutional Church would do well to publicly and explicitly teach that cruelty to other animals, even when it consists simply in our supporting factory farms with money, is seriously sinful behavior.

Both approaches can also work together to expose various cruel and unnecessary practices of non-animal experimentation by corporations, and should also refuse to participate in these sinful social structures by refusing to buy their products. The *Catechism* claims that there should be 'reasonable limits' on such research; presumably, such limits would be based on the values mentioned in the very same passage: treating with kindness, refraining from cruelty, and using animals only when necessary. And imprisoning and experimenting on non-human animals (like primates and dolphins) who are self-aware, are capable of third-order reflection, feel empathy, and have a sense of fairness *seriously wrongs* beings whose moral value is such that they are very close to human persons.

For the Christian who takes their biblical and broader tradition seriously, non-human animals are to be treated with kindness as our kin and companions, not as mere objects to be cruelly raised for their tasty flesh at the cheapest possible price. For we have learned from the prophet Isaiah that one of our most solemn evangelical duties is to help bring

[174] We will explore this concept in more detail in the next chapter.
[175] If one's health or even life were in danger without getting meat to eat (say, if one is starving in the forest), however, then both Singer and the Church would allow for killing and eating the flesh of a non-human animal. Perhaps this would also include those in poverty and with ill health such that they require cheap sources of the nutrition that meat provides.

"knowledge of the Lord" to our violent world with the goal that none will be "harmed or destroyed on God's holy mountain." Happily, despite the overwhelming work looming on this front, there are many different kinds of partnerships available for getting it done. One of those is between Peter Singer and Christian ethics.

CHAPTER 4

Duties to the poor

Our affluence means that we have income we can dispose of without giving up the basic necessities of life, and we can use this income to reduce extreme poverty. Just how much we will think ourselves obliged to give up will depend on what we consider to be of comparable moral significance to the poverty we could prevent: stylish clothes, expensive dinners, a sophisticated stereo system, exotic holidays, a luxury car, a larger house, private schools for our children and so on ... none of these is likely to be of comparable significance to the reduction of extreme poverty.

Peter Singer, *Practical Ethics*

Each man must examine his conscience, which sounds a new call in our present times. Is he prepared to support, at his own expense, projects and undertakings designed to help the needy? Is he prepared to pay higher taxes so that public authorities may expand their efforts in the work of development? Is he prepared to pay more for imported goods, so that the foreign producer may make a fairer profit? Is he prepared to emigrate from his homeland if necessary and if he is young, in order to help the emerging nations?

Pope Paul vi, *Populorum Progressio*

INTRODUCTION

In the last three chapters, despite there being significant and wide-ranging overlap, Peter Singer and the Church generally have come to significantly different final conclusions. But with regard to duties to the poor, the similarities between the two approaches are absolutely striking. There are important differences that we will discuss in due course, but with this topic we will see most clearly how much the two approaches have in common.

Both Singer and the Church, for instance, recognize this as a pivotal time in the history of the battle against poverty. In Singer's recent book *The Life You Can Save: Acting Now to End World Poverty*, he says:

We live in a unique moment. The proportion of people unable to meet their basic needs is smaller today than it has been at any time in recent history. And perhaps at all time since humans first came into existence. At the same time, when we take a long-term perspective that sees beyond the fluctuations of the economic cycle, the proportion of people with far more than they need is also unprecedented. Most important, rich and poor are now linked in ways they never were before ... Not only do we know a lot about the desperately poor, but we have much more to offer them in terms of better healthcare, improved seeds and agricultural techniques, and new technologies for generating electricity ... Economist Jeffery Sachs has argued convincingly that extreme poverty can be virtually eliminated by the middle of this century.[1]

The Church also recognizes the moment currently before us. In preparation for the great Jubilee year 2000, the Pontifical Council *Cor Unum* ('one heart') produced a document called *WORLD HUNGER, A Challenge for All: Development in Solidarity*. Mindful that the Jubilee year as described in the Hebrew Bible was particularly concerned with the poor and least in the community, the document has a goal of "the elimination of hunger and malnutrition and the guarantee of the right of proper nutrition."[2] In addition, as Singer wrote and released *The Life You Can Save*, the United States Conference of Catholic Bishops, teaming up with its international arm of Catholic Relief Services, found itself in the midst of an intense Zero Poverty campaign to mobilize one million people to join the fight against global poverty.[3] In addressing factors like international peace-keeping and peace-building, global trade and agricultural practices, migration patterns and causes, debt relief, and organizational/individual assistance, the Church is aiming squarely at the goal of eliminating absolute poverty. Indeed, the Zero Poverty campaign is motivated in part by the Church's belief that such poverty "is unacceptable in the 21st century."[4]

But this topic is more than simply a focus of the present moment for both approaches. One could argue that Singer arrived as a player on the academic scene with a now famous 1972 article he published in

---

[1] Peter Singer, *The Life You Can Save: Acting Now to End World Poverty*, 1st edn. (New York: Random House, 2009), 206, xii.

[2] Pontifical Council *Cor Unum*, "WORLD HUNGER, A Challenge for All: Development in Solidarity" (Vatican: The Holy See), www.vatican.va/roman_curia/pontifical_councils/corunum/documents/rc_pc_corunum_doc_04101996_world-hunger_en.html (Accessed July 31, 2011), Introduction.

[3] United States Conference of Catholic Bishops, "Catholics Confront Global Poverty." USCCB website. www.usccb.org/sdwp/globalpoverty/ccgp_index.shtml (Accessed April 13, 2009).

[4] "Caritas Launches Zero Poverty Campaign," ZENIT – The World Seen From Rome, www.zenit.org/article-28176?l=english (Accessed July 28, 2011).

Philosophy and Public Affairs called "Famine, Affluence and Morality."[5] This foundational focus on poverty was continually highlighted in future works, and Gerard Maguiness has even argued that this article served as a kind of "early manifesto of themes" that would emerge as his career unfolded.[6] And though *The Life You Can Save* consolidates aspects of arguments he has made over the last four decades, its central argument remains largely unchanged from the 1972 article.

Modern-day Roman Catholic movements to aid the impoverished are absolutely massive in scale,[7] but they go back to the very beginnings of Christianity and are also of foundational importance. Indeed, though Jesus himself rarely speaks of Hell, when he does so it is almost always connected to a failure of one's duties to the poor. In recounting a rich man's refusal to help a poor beggar, for instance, Jesus notes that the rich man ends up in torment in Hell (Luke 16:19–31). He famously said that that love of money is the root of evil and that a rich person will struggle to enter the Kingdom of God (Matthew 19:24). And in one of the most important stories of the Christian tradition, Jesus famously divides the Heaven-bound from the Hell-bound based on whether or not they fulfilled duties to 'the least ones' in their communities (Matthew 25:31–46). The early Christian Church took this message of Jesus so seriously that, when they had the resources to do so, they largely served as the social welfare system of the ancient world. Singer himself built on precisely this historical fact when, in the second edition of *Practical Ethics*, he suggested we give 10 percent of our resources to those in absolute

[5] Peter Singer, "Famine, Affluence and Morality," *Philosophy and Public Affairs*, vol. 1 (Spring 1972), 229–43.
[6] Gerard H. Maguiness, "Assisted Suicide, Self-Love, and a Life Worth Living," Dissertation (Rome: 2002).
[7] For instance, Catholic Relief Services (the poverty-fighting arm of the US Bishops) alone is present in virtually every country on the planet doing things like managing refugee camps, initiating projects to better account for oil revenues, conducting seeds fairs, constructing temporary classrooms and shelters in disaster-hit areas, engaging in peace-building initiatives, micro-financing the other lending/bank initiatives, organizing movements against exploitive child labor and military service, support of orphans and those otherwise affected by AIDS, and so much more. (http://crs.org/publications/showpdf.cfm?pdf_id=29) The *Catholic Aid Directory* (5th edition) has some 1100 entries, but to get a flavor of the international scale of the effort, consider just the member organizations of 'Cor Unum': the International Association of St Vincent de Paul, Caritas Internationalis, the International Union of Superiors General, the Union of Superiors General, Australian Catholic Relief, Caritas Italiana, Caritas Lebanon, Catholic Relief Services, Deutscher Caritasverband, Manos Unidas, Organisation Catholique Canadienne pour le Développement et la Paix, Secours Catholique, Kirche in Not, the Society of St Vincent de Paul, the Secretariat of Caritas in French-speaking Africa, Caritas Aotearoa (New Zealand), Caritas Bolivia, Caritas Spain, Caritas Mozambique, Misereor, Österreichische Caritaszentrale, the Knights of Malta.

poverty, given that this was the tithing percentage required by the social welfare mechanism of the age: the Church.[8]

I will pull from various parts of Singer's writings for his insights on the topic of this chapter, but much of it will obviously be focused on his most recent book on poverty which consolidates much of his thought. Similarly, I will draw on various texts from the Church in building its point of view, but much of it will be focused on a line of reflection within the tradition sometimes called Catholic Social Teaching (CST).[9] CST does have its own distinct 'flavor,' however, and thus it might be worth saying a few introductory words before referencing it in an argument. In many ways CST has quite ancient roots. Its central principles, like the duty to have a particular focus on the poor, certainly go back to Jesus himself – and many go back to the even older Jewish traditions which also focus on the poor. But some of the specifically social aspects of the teaching come out of the tradition in the fourth century and beyond when Christianity becomes formally intercon-nected with the State and therefore bears some responsibility for forming social policy. But in most cases, and generally in the context of this chapter, CST refers to "a limited body of literature written in the modern era that is a response of papal and episcopal teachers to the various political, economic and social issues of our time."[10] Though the beginning of the formal tradition seems to be a new move to emphasize 'the social questions' starting with Pope Leo XIII's *Rerum Novarum* in 1891, there is no official list of documents which 'count' as CST. Kenneth Himes points out:

> Clearly, the expression CST is elastic, sometimes designating an expansive body of material and at other times used in a more constricted sense ... Perhaps we can understand the term *Catholic Social Teaching* as an effort by the pastoral teachers of the church to articulate what the broader social tradition means in the era of modern economics, politics and culture.[11]

CST is sometimes called the Church's "best kept secret." And though there have been concerted efforts in Catholic higher education to make people aware of it, this remains a fair characterization. The Church's positions on the topics of abortion and euthanasia are far more commonly referenced (by

---

[8] Singer, *Practical Ethics* (1993), 246.

[9] Scholars of CST know that there are tensions pulling in various directions through this tradition, and sometimes even within individual documents, but it goes beyond the scope of this chapter to get into these nuances. Here, I am simply highlighting major lines of the tradition as they inform a discussion between Singer and Christian ethics on duties to the poor.

[10] Kenneth R. Himes, *Responses to 101 Questions on Catholic Social Teaching* (New York: Paulist Press, 2001), 115, 5.

[11] *Ibid.*, 5.

Catholics and non-Catholics alike) than its social teachings, but this should not be mistaken for CST having any less normative weight. Indeed, John Paul II specifically refers to it as *doctrine*.[12] Finally, especially in the context of a book like this one, it is worth noting something about the intended audience of CST. Though many aspects of the Church's teachings on ethics are directed at an audience wider than those who are explicitly Catholic, the later documents of CST (beginning with Pope John XXIII in the 1960s) are explicitly directed at an audience consisting of all those of good will. Indeed, the *Cor Unum* document referenced above claims that its spirit is "not based on any particular ideology."[13] It is this aspect, perhaps more than any other, which makes CST a particularly good conversation partner for Peter Singer – who is also attempting to direct his argument about poverty in ways that can appeal to those of many different ideologies.[14]

The methodology of this chapter will be similar to that of other chapters. The first half will draw attention to the remarkable number of ideas and arguments that Singer and the Church have in common on duties to the poor, but the second half will make arguments about some issues where the two approaches diverge. A major bone of contention will involve the conflict between Singer's claim that we must have a nearly dispassionate egalitarianism for the needs of individuals regardless of where they are in the world or their relationship to us, and the Church's view that partial preferences are morally acceptable. CST's emphasis on having a 'preference for the poor' – which goes beyond donations to aid organizations to living with, listening to, and learning from the marginalized – is also at variance with Singer's approach. But in this chapter, perhaps more than in all the others, these exceptions really prove the rule: Peter Singer and the Roman Catholic Church are stunningly similar when it comes to articulating our duties to the poor.

THE ARGUMENTS

In making their arguments about duties to the poor, both approaches appeal to a central narrative analogy. This is Singer's famous 'drowning child' thought experiment:

---

[12] Pope John Paul II, *Centesimus Annus*, 113, 5. The normative force of CST should also be obvious to anyone who examines the title of the document released by the Pontifical Council for Justice and Peace, called the *Compendium of the Social Doctrine of the Church*.
[13] Pontifical Council *Cor Unum*, "WORLD HUNGER, A Challenge for All: Development in Solidarity," Preface.
[14] Singer, *Practical Ethics*, 199–200. This, as we will see in some detail in the final chapter, is especially true of Singer's work in the last decade or so.

On your way to work, you pass a small pond. On hot days, children sometimes play in the pond, which is only about knee-deep. The weather's cool today, though, and the hour is early, so you are surprised to see a child splashing about in the pond. As you get closer, you see that it is a very young child, just a toddler, who is flailing about, unable to stay upright or walk out of the pond. You look for parents or a babysitter, but there is no one else around. The child is unable to keep his head above water for more than a few seconds at a time. If you don't wade in and pull him out, he seems likely to drown. Wading in is easy and safe, but you will ruin the new shoes you bought only days ago, and get your suit wet and muddy. By the time you hand the child over to someone responsible for him, and change your clothes, you'll be late for work. What should you do?[15]

And then, of course, there is Jesus' parable of the Good Samaritan:

Jesus replied, "A man fell victim to robbers as he went down from Jerusalem to Jericho. They stripped and beat him and went off leaving him half-dead. A priest happened to be going down that road, but when he saw him, he passed by on the opposite side. Likewise a Levite came to the place, and when he saw him, he passed by on the opposite side. But a Samaritan traveler who came upon him was moved with compassion at the sight. He approached the victim, poured oil and wine over his wounds and bandaged them. Then he lifted him up on his own animal, took him to an inn and cared for him. The next day he took out two silver coins and gave them to the innkeeper with the instruction, 'Take care of him. If you spend more than what I have given you, I shall repay you on my way back.' Which of these three, in your opinion, was neighbor to the robbers' victim?" (Luke 10:30–36)

Both of these stories are told in order to elicit a particular moral intuition: one should provide aid to those who need it. But both Singer and the Church go further and claim that it is morally wrong *not* to provide aid. Let us look at Singer's argument and then the features it has in common with that of the Church:

1. Suffering and death from lack of food, shelter and medical care are bad.
2. If it is in your power to prevent something bad from happening, without sacrificing anything nearly as important, it is wrong not to do so.
3. By donating to aid agencies, you can prevent suffering and death from lack of food, shelter, and medical care, without sacrificing anything nearly as important.
4. Therefore, if you do not donate to aid agencies you are doing something wrong.[16]

---

[15] Singer, *The Life You Can Save*, 206, 3. [16] *Ibid.*, 16.

When applied to the drowning child thought experiment above, we find that this argument supports the moral intuition that not only is it a good idea to aid the child, but one is morally blameworthy if they do not. The concept of "anything nearly as important" is vague, but virtually no one could argue that ruining one's shoes, getting one's suit dirty, and being late to work could be nearly as important as the life of the drowning child.

Perhaps this argument doesn't even appear to be all that controversial. Yet Singer rightly points out that

> if we were to take it seriously, our lives would be changed dramatically. For while the cost of saving one child's life by a donation to an aid organization may not be great, after you have donated that sum, there remain more children in need of saving, each one of whom can be saved at a relatively small additional cost. Suppose you have just sent $200 to an agency that can, for that amount, save the life of a child in a developing country who otherwise would have died. You've done something really good, and all it has cost you is the price of some new clothes you didn't really need anyway. Congratulations! But don't celebrate your good deed by opening a bottle of champagne, or even going to a movie. The costs of that bottle or movie, added to what you could save by cutting down on a few other extravagances, would save the life of another child. After you forgo those items, and give another $200, though, is everything else you are spending as important, or nearly as important, as the life of a child?[17]

The answer to the question, of course, is obvious. It looks like we must radically rethink how we use our resources, not simply because we want a feather in our cap for being 'charitable,' but because it is our *duty* to do so. We are morally *blameworthy* if we do not sacrifice things of lesser value in order to save the lives of children in this way. For the vast majority of those in the developed world (including almost everyone reading this book), we have income of which we can dispose without giving up the basic necessities of life, and this income should be donated to aid agencies serving the needy. Just how much we will think ourselves obligated to give will depend on what we consider "nearly morally important" compared to the lives we could save. But for most of us it would mean a radical rethinking of our lives.

But *how* blameworthy are we for failing to meet this high ethical demand? Let's consider the person in the drowning child thought experiment who simply walks by and lets the child die because they preferred to keep their shoes from being ruined. Singer wonders about

---

[17] *Ibid.*

the possibility of this being the moral equivalent of murder. Given that presumably the person who lets the child drown does not intend for him to die means that the question of whether it actually should count as murder gets into complex questions regarding how one should think about the relationship between one's intention and the consequences one's actions produce. And though these currently go beyond the scope of this chapter,[18] Singer persuasively claims that even if it doesn't count as murder it still counts as something like unintentional or reckless homicide – the kind of charge that might be leveled at someone who, say, kills another while driving a car irresponsibly. This is still a very serious matter given that the offender is morally responsible for the person's death.

CHRISTIAN OVERLAP WITH SINGER

We have already seen above that Jesus' parable about the Good Samaritan, a central story for every Christian (and even for many outside the faith), also attempts to show that we should aid those in need. We have also seen above that the few times Jesus speaks of Hell it is connected to a refusal to help vulnerable persons in need. But would a Christian agree with Singer that it is *wrong* not to aid? I argue that the answer is yes. Mass-going Catholics will recall the following Penitential Act of Contrition:

> I confess to Almighty God, and to you, my brothers and sisters, that I have sinned through my own fault, in my thoughts and in my words, in what I have done *and in what I have failed to do* [emphasis added].

Sin, then, is not only what we *do*, but also what we *fail* to do.[19]

But what about the seriousness of refusing to aid? Could murder, or something morally close to murder, really be the result of something we fail to do? The *Catechism*, interestingly, discusses this very topic under the fifth commandment of the Hebrew Bible's Decalogue, "Thou Shall Not Kill":

> The moral law prohibits exposing someone to mortal danger without grave reason, as well as refusing assistance to a person in danger.
>
> The acceptance by human society of murderous famines, without efforts to remedy them, is a scandalous injustice and a grave offense. Those whose

---

[18] We will revisit this question in some detail in the chapter on ethical method.

[19] To recall Matthew 25 once again, *all* the sins that separate the goats from the sheep are failures to act rather than sins that directly act against the good of another.

usurious and avaricious dealings lead to the hunger and death of their brethren in the human family indirectly commit homicide, which is imputable to them.[20]

Unintentional killing is not morally imputable. But one is not exonerated from grave offense if, without proportionate reasons, he has acted in a way that brings about someone's death, even without the intention to do.[21]

And just to clear up any confusion about what is being taught here, let us look at an important quote from another normative document for Roman Catholics: Vatican Council II's *Pastoral Constitution on the Church in the Modern World*:

Since there are so many people prostrate with hunger in the world, this sacred council urges all, both individuals and governments, to remember the aphorism of the Fathers, "Feed the man dying of hunger, because if you have not fed him, you have killed him," and really to share and employ their earthly goods, according to the ability of each, especially by supporting individuals or peoples with the aid by which they may be able to help and develop themselves.[22]

The Church has a position, then, that is very nearly identical to Singer's. Not only is it wrong not to aid, but some of the holiest people in the tradition – along with those articulating the current teaching – consider it in the same category as 'homicide' and 'killing.' When there is no explicit intention to kill, a refusal to aid is not considered murder, but one is still guilty of a "grave offense" if one does not have a proportionate reason for not aiding a person in danger. This connects nicely with Singer's point that we are only justified in ignoring the poor if we would be forced to sacrifice something of similar moral importance.[23]

Singer, it turns out, would be one of the least surprised people to find that he has this kind of dramatic overlap with the Christian tradition, for he cites it on several occasions. It is also fascinating to see that, when Singer gives his narrative explaining how our culture derailed into a consumerist marketplace which virtually ignores the poor, he argues that *it was a rejection of Roman Catholic theology* by the secular Enlightenment and Reformation that was the turning point. Indeed, Singer notes that

[20] This middle paragraph quotes the great fourth-century Church father, Bishop Ambrose of Milan.
[21] *Catechism of the Catholic Church*, Paragraphs 904, 2269.
[22] National Catholic Welfare Conference and Donald R. Campion, *Gaudium et Spes*, 138, 69.
[23] It is also yet another clear instance where the principle of double effect does a lot of work. It is never acceptable to intend the death of an innocent person, but one would need a proportionate reason in order to let another die without such an intention. We will look at this principle in more detail in the next chapter on ethical theory.

before then the Church had skepticism with regard to money-making as an enterprise: Pope St. Gregory the Great claimed that it stained one's soul, Pope St. Leo the Great mentioned that it was difficult to avoid sin when buying and selling, and the usurious lending of money at interest was punishable by *excommunication* and even denial of a Christian burial. Lutheran and Calvinist reformers, in rejecting this way of thinking, cleared the conceptual space for what Singer says brought about the real shift: the secular Enlightenment. The attitude that Singer most regrets arriving on the scene, which he attributes to intellectual giants of the age like Adam Smith and Benjamin Franklin, is one which accepts that attaining wealth is the proper goal of life. Far from being skeptical about such a goal, our culture now, according to Singer's narrative, considers it a virtue.[24] And the key turning point for him was a rejection of Roman Catholicism.

RESPONDING TO OBJECTIONS

Few actually share these strong claims about the moral implications of refusing to aid the poor, and while much of the reason is because most have yet to think through these issues, it is nevertheless important to respond to objections. Here I will largely follow those that Singer lays out,[25] and then show overlap with the Church in responding to such objections.

Objection One: There is no black-and-white universal code for everyone. It is better to accept that everyone has a different point of view on the issue and that all people are entitled to follow their own beliefs.

We already saw Singer reject moral relativism in the pro-choice arguments considered in Chapter 1, and Singer's response here is consistent. While certain situations are complicated and we should be tolerant of many points of view, this doesn't mean that everyone is entitled to follow his or her own beliefs. Rather, we should "try to stop people who are cruel to animals, just as we stop rapists, racists and terrorists." And if we reject moral relativism in some situations, then "we should reject it everywhere."[26]

The Church, as we know, also rejects moral relativism. Ethical truths are not mere social constructs, or projections of power by the privileged, but rather are revealed by God via scripture, tradition, nature, and reason. Indeed, the Church's "social doctrine sees ethical relativism,

[24] Peter Singer, *How are we to Live? Ethics in an Age of Self-Interest* (Amherst, NY: Prometheus Books, 1995), 262, 59–74.
[25] Singer, *The Life You Can Save*, 25–41.   [26] *Ibid.*, 25.

which maintains that there are no objective or universal criteria for establishing the foundations of a correct hierarchy of values, as one of the greatest threats to modern-day democracies."[27] Giving to the poor is a matter of *justice* – and duties of justice are not subject to moral relativism. What we owe another does not change simply because we change our minds or because of a majority vote.

But how could anyone think that giving to the poor is a matter of justice or a matter of moral duty? Doesn't the very word we use to describe such giving – charity – imply that it is not a moral duty but rather morally optional? This leads us to another objection:

Objection Two: You work hard for your money; therefore it belongs to you and you have a right to spend it on yourself. While it might be wrong to refuse to give something which belongs to someone else, or to refuse to aid someone we have actively harmed, one cannot be held morally responsible for not giving to the poor. The money does not belong to them – therefore it is morally optional to give it to them.

Leaving aside the question of how much of our money is actually accrued via hard work on our part,[28] Singer instead focuses on what is necessary in addition to hard work. If, say, one has been born into a middle-class situation in a developed country, then one is "fortunate to be born into social and economic circumstances what make it possible for you to work hard and have the right abilities." Indeed, many of us benefit from living

in a society with good institutions, such as an efficient banking system, a police force that will protect you from criminals, and courts to which you can turn with reasonable hope of a just decision if someone breaches a contract with you. Infrastructure in the form of roads, communications, and a reliable power supply is also a part of social capital.

Without these, one would struggle to escape poverty regardless of how hard one worked.[29] Our community creates and sustains the conditions for the possibility of our hard work benefiting us. We have the duty, then, to help create and sustain the possibility of others' hard work to benefit them.

---

[27] Catholic Church. Pontificium Consilium de Iustitia et Pace, *Compendium of the Social Doctrine of the Church* (Dublin: Veritas, 2005), 494, 407.
[28] Many of us are products of generational wealth and/or of wealth generated by interest and investment by others, not hard work. Furthermore, plenty of people get wealthy through jobs which we don't normally think of as involving strenuous labor.
[29] Singer, *The Life You Can Save*, 27.

And perhaps we have also been, at least in part, the *cause* of the situation in which the world's poor find themselves. If we have harmed the poor, then surely we ought to compensate them for what we have done.[30] Industrial fishing and farming practices in the developed world (which often include governmental subsidies that artificially deflate prices such that those living in developing countries cannot compete) have put those who fish and farm in the developing world out of business and thus significantly constrained their capacity for social development. And sometimes, especially in the cases of overfishing, such practices leave developing societies without basic food resources at all. Industrial oil and mineral companies from the developed world also make huge profits from the natural resources of places like Sudan, Equatorial Guinea, the Congo, Angola and dozens of other developing countries – while the people who inhabit such countries continue in absolute poverty. And when developed countries like the United States (along with the international corporations that many of us own in our investment portfolios) profit from dealing with corrupt dictators, they are "akin to people who knowingly buy stolen goods." And if we use goods made from raw materials obtained by these unethical dealings with resource-rich (but money-poor) nations, then we are harming those who live in these countries.[31]

This is a radical argument – and some wonder what it might mean for ownership of property in the first place. At the end of the day, may one even own private property, given our massive and seemingly unending duties to the global poor? Yes, says Singer, for a theory of property rights "can insist on our *right* to retain wealth without pronouncing on whether the rich *ought* to give to the poor."[32] Thus it is not necessarily owning property or having wealth that is the moral problem, but rather when doing so is inconsistent with the duties one has to the poor.

In response to this objection, Catholic Social Teaching (CST) has quite a lot to say which parallels and overlaps with Singer, and the roots of its response are ancient. Indeed, the question of private property and what is owed to the poor goes back specifically to the venerable concept of the aforementioned Jewish jubilee year. The Pontifical Council *Cor Unum* even claims that its legal framework forms the general blueprint for the Church's social teaching. Every 50 years God commands a Jubilee in which land is returned to its ancestral-family roots, all debts are canceled, and all slaves are freed. Even the land is to lay fallow. Here, then, is one of

---

[30] *Ibid.*, 29.   [31] *Ibid.*, 31.   [32] Singer, *Practical Ethics*, 204.

the key bases for a central principle in CST: the universal destination of goods. Land, money, and even labor do not belong to anyone but God who desires that they be used for the common good of all. Indeed, of the Julibee regulation *Cor Unum* says:

> [the] social lien on the right to private property was thereby regularly expressed in public law in order to make up for individual failures to comply with this demand [of the Universal Destination of Goods]. These failures include: the excessive desire for wealth, ill-gotten profits and so many other ways of exercising ownership, possession, and knowledge, along with the denial of the fact that created good must always serve everyone equitably.[33]

The claim that the goods of the Earth are meant to be used for the common good of all is an axiom necessary to build a society based on justice, peace, and solidarity. It also means that the right to private property, while legitimate, "is not absolute."[34]

In light of the universal destination of goods, CST claims that not only do all have a right to have their basic needs met, but that this right is of supreme foundational importance:

> Each person must have access to the level of well-being necessary for his full development. The right to the common use of goods is the 'first principle of the whole ethical and social order' and 'the characteristic principle of Christian social doctrine.' For this reason the Church feels bound in duty to specify the nature and characteristics of this principle. It is first of all a *natural* right, inscribed in human nature and not merely a positive right connected with changing historical circumstances; moreover it is an 'inherent' right. It is innate in individual persons, in every person, and has *priority* with regard to any human intervention concerning goods, to any legal system concerning the same, to any economic or social system or method: 'All other rights, whatever they are, including property rights and the right of free trade must be subordinated to this norm [the universal destination of goods]; they must not hinder it, but must rather expedite its application. It must be considered a serious and urgent social obligation to refer these rights to their original purpose.'[35]

This is *very* strong language – and the implications that it has for our moral obligations are even stronger. For the principle affirmed above "requires a common effort to obtain for every person and for all peoples the conditions necessary for integral development, so that everyone can contribute to making a more humane world."[36] While private property is

---

[33] Pontifical Council *Cor Unum*, "WORLD HUNGER, A Challenge for All: Development in Solidarity," 54.
[34] *Ibid.*, 24.   [35] Catholic Church. *Compendium of the Social Doctrine of the Church*, 172.
[36] *Ibid.*, 175.

"an essential element of an authentically social and democratic economic policy, and it is the guarantee of a correct social order ... *The Church's social doctrine requires that ownership of goods be equally accessible to all,* so that all may become, at least in some measure, owners."[37]

But what does all of this mean specifically about our duties to the poor? CST is very clear on this question:

The principle of the universal destination of goods requires that the poor, the marginalized and in all cases those whose living conditions interfere with their proper growth should be the focus of particular concern.[38]

Indeed, the Roman Catholic Bishops teach that developed peoples "are obliged to come to the relief of the poor and to do so not merely out of their superfluous goods." They even go so far as to say that if one is in extreme necessity, "he has the right to procure for himself what he needs out of the riches of others."[39] Both of these remarkable claims have solid backing in the intellectual and spiritual giants of the Church. Consider the following passages from Gratian's *Decretum,* a Christian jurisprudential document from the Middle Ages:

A man who keeps for himself more than he needs commits theft.

The use of all things that are in the world ought to be common to all.

No one may call his own what is in common, of which if he takes more than he needs, it is obtained by violence[[40]] ... The bread that you hold back belongs to the needy, the clothes that you store away belong to the naked.[41]

St. Ambrose of Milan, Bishop and mentor to the great St. Augustine, claims:

Nature created everything for common use. If, then, there are men who are excluded from the products of the earth, it is contrary to nature. The unequal division of this wealth is the result of egoism and violence.[42]

---

[37] *Ibid.,* 176.   [38] *Ibid.,* 182.
[39] National Catholic Welfare Conference and Donald R. Campion, *Gaudium et Spes,* 69.
[40] That this is considered a form of violence (both by Gratian here and by Ambrose below) is important in its own right, but also for the following line of argument made in the conclusion of this book. Much of what links the four different kinds of practical issues, in addition to consumerism and autonomy, is a kind of violence.
[41] Quoted in Brian Tierney, *The Idea of Natural Right: Studies on Natural Rights, Natural Law, and Church Law, 1150–1625,* Vol. 5 (Atlanta, GA: Scholars Press, 1997), 380, 70.
[42] Quoted in William Dwight Porter Bliss and Rudolph Michael Binder, *The New Encyclopedia of Social Reform, Including all Social Reform Movements and Activities, and the Economic, Industrial, and Sociological Facts and Statistics of all Countries and all Social Objects,* New edn. (New York: Funk & Wagnalls Company, 1908), 3, 265.

Finally, let us look at Thomas Aquinas:

Hence whatever certain people have in superabundance is due, by natural law, to the purpose of succoring the poor.

Nevertheless, if the need be so manifest and urgent, that it is evident that the present need must be remedied by whatever means be at hand (for instance when a person is in some imminent danger, and there is no other possible remedy), then it is lawful for a man to succor his own need by means of another's property, by taking it either openly or secretly: nor is this properly speaking theft or robbery.[43]

The Church teaches, then, that not only do we have a moral duty to give to the poor because we owe them access to the level of well-being necessary for their full development, but they have the right to *take it from us* should we fail to provide it for them. The principle of the universal destination of goods, and all that follows from it, obviously contains substantial overlap with what Singer argues above.

CST also agrees with Singer's suggestion that most of us are at least partially responsible for the situation of the poor. It recognizes, for instance, that globalization has brought about *de facto* interdependence such that the choices of the developed world necessarily (and often disproportionately) affect developing peoples.[44] Pope John xxiii recognized this as early as 1960 when he wrote the following in *Mater Et Magistra*:

As the mutual relations of peoples increase, they each become daily more dependent upon the other ... One of the principal characteristics of our time is the multiplication of social relationships, that is, daily more complex interdependence of citizens, introducing into their lives and activities many and varied forms of association.[45]

The US Bishops specifically relate these concepts to some of what Singer has in mind when they note that trade policy "illustrates the conflicting pressures that interdependence can generate" and that the United States should do all it can to ensure that the trading system treats the poorest segments of developing countries fairly and does not lead to human rights violations. "In particular, the United States should seek effective special measures under the General Agreement on Tariffs and Trade (GATT) to

---

[43] Thomas and Dominicans. English Province, *Summa Theologica*, 3057, ii:ii, Q66, Art 7.
[44] For an important detailing of this, see Todd Whitmore's chapter 'Catholic Social Teaching: Starting with the Common Good' in Kathleen Maas Weigert and Alexia K. Kelley, *Living the Catholic Social Tradition: Cases and Commentary* (Lanham, MD: Rowman & Littlefield Publishers, 2005).
[45] Catholic Church, Pope John xxiii, *Mater Et Magistra: Encyclical Letter: Christianity and Social Progress* (New York: Paulist Press, 1961), 96, 59.

benefit the poorest countries."[46] Pope Paul VI takes this concern directly to the individual by asking him the following direct question: "Is he prepared to pay more for imported goods, so that the foreign producer may make a fairer profit?"[47]

The larger problem behind what Singer points out is what CST has described as social or structural sin. This, though "always connected to concrete acts" of individuals, consolidates such actions and makes their effects difficult to remove. Indeed, they make the sin "grow stronger, spread and become sources of other sins, conditioning human conduct."[48] Insofar as we are participating in sinful social structures which contribute to the poverty and other harms inflicted on the vulnerable – and it is difficult to imagine how a functioning member of a developed country in a globalized world could not be – we have a special moral duty to aid them. In fact, the interdependence of peoples is not necessarily a bad thing because it can be transformed by the virtue of solidarity: a firm and preserving determination to see all human beings as brothers and sisters and to lose oneself for the sake of the other instead of exploiting him, and to serve him instead of oppressing him for one's own advantage.[49] Repeating a theme that echoes throughout the Church's history, here is yet another case where the source of our sin can also be the source of our redemption.

So perhaps we should have the poor's best interests in the front of our minds. And perhaps because of something like solidarity, maybe it is even a duty to do so. However, isn't it an open question whether or not philanthropic responses on the part of individuals actually serve the best interests of the poor? This leads us to a third objection.

Objection Three: Philanthropic responses on the part of individuals actually hurt the poor by creating dependency and often undermining the need for the correct kind of political and structural change.

It does seem likely that some resources given directly to the poor create dependency, and that a certain kind of philanthropy also runs the risk of what Singer refers to as "political quietism" and a deflection of attention away from the institutional and structural causes of poverty.[50] Singer

---

[46] Catholic Church. National Conference of Catholic Bishops and Catholic Church. National Conference of Catholic Bishops, *Economic Justice for All: Pastoral Letter on Catholic Social Teaching and the U.S. Economy*, Vol. 101 (Washington, D.C.: Office of Publishing and Promotion Services, United States Catholic Conference, 1986), 268–269.

[47] Pope Paul VI, *Encyclical Letter of His Holiness Pope Paul VI on the Development of Peoples* (New York: Paulist Press, 1967), 80, 47.

[48] Catholic Church, *Compendium*, 119.   [49] *Ibid.*, 193.

[50] Singer, *The Life You Can Save*, 35.

doesn't have as much to say about this objection as others, but he does claim to be "open-minded" about the ways in which we fulfill our duties to the poor. Though we should certainly give food and money in disaster situations, he also says that if, after investigating the causes of global poverty and considering what approach is more likely to reduce it, one really believes that more revolutionary change is needed, then it would make sense to put one's time, energy, and money into organizations promoting that revolution in the global economic system.[51] Apparently skeptical about the possibility of such broad-based change, Singer is more positive about the kind of structurally aware aid that will make people less dependent. Huge shipments of food can indeed destroy local markets and reduce incentives for local farmers to produce a surplus to sell, but we should instead give to organizations which will work to develop social structures "to make it possible for people to earn their own money, or to produce their own food and meet their other needs in a sustainable manner and by their own work."[52]

CST agrees with the basic thrust of Singer's response here, but goes into significantly more detail:

To satisfy the demands of justice and equity, strenuous efforts must be made, without disregarding the rights of persons or the natural qualities of each country, to remove as quickly as possible the immense economic inequalities, which now exist and in many cases are growing and which are connected with individual and social discrimination. Likewise, in many areas, in view of the special difficulties of agriculture relative to the raising and selling of produce, country people must be helped both to increase and to market what they produce, and to introduce the necessary development and renewal and also obtain a fair income. Otherwise, as too often happens, they will remain in the condition of lower-class citizens. Let farmers themselves, especially young ones, apply themselves to perfecting their professional skill, for without it, there can be no agricultural advance.[53]

This is embodied in CST's principle of subsidiarity which works from the following assumption:

It is impossible to promote the dignity of the person without showing concern for the family, groups, associations, local territorial realities; in short, for that aggregate of economic, social, cultural, sports-oriented, recreational, professional and political expressions to which people spontaneously give life and which make it possible for them to achieve effective social growth.[54]

---

[51] *Ibid.*, 36.   [52] *Ibid.*, 36.
[53] National Catholic Welfare Conference and Donald R. Campion, *Gaudiem et Spes*, 66.
[54] Catholic Church, *Compendium*, 185.

It is therefore "gravely wrong" to take from individuals "what they can produce by their own initiative and industry" and "a grave evil and a disturbance of right order to assign to a greater and higher association what lesser and subordinate organizations can do."[55] A key value is participation: not just for the sake of the individual, but because this is the best way of aiming at the common good of all.[56]

By way of example, it might be helpful to look at Catholic Relief Services (CRS) as they work with the worldwide poor. They limit 'handouts' to their disaster-relief efforts, and focus on economic and political structures in most of their other work. Here are just a few examples:

- Conferences pushing for accountability for oil revenue
- Seed Fairs
- Trafficking seminars for border police
- Conferences on fighting child labor
- Microfinance Programs
- Peacebuilding Curriculum
- Classroom Construction
- Development of bank contracts for community development
- Six-Year RAPIDS (Reaching AIDS-affected People through Integrated Development and Support) consortium project

And though the above work is impressive from the standpoint of changing structures, this kind of approach doesn't produce the best results unless it is disciplined by subsidiarity. And CRS found this out the hard way.

The aftermath of the 1994 Rwandan genocide was something which CRS Executive Vice-President Michael Wiest described as "almost crushing the agency."[57] This unspeakable tragedy happened despite CRS having worked in the country since 1960 and having spent millions of dollars on education, maternal and child health, and in agricultural development work. CRS workers were so close with the people that several even married Rwandans. The utter failure of their aid effort to avoid the genocide caused the agency to engage in a "prolonged period of prayer, reflection, planning and policy development." What they found was that their top-down focus and "limiting the terms of human development to economic and public health considerations" left out

---

[55] *Ibid.*, 186.   [56] *Ibid.*, 189.

[57] The Wiest quotes here and below are cited from a transcript and notes of a talk he gave at Fordham University in April 2009 entitled 'Faith, Justice and Solidarity in the 21st Century.' See Michael Wiest, "Faith, Justice and Solidarity in the 21st Century," Talk at Fordham University (April 2009).

broader issues of justice and subsidiarity. Instead of parentally imposing the 'best and newest' development plan onto a culture, CRS shifted strategy and used their best resource – the local bishops, priests, and parishioners – to find out what local populations needed and the best way CRS could help them. This shift "changed the DNA" of CRS, and took it from being on the brink of moral and financial collapse to perhaps the most flourishing international aid organization in the world.

So, while objection three helpfully reminds us that we need to be smart about how we discharge our obligation to the poor, it does not undercut our duty to give to organizations which promote authentic development. But what about this final objection?

Objection Four: Because a major factor in poverty is overpopulation, and giving to those in need will increase population, helping the impoverished only assures that there will be more people born into poverty.

This line of thought, Singer notes, is not new. Everyone from eighteenth-century English economist Thomas Malthus to 1960s entomologist Paul Ehrlich have claimed that the human race was headed for a catastrophic famine because population growth was going to outstrip resources. Ehrlich, for instance, famously claimed that by 1985 hundreds of millions of people would starve to death. But as Singer points out, he and others like him could not have been more wrong:

> Food production grew strongly, on a per capita basis, in the three decades after he made his dire prediction, and the proportion of people living in developing countries who were not getting 2200 calories per day – a basic sufficiency – declined from more than one in two to just one in ten.[58]

Singer observes that we saw similar worries in 2008 with a dramatic increase in food prices, but the problem with these kinds of arguments is that they fail to realize that "the problem is not that we are producing too little food; rather, we are not eating the food we grow."[59] And the solution is not simply better distribution, for a major part of the problem (which was also partly responsible driving up food prices) is the *100 million tons of corn* annually turned into biofuel for American gas tanks. Furthermore, as we saw in the previous chapter, we spend even more resources creating food via the notoriously inefficient method of feeding livestock.[60] Especially with the rise of prosperity in India and

---

[58] Singer, *The Life You Can Save*, 121. [59] *Ibid.*, 121.
[60] Singer points out that in the case of cattle, for instance, we get back only 1 pound of beef for every 13 pounds of grain used in feed. And these figures underestimate the waste because meat has a higher water content than grain.

China (which has brought with it even more dramatic levels of meat-eating), the world now uses more than *757 million tons of grain* to feed its livestock.[61] Singer puts this in perspective by asking us to

imagine it was equally divided among the 1.4 billion people living in extreme poverty. It would give each of them more than half a ton of grain, or about 3 pounds per day, which gives you twice as many calories as you need ... The difference between the present situation and the one Malthus predicted is that while he envisaged the growth of populations leading to mass famines, so far the only looming "danger" is mass vegetarianism. The grain and soy we feed to animals gives us a handy buffer against starvation, should we need it. We do produce enough to feed everyone on the planet, and even enough for the additional 3 billion people we can expect to be sharing it with by 2050.[62]

The Church agrees with Singer's general trajectory on so-called overpopulation. Pope John XXIII, for instance, claimed that the problems facing poor nations "are caused, more often than not, by a deficient economic and social organization, which does not offer living conditions proportionate to the increase in population." Therefore, "the real solution of the problem is not to be found in expedients ... which attack human life at its very source, but in a renewed scientific and technical effort on man's part to deepen and extend his dominion over Nature."[63] Despite being made before knowing what we know today, the Pope's prediction – very unpopular at the time – turned out to be exactly right. Archbishop Celestino Migliore, former Observer of the Vatican at the United Nations, had the following to say in addressing his colleagues on population issues:

Prior to the International Conference on Population and Development, many demographic experts and politicians warned that an increasing world population would create an overwhelming burden upon the world with dire possible consequences including food shortages, mass starvation, environmental destruction and resource-driven conflict. Now, fifteen years later, the population growth has begun to slow, food production continues to rise to the point where it is capable of supporting a larger global population and is even being diverted to the production of fuel.[64]

Where Catholic Social Teaching (CST) goes beyond Singer, and perhaps even contrasts with him,[65] is on the question of the population growth

---

[61] The figures do not include soy products.   [62] Singer, *The Life You Can Save*, 123.
[63] Catholic Church, Pope John XXIII, *Mater Et Magistra*, 96, 189–190.
[64] www.holyseemission.org/1Apr2009.html (Accessed May 9, 2009).
[65] Singer does seem to indicate that he is open to the idea of population-control measures which the Church would not support, but he does not call outright for their implementation. See Singer, *The Life You Can Save*, 124.

rate. Both approaches note and agree that we have the resources to deal with a significant rise in population. And while Singer does admit "the well-established fact that reducing poverty also reduces fertility," he doesn't go much beyond this. CST makes this bold claim:

Although it is true that an uneven distribution of the population and of available resources creates obstacles to development and a sustainable use of the environment, it must nonetheless be recognized that demographic growth is fully compatible with an integral and shared development.[66]

Not only is a pro-life policy fully compatible with authentic development, but the 'population reduction' mentalities of many UN-affiliated non-governmental organizations (NGOs) (which often involve promotion of abortion, sterilization, and contraception) have actually been shown to *hurt* development. For instance, in a developed country where this mentality has taken hold, "there is a drop in the birth-rates, with repercussions on the aging of the population, [and it is] unable even to renew itself biologically."[67] And the current drop in birth rates in the developed world has been absolutely astounding; virtually no European country is able to replace the population it already has, and some have such serious depopulation problems that they are beginning to panic. The BBC recently reported, for instance, that a German government minister suggested that it would be time to "turn the lights out" if something isn't done.[68] Russia, in a desperate attempt to repopulate itself, has instituted *Give Birth to a Patriot* day where Russian workers in various areas are given time off of work to go home, have sex, and (hopefully) procreate.[69] Why is this kind of depopulation a problem? One answer comes in another point raised in the BBC article: "The dependency ratio of those aged 65 and over to those of working age looks set to double from one-to-four to one-to-two in 2050." This puts tremendous economic pressure on these countries – especially for those with significant public social commitments to their retired citizens. However, it also creates a tremendous *opportunity* for those countries who are not suffering from the population reduction mentality. Again, Archbishop Migliore:

Further, the increased birth rates in Africa over the last decades have been identified by experts as lowering the elderly dependency ratio and presenting

---

[66] Catholic Church, *Compendium*, 483.   [67] *Ibid.*, 483.
[68] "The EU's baby blues," BBC News, http://news.bbc.co.uk/2/hi/europe/4768644.stm (Accessed May 9, 2009).
[69] Associated Press, "Russia Marks Day of Conception," MSNBC.com, www.msnbc.msn.com/id/20730526 (Accessed May 9, 2009).

the population with a plentiful workforce capable of providing the Continent with an unprecedented advantage in economic terms over regions whose aging populations show growing economic challenges. To capitalize on this opportunity, for Africa and ultimately for the whole world, greater commitment must be made to provide economic assistance and investment in human capital and infrastructure to support economic growth. Consequently, additional funding programs which focus upon lowering population growth rather than fostering an environment for development will slow, not expedite, the achievement of the [millennium development goals].[70]

But won't the world's population continue to grow exponentially such that all of these arguments become moot? Not according to the United Nations – which had predicted that the world's population will start declining in two, or at most three, generations.[71] History is repeating itself once again: reports of a supposed imminent overpopulation disaster are wildly exaggerated. Indeed, those of us with privilege in the global North should be far more worried about our own consumerist lifestyles than controlling the numbers of children born to poor people of color in the global South.

At any rate, the Church refuses to make a false choice between the dignity of the human person and authentic economic development. Indeed, far from a harm to developing countries, a growing population (combined with a building up of social structures and a commitment of solidarity from developed peoples) is actually an important economic resource which will help them compete with other countries burdened with economic stagnation due to lack of workforce.

COMMON OBJECTIVES

Identifying and connecting with the victim

Singer spends some time reviewing studies which show something that might seem like common sense: finding a connection with the persons in need (seeing a picture of them, for example) dramatically influences one's giving behavior. He claims that this "identifiable victim effect" leads to "the rule of rescue": for human beings will generally spend far more to rescue an identifiable victim than we will to save a "statistical life."[72] He

---

[70] www.holyseemission.org/1Apr2009.html (Accessed May 9, 2009).
[71] "World Population in 2300," Welcome to the United Nations: It's Your World, www.un.org/esa/population/publications/longrange2/longrange2.htm (Accessed April 10, 2011), 1.
[72] Singer, *The Life You Can Save*, 47.

uses the powerful example of the 1987 case of 18-month-old Jessica McClure falling into a dry well in Midland, Texas to illustrate the point. CNN broadcast images of the two-and-half-day recue – and donors sent in so much money that she is now a millionaire. But Singer points out that during the time spent to rescue her, 67,000 children worldwide died from avoidable, poverty-related diseases. This is strong evidence that deliberative, rational calculation will only go so far in convincing people to give, and so he emphasizes the need to "put a face on the needy" – in effect, allowing potential givers to connect to their stories – and praises institutions who appeal to people in terms of having personal relationships with the children they support. Sending pictures and other information which will create an "emotional affective response" helps transcend the barriers of indifference and of distance, and encourage substantial giving.[73]

Christian theology is generally very interested in this kind of personalization. Christians believe that our central figure, Jesus Christ, is the 'Word of God.' Without getting into the complex Christological questions this concept raises, suffice it to say that the tradition claims that the Word became *flesh* and not merely an abstract proposition or idea.[74] God's word was personalized in the historical figure of Jesus Christ – and it was the *personal encounter* with Jesus that was convincing to those who interacted with him both before and after his death.[75] Indeed, Christians believe that this face-to-face encounter happens with Jesus in a special way when we have personal encounters with the poor. For Jesus tells us that, in some mysterious way, whatever we do for the poor we do for *him*:

Then the king will say to those on his right, "Come, you who are blessed by my Father. Inherit the kingdom prepared for you from the foundation of the world.

For I was hungry and you gave me food, I was thirsty and you gave me drink, a stranger and you welcomed me, naked and you clothed me, ill and you cared for me, in prison and you visited me."

---

[73] One of the problems with this approach, as Singer points out, is that actually setting up a system in which individuals give to a specific child can be an inefficient use of resources – and thus most organizations who send pictures and letters admit that the money is pooled with contributions from other sponsors to support programs benefiting communities worldwide. Nevertheless, this method moves in the helpful direction of 'personal connection' and away from 'faceless statistic.'

[74] I owe this insight to an e-mail conversation with my colleague, Dr. John Perry of Oxford University.

[75] St. Paul, for instance, claims that it was his personal encounter with Jesus that changed his life – and many others, even today, emphasize their personal relationship with him as the reason for their faith.

Then the righteous will answer him and say, "Lord, when did we see you hungry and feed you, or thirsty and give you drink? When did we see you a stranger and welcome you, or naked and clothe you? When did we see you ill or in prison, and visit you?"

And the king will say to them in reply, "Truly I say to you, whatever you did for one of these least brothers of mine, you did for me." (Matthew 25:34–40)

Christians, then, have a special duty to have and promote a personal connection to the poor, in part, because it is in them that we find Jesus.[76]

But CST goes even further than this. Because the Church starts with the dignity of the human person in her social relationships, and builds much of its ethic off of this relational understanding of the human person, the principle of *solidarity* is of utmost importance. This principle highlights the many relationships and interconnections that the whole human family shares. We are all connected – in fact, we are all brothers and sisters – due to our all being children of the same God. And because of globalization, there has perhaps never before "been such a widespread awareness of the bond of interdependence between individuals and peoples, which is found at every level."[77] But solidarity is more than just a vague social principle; it also implies a moral duty:

The commitment to this goal is translated into the positive contribution of seeing that nothing is lacking in the common cause and also of seeking points of possible agreement where attitudes of separation and fragmentation prevail. It translates into the willingness to give oneself for the good of one's neighbor, beyond any individual or particular interest.[78]

Solidarity means that, even apart from personal connections like pictures and letters, we are all personally connected to each other in a very intimate way – whether we live next door or on the next continent. Truly, "we are *all* really responsible *for all*."[79]

Creating a culture of giving

Singer makes another important psychological point that our sense of fairness makes us less likely to give when others are not doing so, but "the converse also holds: we are more likely to do the right thing if we think others are already doing it."[80] This phenomenon can be seen in many

---

[76] And this might also mean a special duty to go and serve the poor directly. We will look at this in more detail in the next section of the chapter.

[77] Catholic Church, *Compendium*, 192.   [78] *Ibid.*, 194.

[79] *Ibid.*, 193.   [80] Singer, *The Life You Can Save*, 64.

contexts: from National Public Radio fund drives to the Church collection plate. Singer therefore wants to encourage those who give to make it public to put positive social pressure on other people to give – or at least take away the negative social pressure to remain self-centered.

But because we are still attempting to highlight common ground between Singer and the Church, it looks like this discussion might be out of place. For, as Singer points out:

Jesus told us not to sound a trumpet when we give to the poor "as the hypocrites do in the synagogues and in the streets, so that they may be honored by men." Instead, he advised, we should give so secretly that not even our left hand knows what our right hand is doing. Only then would we be rewarded in heaven, rather than on earth.[81]

Perhaps 'getting giving out in the open' is working at cross-purposes with the Christian tradition, and this is not something that it has in common with Singer. But this is yet another point where one needs to be careful in interpreting ancient theological texts. The Christian tradition has generally interpreted this as an injunction against giving to the poor *for reasons of self-promotion*. In other places, for instance, Jesus also tells us that we

are the light of the world. A city set on a hill cannot be hidden. Nor does anyone light a lamp and put it under a basket; but on the lampstand, and it gives light to all in the house. Just so, your light must shine before others, that they may see your good deeds and glorify your heavenly Father. (Matthew 5:14–16)

They key factor is the *reason* we are publicly giving. Doing good works out of love for God and neighbor means that one will not hide them away, but rather – like Singer advocates – let them shine for all to see. And CST understands and advocates doing so for exactly the same reason. Though "those freed from fears and purely material ambitions" might be working "discreetly and in depth," nevertheless

their work will take on the character of a mission in which their talents must be exercised and developed. A mission where they are called to contribute towards reforming structures and institutions. This exemplary behavior will then encourage their neighbors to do likewise and to be essentially devoted to serving the dignity of all men and women and their common good.[82]

We have just mapped out remarkable overlap between Peter Singer and Christian ethics on the matter of duties to the poor. However, there are at

[81] *Ibid.*, 65.
[82] Pontifical Council *Cor Unum*, "WORLD HUNGER, A Challenge for All: Development in Solidarity," 69.

least two ways in which the two approaches have significant differences on this question, and the first connects to a third goal which Singer thinks is necessary to achieve in order to meet our duties to the poor: namely, the end of parochialism.

IMPARTIALITY IN DUTIES TO THE POOR?

Singer challenges us to stop what he considers unjust giving that disproportionately favors those in closer blood, social, and spatial relationships. The poverty of the developed world must be distinguished, he says, from that of the developing world:

> In the United States, 97 percent of those classified by the Census bureau as poor own a color TV. Three quarters of them own a car. Three quarters of them have air-conditioning. Three quarters of them have a VCR or DVD player. All have access to health care [at least through emergency rooms and free clinics].

These individuals might be considered poor by a standard relative to the rest of the US population, but in contrast:

> The 1.4 billion people living in extreme poverty are poor by an absolute standard tied to the most basic human needs. They are likely to be hungry for at least part of each year. Even if they can get enough food to fill their stomachs, they will probably be malnourished because their diet lacks essential nutrients. In children, malnutrition stunts growth and can cause permanent brain damage. The poor may not afford to send their children to school. Even minimal health services are usually beyond their means.[83]

Singer points out that this kind of poverty is deadly. In relation to the developed world, poor countries have three decades less of life expectancy, twenty times the infant mortality rate, and have nearly 10 million more of their children die each year from avoidable, poverty-related diseases.

Especially in light of this dramatic difference in need, he claims that we give far too much to the poor in our own countries relative to those in absolute poverty. For instance, the tsunami which devastated Southeast Asia in late 2004 killed over 220,000 people and made millions homeless and destitute. Americans responded by giving $1.54 billion for disaster relief – by far the most ever given for such work outside of the United States. However, "this was less than a quarter of the $6.5 billion Americans gave the following year to help those affected by hurricane Katrina, which killed about 1,600 people and left far fewer homeless than

[83] Singer, *The Life You Can Save*, 8.

the tsunami."[84] After the 9/11 terrorist attacks in New York, "an avalanche" of aid was given to the victims, and in only three months a whopping $1.3 billion had already been raised. Nearly a million dollars went to each family of uniformed personnel killed in the attacks, but Singer points out that because of pensions and scholarships the "families of the firefighters killed would have been adequately provided for even if there had been no donations at all."[85] We can contrast this response with the "earthquake in Pakistan in October 2005 that killed 73,000 people elicited a comparatively small $150 million in donations from Americans."[86]

But what about total aid given to the developing world? Singer cites and supports the seemingly modest UN goal of developed countries giving 0.7 percent of their Gross National Product (GNP). Though very few countries have actually met this goal, "none fails so miserably to meet the United Nations target as the United States, which in 2000, the last year for which figures are available, gave 0.10 percent of GNP, or just 10 cents in every $100 its economy produces, one-seventh of the United Nations target."[87] It turns out that this is even less in total US dollars than Japan gives – despite an economy that is half the size. It is true that US aid is not as government-focused as it is for many developed countries, but even when non-government aid is added, this "takes the United States aid total only from 0.10 percent to 0.14 percent of GNP. This is still only one-fifth of the modest United Nations target, and not enough to get the United States off the very bottom of the table."[88] And as this book goes to press, the United States Congress is considering cutting this aid to an even *lower* percentage of GNP. Perhaps Singer would have been more fair-minded to consider the good that other government-funded institutions like the US military, Centers for Disease Control, etc., do in terms of disaster relief and development, but even with that caveat (and especially in light of the very high standard just set by Singer and the Church) the United States does not give nearly enough aid to the vulnerable poor overseas.

Though these facts might be discomforting to us, Singer does not find them difficult to understand: they come from attitudes which are the products of evolution. He cites Adam Smith's claim that this bias seems "wisely ordered by nature" since those far from us are people "we can neither serve nor hurt." Singer is not impressed:

---

[84] *Ibid.*, 51.
[85] Peter Singer, *One World: The Ethics of Globalization* (New Haven, CT: Yale University Press, 2002), 235, 150–151.
[86] Singer, *The Life You Can Save*, 51.   [87] Singer, *One World*, 181.   [88] *Ibid.*, 181–182.

Today these words are as obsolete as the quill with which Smith wrote them. As our response to the tsunami vividly demonstrated, instant communication and rapid transport mean that we *can* help those far from us in ways that were impossible in Smith's day.

But philosophers like Bernard Williams claim that a rational defense of partial treatment for one's spouse, children, friends, and local needy demands "one thought too many."[89] Singer concedes that while this is perhaps correct for everyday decision-making, it is not correct at the level of critical thinking at which people should be examining their biases.[90] Indeed, he claims preferences for friends or kin can be analogically connected to preference for race: an idea that had, in its time, "an intuitive appeal similar to the intuitive appeal of the idea that we have obligations to favor family and friends."[91] Thus, Singer claims, if we let our intuitions go unchallenged we risk the result of a bad moral outcome and have one thought *too few*. That our intuitions are shared by others or come naturally is not evidence that they are justified.[92]

But what kind of friend, parent, lover, spouse, etc., would one be without partial preferences? One could argue that the very meaning of the relationships themselves *presupposes* that one will have preferences for some over others. What would it mean, for instance, to say that "*x* is the spouse of *y* but not of *z*" if *x* must treat *y* and *z* exactly the same? If marriage requires a partial relationship, and partial relationships are immoral, does it follow that getting married is immoral? No, says Singer, we do not need to be impartial in every aspect of our lives. Indeed, acting partially toward some – like one's spouse or child – can actually help us develop virtues of compassion and other-centeredness which prepare us for more impartial preferences at other times. They help us become other-centered rather than self-centered.

But not all partial relationships are created equal in this regard, and Singer wonders if "any of these survive the demand for impartial justification, and if so, which ones?"[93] Before considering the ethical significance of the nation-state and partial preference for our fellow citizens, Singer considers partiality for family, lovers, and friends.[94] Ultimately, these relationships should make everyone involved more likely to engage in impartial consideration. So, with regard to parents showing partiality for children, for example, he says such preference

---

[89] *Ibid.*, 162.
[90] This is a classic example of Singer's 'two-level' utilitarianism, a theory that will be discussed in some detail in the next chapter.
[91] Singer, *One World*, 163.   [92] *Ibid.*, 164.   [93] *Ibid.*, 160.   [94] *Ibid.*, 164.

must extend to providing them with the necessities of life, and also their more important wants, and must allow them to feel loved and protected; but there is no requirement to satisfy every desire a child expresses, and many reasons why we should not do so. In a society like America, we should bring up our children to know that others are in much greater need, and to be aware of the possibility of helping them, if unnecessary spending is reduced.[95]

The same is true, Singer claims, of lovers and friends. Such relationships require partiality, but are justified only where the friendship includes and fosters a shared impartial concern and compassion for the welfare of others.

But what of other categories like 'neighbor' or 'kin'? With regard to the former, Singer claims geographical proximity is not of itself of any moral significance, but "it may give us more opportunities to enter into relationships of friendship and mutually beneficial reciprocity"[96] – a virtue certainly worth cultivating for impartial reasons. With regard to kin, it is sometimes the case that relatives "are important sources of love, friendship, and mutual support, and then will generate impartially justifiable reasons for promoting these goods."[97] But if a distant cousin from whom you have not heard in decades asks you for a home-improvement loan, the fact that you are kin should not be a factor in your decision.

But what about our fellow citizens? Singer spends significant time addressing this question, and begins by claiming that if we reject preference for 'race' or 'blood' then we should do the same for preference of members of our nation-state. For instance, my own family recently explored the idea of getting Italian citizenship through a program that grants it to those related to an Italian citizen within the last three generations. Of course, my brother and sister and I have no current ties to Italy, but because of our ancestry, the Italian government might grant it anyway. This kind of preference, for Singer, is just too close to racial preference to be justified.

But suppose we think of our preference for our fellow citizens as based on something other than race or blood? Perhaps it is instead based on the fact that we are "a community of reciprocity" engaged in a collective enterprise of some sort. Wouldn't that meet Singer's criteria for a justified partiality? No, for favoring one's fellow citizens ahead of citizens of other countries whose needs are more pressing requires more than the kind of reciprocity and shared values that the average citizens of a nation-state have in common:

[95] *Ibid.*   [96] Singer, *One World*, 166.   [97] *Ibid.*

Most citizens are born into a nation, and many of them care little for the nation's values and traditions. Some may reject them. Beyond the borders of the rich nations are millions of refugees desperate for the opportunity to become part of those national communities. There is no reason to think that, if we admitted them, they would be any less ready than native-born citizens to reciprocate whatever benefits they receive from the community. If we deny admission to these refugees, it hardly seems fair to then turn around and discriminate against them when we make decisions about whom we will aid, on the grounds that they are not members of our community and have no reciprocal relationships with us.[98]

Singer believes that the supposed community of the nation-state is imagined rather than real, and therefore it cannot ground a moral argument for preferring one's fellow citizen over someone overseas.[99] Based on the extreme need in communities outside our borders, we should "begin to consider ourselves as the imagined community of the world ... Our problems are now too intertwined to be well resolved in a system of nation-states in which citizens give their primary, and near exclusive, loyalty to their own nation-state rather than to the global community."[100] So, once again, preferring our nation-state is fine when it furthers the ultimate goal of broadening our concern beyond self-interest, but insofar as it turns us away from the dramatic need of the developing world, such preferences should be rejected. But, Singer warns, when subjected to the test of impartial assessment, there are few strong grounds for giving preference to the interests of one's fellow citizens, and "none that can override the obligation that arises whenever we can, at little cost to ourselves, make an absolutely crucial difference to the well-being of another person in real need."[101]

THE CHURCH ON PARTIAL PREFERENCES

As noted above, the Church has important disagreements with Singer's position, but there are areas of overlap even here. First, and perhaps most importantly, the Church agrees with Singer that we need to imagine ourselves as a world community, not just for the reasons Singer advocates, but because we *really are* part of a world community. Globalization simply highlights this already existing relationship. The principle of solidarity implies that what is at stake is not some abstract "ideological internationalism," but rather a genuine commitment as "members of

[98] Singer, *One World*, 169–170.   [99] *Ibid.*, 170.   [100] *Ibid.*, 171.   [101] *Ibid.*, 180.

the whole human family."[102] Whether in the Bronx, Botswana or Bolivia, all human beings are our brothers and sisters, and all really are responsible for all.

Though the Church claims that partial preferences are more valuable than Singer does, both approaches claim that there are many values which trump partial preference for the nation-state. Tellingly, the great commission of Jesus specifically mentions going out to preach the Gospel in *all* nations.[103] CST criticizes "nationalistic ideologies that contradict the values of the person integrally considered in all his various dimensions, material and spiritual, individual and community."[104] Indeed, the Church hardly needs to 'imagine' the concept of a transnational community, because the Church itself *is* such a community.[105] Therefore, it is not surprising when the Church insists "on the need to establish some universal public authority acknowledged as such by all and endowed with effective power to safeguard, on behalf of all, security, regard for justice, and respect for rights."[106] Indeed, as we saw above, a compelling case can be made that Roman Catholicism is the source for our modern understanding of international law.[107]

The Church makes several specific claims about preference for the international community over that of the nation-state. Consider the following principle: "rejection of war as a means for resolving disputes" is "prior to and superior to the internal law of States."[108] The *Compendium* also makes the following claim, now prophetic in light of the global financial meltdown of late 2008:

> *In particular, intergovernmental structures must effectively perform their functions of control and guidance in the economic field* because the attainment of the common good has become a goal that is beyond the reach of individual States, even if they are dominant in terms of power, wealth, and political strength.[109]

Catholic Social Teaching (CST) also considers the situation of migrants and refugees as another example in which a more important value trumps

---

[102] Catholic Church, *Compendium*, 432.   [103] Matthew 24:14.
[104] Catholic Church, *Compendium*, 433.
[105] For instance, I have had the fortunate experience of attending two worldwide conferences on Roman Catholic ethics in Padova and Trento, Italy. The experience of those attending as part of a worldwide community (especially in our common commitment to the Catholic moral tradition) was palpable and moving.
[106] Catholic Church, *Compendium*, 441.
[107] See especially chapter seven of Thomas E. Woods, *How the Catholic Church Built Western Civilization* (Washington, D.C.; Lanham, MD: Regnery Publishing; Distributed to the trade by National Book Network, 2005), 280.
[108] Catholic Church, *Compendium*, 437.   [109] *Ibid.*, 442.

preference for the nation-state. Indeed, "No person must be sent back to a country where he or she fears discriminatory action or life-threatening situations." Solidarity demands that we overcome selfishness and fear of the other so that the "condition of refugees that reaches to the very limits of human suffering becomes a pressing appeal to the conscience of all."[110] And the right to transcend boundaries, and the duty of nation-states to receive displaced persons, is not limited to situations of war or natural disaster. The universal destination of goods means that if one's state "suffers from great poverty combined with great population and cannot supply such use of goods to its inhabitants" then the inhabitants of that state "possess the right to emigrate, to select a new home in foreign lands, and to seek conditions of life worthy of [humanity]."[111]

Divergence from Singer

In a book chapter called "Incarnation and Patriotism," Christian ethicists Michael and Kenneth Himes take on a "fundamental issue in Christianity" which they call "the scandal of particularity."[112] How are we to think about the value accorded to being rooted in a given place and with a given people? They begin with a quick analysis of love in the Christian tradition. *Agape* is "the gift of the self to the other purely for the other's good." This is the love that the Gospel of John has in mind when it claims that God is love. God is pure "self-gift."[113] But they go on to say, "No human act of love has the purity of divine agape; it is always more or less debased by the selfishness of *eros* or *philia*."[114] *Eros* is a feeling or movement toward the beloved because of a desire for fulfillment, and *philia* is a particular example of *eros* in which fulfillment comes specifically from the company of the beloved. Through grace we can participate in a life of God's love,[115] but we need a moral realism which acknowledges that

[110] Catholic Church. Pontifical Council for the Pastoral Care of Migrant and Itinerant People and United States Catholic Conference, *Refugees: A Challenge to Solidarity*, Vol. 576–3 (Washington, D.C.: United States Catholic Conference, 1992), 18.
[111] *Instruction on the Pastoral Care of People Who Migrate* (1969), quoted in Terry Coonan, "There Are No Strangers Among Us: Catholic Social Teachings and U.S. Immigration Law," 40 *Catholic Lawyer* 105, n. 62 (2000).
[112] Michael J. Himes and Kenneth R. Himes, *Fullness of Faith: The Public Significance of Theology* (New York: Paulist Press, 1993), 213, 126.
[113] Himes and Himes, *Fullness of Faith*, 131. [114] *Ibid.*, 131–132.
[115] This point will become important in Chapter 5 when John Hare presses Singer and other utilitarians on how it is possible, without God's grace, to overcome our limitations and take the point of view of the universe.

agape is realized in and through our human eros and philia. Love for those closest to us – husband, wife, parent, child, brother, sister, friend, colleague, fellow citizen – is a sacrament of charity, universal love for all the creatures of God.[116]

And while Himes and Himes think this is consistent with a Singer-like universalist perspective insofar as particular kinds of love do foster a "concern for others beyond themselves," Singer's attempt to ascend above the particular in pursuit of the universal is nevertheless thoroughly out of accord with the realism of the Catholic tradition at large.[117] The central idea behind this claim is the phenomenology of moral experience – arising not from an abstract theory, but instead from being in the actual presence of the other. The human person finds herself immersed in a sea of relationships which are simply *there*.[118] And this phenomenological reality of particular personal relationships and local communities is directly connected, they say, to CST's preference for local communities in the principle of subsidiarity mentioned above.

Singer might agree with this claim as far as it goes and still press the point of moral implication. No doubt Himes and Himes describe the moral psychology and experience of most people quite correctly (Singer emphasizes something similar in his desire to 'identify the victim' of poverty), but one could have made a widely accepted and similar claim about preference for race even just one or two generations ago. The preference for race was (and, sadly, still is) also "simply there." To give it some normative weight simply on that basis is one thought too few, and the same might be said of the argument about moral experience above. Singer's point is well taken, but experience is a good place to start, and the Church has a heavy hitter who can push the idea further.

We have already seen how Thomas Aquinas' thought serves as a source for CST's universal destination of goods, but his 'order of *caritas*' is absolutely essential to this discussion as well. Here I will draw from the important work of Stephen Pope,[119] and present the idea as a key challenge to Singer's impartial ethic. Thomas starts with the nature of what it means to be a person: a reality that goes beyond willed relationships, but, for human beings anyway, is grounded in having a body and an integrated place in the natural world.[120] One of the features of our nature is the inclination to live in society. This is good insofar as it moves the

---

[116] Himes and Himes, *Fullness of Faith*, 133. [117] *Ibid.*, 135. [118] *Ibid.*, 134.
[119] Stephen J. Pope, *The Evolution of Altruism and the Ordering of Love* (Washington, D.C.: Georgetown University Press, 1994), 160.
[120] *Ibid.*, 50.

person toward an appropriate end. The ideal of love for Thomas, then, "is not that of moral duty overcoming natural inclinations" but rather that of an "integral personal response *ordering* and *incorporating* the appetites as well as the intellect."[121] Therefore, it is no accident that human beings "flourish through political association, assistance, cooperation, and friendship." This is one of the ends to which our natures as social persons draw us.

Still, we have yet to see an argument about specific preferences, and this is where the order of *caritas* comes in. In ordering preferences, Thomas begins with love of *self.* Far from being antithetical to love of the other, love of self *is presumed* by love of the other – at least if one accepts the golden rule of 'do unto others as you would have them do unto you' and Jesus' command to love your neighbor as yourself. Pope points out that love of self, something that is underscored in contemporary psychology, is the starting point and a legitimate partial preference.

Thomas Aquinas also believes that charity is universally benevolent insofar as it desires flourishing and salvation for all people, but is partial in its intensity and in its beneficence. Natural and family relations "are given a general priority over all other kinds of union by Thomas, for two reasons: first, they are more stable and permanent than other bonds; second, they coincide with other bonds that together offer more reasons for loving."[122] Thomas notices that relationships based on virtue and even sanctity can "progress and recede, wax and wane," but the relationships of blood relatives, above and beyond being logically and naturally prior to other kinds of relationships, are generally more stable because they spring from "the very substance of the human person."[123] He also notes that "people tend to love family members in more ways than they love others," insofar as the family is based on relationships surrounding shared goods.[124]

This defense of partiality pushes against Singer's approach, but Thomas did not view the order of charity as a simple collection of concentric circles "in which family and members of one's own household come first, next close friends, neighbors and associates, and finally others in an outwardly radiating gradation of various relations to the self."[125] Thomas' sense of the pluralism of human goods and relationships complicated

---

[121] *Ibid.,* 57.   [122] *Ibid.,* 62.
[123] Perhaps Aquinas has in mind the parable of the Prodigal Son, in which the child's last hope, after other kinds of relationships have withered away, is coming home to his father who welcomes him.
[124] Pope, *The Evolution of Altruism, 63.*   [125] *Ibid.,* 64.

matters and actually draws him closer to Singer's position. The priority of family members, for instance, was not assigned absolutely, and only trumped other claims "in the area of material well-being – and even here they have priority only when the degree of need is roughly comparable."[126] Thomas' general principle that we ought to do good first to those who are most closely connected with us has a *very* important qualification: "other things being equal."[127] Thus

in a particular case because of their greater need, strangers may have a greater claim to be assisted than one's family members, as in the case of the person who is bound to give aid to a stranger in extreme need rather than to his or her own parent who does not happen to be in such dire straits. Cases of conflict are adjudicated through the exercise of the cardinal virtue of prudence, which carefully weighs degrees of need and connection.[128]

At first, this doesn't seem all that different from Singer's prudential judgment about when a partial preference is working for or against impartial preferences. But there are important differences between the two, and perhaps most important is at what the prudential judgment is aiming. Singer puts his emphasis on making impartial judgments, but for Thomas there are legitimate instances in which one is able to act for the objective good of oneself and partially toward one in closer proximity. Love of self and love of one's friends and family have their own internal goods that need not be connected to the good of the larger human family. This is what is able to be rescued from Bernard Williams' claim above: surely if I have to think about *why* I love my friends and family that is one thought too many.[129] But even Thomas would agree that if one prefers them *over others in greater need* simply because 'this is the situation in which I find myself' that is indeed one thought too few.

Another point which Thomas Aquinas helps illustrate is that Singer, primarily in his single-issue consideration of racism, dismisses nature too quickly. The Church is, of course, prepared to admit that human nature is flawed in significant ways, but our nature can also tell us quite

---

[126] *Ibid.*   [127] The Latin here is *ceteris paribus.*   [128] Pope, *The Evolution of Altruism*, 64.
[129] Indeed, Singer's position (and perhaps that of all utilitarians) forces him into responding to certain questions with counter-intuitive and quite awkward answers. If Singer was asked by his friend how the time they spend together could be justified ethically, I suppose Singer would be forced to say something like, "Because our friendship helps cultivate the values which produce impartial giving to others." But as we will see in the final chapter, Singer may be in a position to explore concepts that would afford him a different answer.

a bit about the morally proper goods of human life. Singer is likely not convinced by this – and the full argument is surely far too complex to make here.[130] But it is worth at least pointing out that both Singer and the Church want to valorize certain aspects of human nature over others. And even if nature does not have normative weight for Singer, it does have practical weight. Parents naturally favor their children, and even if this is undesirable in the big picture, Singer thinks that any attempt to eradicate this preference would have "high costs and would require constant supervision or coercion." In addition, the evidence seems to indicate that children are less abused and better cared for by their parents. Singer considers this one of the "unavoidable constraints of human nature" and concludes that on this basis alone parents should be allowed to show some level of partiality toward their children.[131] Especially because he seems to equate the two, it is interesting that Singer does not push for us to take the same kinds of difficult and culture-changing steps with regard to the family that were necessary to counteract biased preference on the basis of race.[132] But if he is right that (unlike racial ones) partial family preferences are unavoidable, this does give us an important practical reason to pay attention to human nature – and perhaps even to wonder if such an overwhelming impulse does carry normative weight with it, given that it seems so connected to the flourishing of the human person.

A BROADER UNDERSTANDING OF POVERTY?

Singer spends almost all of his focus on situations of "absolute poverty" where the poor cannot meet basic needs like food, shelter, and medical care. But is it possible that this narrow focus is a limitation of his work? There is 'objective' poverty (physical needs, know-how, skill, etc.) and 'relative' poverty (the rich/poor gap, etc.) – both of which Singer acknowledges in his writings. But a third consideration is missing which is a very important emphasis for the Church, and CST describes it as lacking the

[130] For a superb and important attempt see Jean Porter, *Nature as Reason: A Thomistic Theory of the Natural Law* (Grand Rapids, MI: William B. Eerdmans Publishing Co., 2005), 420. We will examine part of her argument in Chapter 5 – which also considers the fact that Singer is currently shifting his views on objective goods in ways which might make him more open to considering a natural law argument like Porter's.
[131] Singer, *One World*, 162.
[132] One might argue that if we put the necessary institutions in place, and coercively changed our child-rearing practices, eventually biological parents would feel no such guilt.

ability to participate in society. Surely if one cares about the poor, one must consider the material needs of an individual. But such material goods are not ends in themselves. They exist to promote the broadly understood flourishing of human beings who, as intrinsically social creatures, can flourish only when participating in a communal life. Therefore, though this consideration would not, of course, totally determine where our support should go, it should be factored into the calculus.

Imagine a scenario in which person A is more objectively poor than person B. Perhaps A eats 800 calories a day, lives in a slum area in east Africa, and has unpredictable access to medical care, while B eats 3,600 calories a day (of mostly unhealthy food), lives in air-conditioned government housing in the Bronx, New York, and can walk into the emergency room whenever they wish. In Singer's paradigm, there is no question where our resources belong: with person A. But CST, in addition to considering the kind of partiality explored above, wants to ask further questions about participation. Given the social structures present in each situation, what is the relative ability of A and B to participate and flourish in their communities? Isn't it possible that B has less opportunity to participate and flourish than A and thus may deserve more of our attention and resources?[133] We should ask this question especially if we have more directly participated in or benefited from the sinful social structures which have caused the marginalization of person B.

CST's preferential option for the poor emphasizes participation in another way that Singer does not: by articulating a duty *for us to participate* in the lives of the poor. As the US Catholic Bishops remind us, paternalistic programs that do too much *for* and too little *with* the poor are to be avoided.[134] The Pontifical Council *Cor Unum* makes the direct point that "everyone is called" to take part in work to "help organize better living, and draw people out of resignation and subjugation."[135] And recall Pope Paul VI linking a duty to give monetary resources with a duty to emigrate from one's homeland in order to help

---

[133] This might be especially true because of racism, access to health-food markets, and just the general cost of things like education, entertainment and other things which form the basis of community life in New York.

[134] Catholic Church. National Conference of Catholic Bishops and Catholic Church. National Conference of Catholic Bishops, *Economic Justice for All: Pastoral Letter on Catholic Social Teaching and the U.S. Economy*, 188.

[135] Pontifical Council *Cor Unum*, "WORLD HUNGER, A Challenge for All: Development in Solidarity," 70.

emerging nations. When we work with the poor we "look the hungry in the eye" and it is in this look that the Church, referencing God's anger at Cain having killed his brother Abel, claims that we find "the blood of our brothers and sisters crying out" to us.[136]

And we are not only called to meet the gaze of the poor, but CST also insists that we listen to them as well. For "they have something specific to tell us. They have their own opinions and experiences with regard to real daily life about which the better-off know nothing."[137] We have already seen an example of how a top-down approach to aiding the poor, one which did not respect subsidiarity, failed to listen to the poor in the Rwandan case with Catholic Relief Services. *Cor Unum* notes that this same mistake has been made in the lending practices which now have the developed world under a crushing debt. "If the lenders and the borrowers had heeded the personal opinions of the poorest people," this would have meant "greater caution and in very many countries the adventure would have not turned out so badly, or might have turned out well."[138] The move to microfinance loans, the lenders of which get to know the specific local situations of the borrowers, is a similar move which acknowledges the need to actually be with and listen to the people one wishes to help.[139]

HOW SERIOUS ARE OUR DUTIES TO THE POOR?

Given its virtual treasure-trove of insights surrounding poverty, the Church is able to speak movingly about the duties we have to the poor. For instance, the kind of authentic listening discussed above, little by little, opens a person to question their own habits of life and

urges one to question the meaning and the value of daily actions, to seek out the immediate and sometimes more remote consequences of professional and voluntary work, handicrafts and domestic work. Further, one must gauge the magnitude, which is much more concrete and wide-ranging than could be imagined, of the consequences of all one does, even the most ordinary things, and hence appraise real responsibility. Christians must question the way time is managed, which in the modern world often suffers by default or by excess

---

[136] *Ibid.*, 60. The biblical reference is Genesis 4:10.
[137] *Ibid.*, 26.   [138] *Ibid.*
[139] Of course, real participation will go beyond a growing movement of 'poverty tourism' where privileged Westerners spent a short amount of time taking quick vacations to poor areas. Authentic participation (born of true solidarity with the poor) takes a broader and more serious commitment.

because of unemployment, which causes such destruction. The eyes of the spirits and hearts of Christians will be opened if they know how to accept this invitation from God, which is extended to all men and women, to go out as a matter of routine, discreetly and humbly to listen to and serve anyone in need.[140]

But the Church's current approach to the *gravity* of the duties we have to the poor is much less direct than that found in its broad tradition. Singer, in both his latest book on poverty and in his previous writings, is willing to say that, given a fairly routine standard of living in the developed world, giving 10 percent of one's resources is morally required. Anything less than that and one is morally blameworthy. In addition, Singer is perfectly comfortable being direct about the seriousness of the blameworthiness. He stops short of saying it should be considered murder for such a person to give less than 10 percent, but it should be considered something like reckless homicide, and thus the person who gives less is nevertheless morally responsible for the deaths of those he has failed to aid.

The current leadership in the Roman Catholic Church, with a few important exceptions, generally refuses to publicly teach that avaricious hoarding of wealth is anything close to the moral seriousness of homicide. This is despite the fact that the *Catechism of the Catholic Church* refers to it with precisely this noun, and that multiple sources of the tradition (including Jesus himself) understand a failure to aid the poor as being the kind of thing that most endangers one's ultimate relationship with God. As shown above, the Church's tradition mirrors Singer almost exactly, affirming the utter moral seriousness of refusal to aid. In this respect, current Church leadership has a lot to learn from Peter Singer. Given the importance of clearly standing for certain non-negotiable values (like having a particular and broad respect for vulnerable, innocent human life), the rejection of which puts one outside the Church in various ways and to various degrees, the current leadership understandably requires public fidelity to certain central teachings that go to the heart of the faith. Though a particular emphasis on the unimaginably vulnerable prenatal lives killed in abortion is essential, current Church leadership would do well to consistently apply the tradition's respect for vulnerable human life by publicly reaffirming for our contemporary age that those who commit the sins of avarice and usury are, in fact, guilty of *indirect homicide* of the desperately poor and seriously imperil their own salvation. This would mean that those who publicly teach or stand for something

---

[140] Pontifical Council *Cor Unum*, "WORLD HUNGER, A Challenge for All: Development in Solidarity," 66.

contrary to official Roman Catholic teaching on these matters – and who as civil and political leaders promote avaricious and usurious public policies – should be subject to similar sanctions as those who publicly support policies which abandon prenatal human persons.[141]

Connecting these issues in this way would not be a new phenomenon in the Church. Joseph Cardinal Bernardin, the former Archbishop of Chicago, tirelessly championed the "consistent ethic of life" – an ethic which pays close attention to the Church's values of respect for persons, a preference for the marginalized and vulnerable, and presumption against violence. Using these values to make analogical connections between issues, Bernardin courageously linked together the Church's views on abortion, embryo destruction, euthanasia, the death penalty, the majority of war and duties to the poor into the ethic.[142] The time has come, without hesitancy or undue qualification, for Christians to see our duties to the poor as part of a consistent ethic of life. Our disproportionate hoarding and consumption of wealth withholds resources from the vulnerable poor which we owe to them. And, at least if we take Gratian, Ambrose, and the *Catechism* seriously, this withholding *does violence*: not only to their dignity, but often to their health and even their very lives.

CONCLUSION

Given all the overlap we saw between Singer and the Church on duties to the poor, the differences noted in the last part of this chapter might seem to pale in comparison. Both approaches react strongly against the violence and injustice that our consumerist and hyper-autonomous culture inflicts on the vulnerable poor. The enormity of what is in common might also suggest yet another duty: taking advantage of the resources and loyalties proper to each approach and unleashing their combined power toward the mutual goal of ending absolute poverty and restoring broad social partici-pation for the poor. The Church, for its part, "knows that she can share

---

[141] It is sometimes argued that the issue of duties to the poor involves a 'prudential judgment' as to how best to help them, and that this would mean putting the issue into a different moral category than abortion. Most pro-choice Roman Catholic teachers and leaders do not argue *against* the dignity of the fetus (those who do would be in a different category, to be sure), but rather claim that they are also making a 'prudential judgment' about how best to defend such dignity – especially in light of the chances that a law banning abortion would 'work' in light of public policy realities. If the prudential judgment argument fails for abortion, it also fails for duties to the poor.

[142] For specifics on the Cardinal's proposals and arguments, see Joseph Bernardin and Thomas G. Fuechtmann, *Consistent Ethic of Life* (Kansas City, MO: Sheed & Ward, 1988), 258. More will be said about the consistent ethic of life in the conclusion to this book.

this commitment with other Christian Churches and religious communities, and with all men and women of good will."[143] The blood of our
impoverished sisters and brothers cries out to us, and it is therefore long
past time to put differences aside (which, if my central argument is
correct, are not as serious as one might think) and work with all persons
of good will toward fulfilling our duties to the poor.

---

[143] Pontifical Council *Cor Unum,* "WORLD HUNGER, A Challenge for All: Development in
Solidarity," 70.

CHAPTER 5

Ethical theory

The ethical point of view does, as we have seen, require us to go beyond a personal point of view to the standpoint of the impartial spectator. Thus, looking at things ethically is a way of transcending our inward-looking concerns and identifying ourselves with the most objective point of view possible – with, as Sidgwick put it, "the point of view of the universe."

> Peter Singer, *Practical Ethics*

By common good is to be understood "the sum total of social conditions which allow people, either as groups or as individuals, to reach their fulfillment more fully and more easily." The common good concerns the life of all ... Human interdependence is increasing and gradually spreading throughout the world. The unity of the human family, embracing people who enjoy equal natural dignity, implies a *universal common good*.

> *Catechism of the Catholic Church*

INTRODUCTION

Some more traditional approaches to academic ethics might have *begun* a book like this by exploring the topic of this chapter. In comparing Peter Singer and Christian ethics, one of the first things that will likely spring to mind (at least for an academic ethicist) is what appears to be a substantial difference in ethical theory. After all, as a utilitarian, Singer's goal is to maximize preference satisfaction, while the Church has moral rules which seem to directly contradict this way of approaching ethics. But there are good reasons to leave discussion of the theoretical approaches of both Singer and the Church until after applied issues have been examined. If we had begun with the differences in ethical theory this might have made it more difficult to see the broad-based agreement in how each approach applies their theory in the practical world. In addition, seeing the overlap in the realm of the practical can help us clear the conceptual space

178

for understanding how the ethical theories of Peter Singer and the Church might not be as far apart as one might imagine.[1] And especially in his more recent writings, Singer's approach attempts to downplay differences in ethical theory with the goal of getting many different kinds of people, with many different approaches to ethics, to agree with his practical conclusions. Indeed, we know that historically there have been times where those participating in discussions about ethics disagree deeply about theory, but nevertheless come to important and even broad agreement about applied or practical ethics; the classic example being the National Commission for the Protection of Human Subjects – a diverse group of thinkers who, at first, couldn't agree on a set of principles. Agreement at this level was only possible once they looked at the practical cases first.[2]

All this being said, Singer is (for now) a preference utilitarian and this has implications for any comparison of his ethic to that of the Church.[3] Furthermore, we have already seen that he understands himself to be leading a 'Copernican revolution' in ethics – directed largely against what he takes to be the Church's moral tradition – and it would be strange if this was not reflected in his ethical theory. Indeed, even those marginally familiar with these two theoretical approaches to ethics might point to several things which seem to make fruitful exchange on this topic unlikely. We will see below that the Church wants to uphold the inherent dignity of the individual person in a way that seems to be incompatible with a utilitarian approach – especially one which reduces the value of a person to merely part of a larger moral calculation determining what will maximize good consequences in any given situation. Part of this inherent dignity requires valuing the concept of *justice*: that, broadly speaking, individuals are due certain kinds of things regardless of the broader consequences for others. But Singer and other utilitarians must claim that justice, while maybe helpful as a working principle, must ultimately be subordinate to what will produce the best consequences in the end – even if that means having a wide disparity in income distribution between rich

---

[1] One important reason is that, at least in my experience, most are not ultimately driven by an ethical theory. Instead, people generally begin with certain intuitive conclusions about practical ethics and *then* decide what theoretical positions to adopt. Indeed, I have a difficult time finding people who hold practical conclusions about ethical issues with which they are uncomfortable because they are being driven by an ethical theory.

[2] Albert Jonsen and Stephen Toulmin, *The Abuse of Casuistry: A History of Moral Reasoning* (Berkeley, CA: University of California Press, 1988), 18.

[3] Chapter 6 will explore Singer's shifting thought on matters of ethical theory.

and poor, punishing an innocent person to stop a riot, or other examples of injustice which seem to produce better consequences overall. Furthermore, the Church wants to uphold the importance of the intention of the agent,[4] while Singer claims that intention is largely unimportant and what matters are the consequences one produces. Perhaps, in light of this deep theoretical disagreement, we should say that what has been going on in the previous four chapters has been nothing more than an exercise in finding Rawlsian overlapping consensus. Perhaps there are interesting agreements on some practical issues, but they are accidental given that the heart of one theory is incompatible with that of the other.

But there are indicators that push against this analysis. An interesting one is that Singer's mentor in graduate school at Oxford was the analytic philosopher and ethicist R.M. Hare. This is a man about whom Singer says "when the history of twentieth-century ethics comes to be written, I believe it will be Hare's own work that will be seen as having made the most important contribution."[5] Undoubtedly, one reason why this dramatic claim is plausible is because of the radical influence Hare had on Singer – and in particular on Singer's ethical theory. As we will see in some detail below, each has a 'two-level' utilitarian ethic which, in part because it makes room for moral rules, is more compatible with a Christian ethic than the act-utilitarianism of classic thinkers like Bentham and Mill. Furthermore, Singer's mentor and role-model as an academic ethicist turns out to be a Christian. Consider this line written by Hare shortly before his death:

My work for the Church did not include any of the study of philosophy of religion; but I had always, *as a Christian* [emphasis added], had an interest in this, and in 1964 was elected as Wilde Lecturer in Natural Religion for that year.[6]

Though there is debate about how 'traditional' he was, multiple people knew him to show up at Church on a weekly basis.[7] Nor was Hare the

---

[4] We saw this most clearly in Chapters 1 and 2 when the Church makes a distinction between (either by action or omission) intending the death of an innocent person in abortion or euthanasia, and removing support (of the mother's body or of some kind of medical intervention) such that death is foreseen but unintended. Much more on this distinction to come in this chapter.

[5] Peter Singer, "R.M. Hare's Achievements in Moral Philosophy: A Talk for the Memorial Service at St. Mary's Church, Oxford, 25 May, 2002," *Utilitas* 14:3 (November 2002), 309.

[6] R.M. Hare, "A Philosophical Autobiography," *Utilitas* 14:3 (November 2002), 295.

[7] His son, John Hare (himself an explicitly traditional Christian), implies that R.M. Hare was not a 'traditional' Christian. This despite the fact, as we will see in Chapter 6, that John Hare believed his father's moral theory required something like traditional Christianity to be true. J. E. Hare, *The Moral Gap: Kantian Ethics, Human Limits, and God's Assistance* (Oxford; New York: Clarendon Press; Oxford University Press, 1996), 292, 15.

type of Christian philosopher to keep theological ideas hidden in his work. Time and time again he would invoke concepts like 'providence' and 'archangel' at important places in his arguments.

Of course, those who have read the previous four chapters might not be all that surprised to find out that Singer's mentor was a Christian philosopher. Indeed, we have already learned that both Singer and the Church uphold the following theoretical claims:

1. Ethics is not relative to the society in which one lives.
2. One is morally responsible not only for what one does, but for what one fails to do.
3. The common good of all people, not just one's close family, friends or neighbors, is a central moral consideration.
4. One should live largely by following moral rules and not simply calculate the consequences for each act.
5. Important moral value can be found outside the species *Homo sapiens.*
6. Preservation of the lives of persons can be trumped by other values in certain situations.

This chapter, like the previous four, will map both the areas of overlap and of disagreement. But it will also argue that while Singer helps push the Church to understand the consequentialist aspects of its own approach, a nuanced understanding of the Church's moral tradition will see that it already contains much of what is strong about Singer's ethical theory while avoiding many of its pitfalls and problems. The first section will examine several areas in which Singer and the Church share aspects of their ethical theory: consequence-based reasoning, rules-based reasoning, and a teleological method. The second section will explore areas of theoretical divergence: especially when it comes to rules 'without exceptions' or acts that are 'intrinsically evil.' Singer rejects these concepts. And while the Church does make room for them, I will show that exceptionless moral norms are understood to be such by the Church precisely in a teleological framework. The final section of the chapter explores in some detail the Church's attempt (in the face of criticism from Singer and others) to consistently combine a teleological ethic with exceptionless moral norms.

Before we begin, however, let me define some terms that might cause confusion among various readers who may use the terms in different ways.[8]

---

[8] Experience tells me that some philosophers use these terms differently from many theologians. In defining the terms the way I do, I was influenced by Lisa Cahill's "Teleology, Utilitarianism, and Christian Ethics," *Theological Studies* 42, no. 4 (1981).

When I speak of 'consequentialism' I am simply using it as an umbrella term for approaches to ethics which locate a primary moral concern in the consequences of one's actions. 'Teleology,' as I use the term, is a subset of consequentialism in that it is concerned with achieving an end or ends. 'Utilitarianism' is a subset of teleology in that it claims that the moral life consists in achieving the end of maximizing utility (pleasure, preferences, etc.). But, as we will see, a *Christian* teleology differs from most kinds of utilitarianism in that the ends pursued are based on the objective and normative *telos* of various entities (and of creation more broadly), thus opening up the possibility that certain means are incompatible with achieving our ends. Consequentialists, of course, are to be distinguished from deontologists who believe morality is characterized primarily by following certain rules. Now, as we will see below, some consequentialists make room for rules as well, but they are "at the service"[9] of achieving various ends. A deontologist most often follows moral rules simply based on authority of the rule-giver: reason, God, etc.[10] This may seem confusing in the abstract, but it will become clearer as we move through our discussion below.

CONSEQUENCE-BASED REASONING

Singer, of course, is well known for focusing on consequence-based reasoning as a preference utilitarian. The moral life is about producing the most utility by maximizing all available preferences. And we have also seen that Singer wishes to consider 'preferences' in the broadest possible terms. Indeed, in doing our preference calculations, he insists that we take "the point of view of the universe."[11] What is perhaps less well known is that the Church makes consequence-based reasoning a locus of its ethical concern as well – and in ways strikingly similar to that of Peter Singer. Consider this from the *Catechism* on the common good:

By common good is to be understood "the sum total of social conditions which allow people, either as groups or as individuals, to reach their fulfillment more fully and more easily." The common good concerns the life of all ... Human interdependence is increasing and gradually spreading throughout the world.

---

[9] As we will see below, John Paul II uses this phrase to describe even the most serious moral rules the Church has.
[10] Of course, there is nothing inconsistent with believing *both* that we should follow rules because of the authority of the rule-giver *and* that such rules are teleological in nature.
[11] This also means taking into account future preferences – something that, as we will see in the next chapter, will cause a major problem for his theory.

The unity of the human family, embracing people who enjoy equal natural dignity, implies a *universal common good.*[12]

And this from the *Compendium of the Social Doctrine of the Church*:

> The common good of society is not an end in itself; it has value only in reference to attaining the ultimate ends of the person and the universal common good of the whole of creation.[13]

It is this understanding of the common good, as the reader will recall from the previous chapter, which leads the Church to argue for the "Universal Destination of Goods."

The Church's Singer-like focus on the fulfillment of all persons[14] – and even creation more broadly speaking – has a strong precedent in the thought of Thomas Aquinas who argued that

> a man's will is not right in willing a particular good, unless he refer it to the common good as an end: since even the natural appetite of each part is ordained to the common good of the whole.

Indeed, the will of the human person is to be conformed to the will of God, which Thomas describes in the following way:

> Now the good of the whole universe is that which is apprehended by God, Who is the Maker and Governor of all things: hence whatever He wills, He wills it under the aspect of the common good; this is His own Goodness, which is the good of the whole universe.[15]

And we have just seen this broad interest in the fulfillment of all the created universe play out in the preceding chapters – whether we were talking about the good of vulnerable human populations very far away or the good of non-human animals in factory farms. Much more will be said about Thomas Aquinas' teleological approach below.

In addition, the Church often uses a consequence-focused concept, proportionate reasoning, in making its ethical arguments. We have already seen in Chapter 2 how the Church permits withdrawal or refusal of even life-sustaining treatment if a proportionate reason is provided for doing so. That is, the good of the thing being aimed at (removing of

---

[12] Catholic Church, *The Catechism of the Catholic Church*, paragraphs 1906 and 1911.
[13] Catholic Church, *Compendium of the Social Doctrine of the Church*, 170.
[14] As we will see in the next chapter in more detail, both Singer and the Church are concerned with *future* people as well as people who are alive today. Utilitarianism is well known for this focus, but, especially in the ecological thought of Pope Benedict xvi, the Church also stands strongly for intergenerational solidarity.
[15] Thomas and Dominicans, *Summa Theologica*, ii:i, 19:10.

burdensome treatment) must be significant enough to warrant the
foreseen but unintended loss of life. The concept is also used, as we
saw in Chapter 1, when making decisions about whether an indirect
abortion is justified. One might remove a fetus from her mother's body
only if there is a proportionate reason that is significant enough to
warrant the foreseen but unintended loss of life. It is also worth mentioning that Christian Just War theory requires a proportionate reason
both to go to war in the first place, and also for any violent act within
the waging of the war itself. If the destruction of property or persons
would be disproportionate to the expected positive results, then it would
be immoral to proceed. Again, we will explore the Church's tradition on
proportionate reasoning in more detail below. Suffice it to say at this
point that we can already see overlapping examples of consequence-
based reasoning.

RULES-BASED REASONING

If there is one thing about which most are sure when it comes to
Roman Catholicism, it is that the Church likes rules. And despite Jesus
claiming that "all the law and the prophets" depend on a more general
duty to love God and neighbor (Matthew 22:34–40),[16] the Church does
indeed acknowledge the important place of moral rules. For instance,
while a state can go to war for a proportionate reason, it is also the case
that a war of *aggression* is intrinsically immoral and may never be
executed for any reason.[17] Both John Paul II and the Bishops of Vatican
Council II noted that there are several other examples of "intrinsically
immoral" acts:

Whatever is hostile to life itself, such as any kind of homicide, genocide,
abortion, euthanasia and voluntary suicide; whatever violates the integrity of
the human person, such as mutilation, physical and mental torture and attempts
to coerce the spirit; whatever is offensive to human dignity, such as subhuman
living conditions, arbitrary imprisonment, deportation, slavery, prostitution and
trafficking in women and children; degrading conditions of work which treat
labourers as mere instruments of profit, and not as free responsible persons: all
these and the like are a disgrace, and so long as they infect human civilization

---

[16] Much more will be said about this passage below – especially what (if any) insight it gives us as to
the relationship between rules and the Church's ethical theory.
[17] Catholic Church, *Compendium of the Social Doctrine of the Church*, 500. Admittedly, a 'war of
aggression' already has reasons built into the description of the act. The complexities of what kinds
of acts can count as intrinsically immoral will be discussed in detail below.

they contaminate those who inflict them more than those who suffer injustice, and they are a negation of the honour due to the Creator.[18]

Such acts have an object which is so evil that it cannot be offered to God and therefore articulates a moral rule prohibiting them in every circumstance.

However, the Church also has rules which may or may not be followed, depending on the particular circumstances. In general, for instance, the Church claims that one must keep one's promises, but this principle may be overruled in certain circumstances:

Professional secrets – for example, those of political office holders, soldiers, physicians, and lawyers – or confidential information given under the seal of secrecy must be kept, save in exceptional cases where keeping the secret is bound to cause very grave harm to the one who confided it, to the one who received it or to a third party, and where the very grave harm can be avoided only by divulging the truth. Even if not confided under the seal of secrecy, private information prejudicial to another is not to be divulged without a grave and proportionate reason.[19]

Certain rules are to be followed in principle; but they may conflict with some other rule which takes precedence, or there may be circumstances in which a proportionate reason exists such that the rule may be violated.

Peter Singer's ethic also has an important place for rules. Some might find this surprising for a preference utilitarian,[20] but he is quite clear about the necessity of rules for his ethical theory:

There is something to be said, however, against applying utilitarianism – whether classical hedonistic utilitarianism or preference utilitarianism – only or primarily at the level of each individual case. It may be that in the long run, we will achieve better results – greater overall happiness – if we urge people not to judge each individual action by the standard of utility, but instead to think along the lines of some broad principles that will cover all or virtually all of the situations that they are likely to encounter ... These principles should include those that experience has shown, over the centuries, to be generally conducive to producing the best consequences ... for example, telling the truth, keeping promises, not harming others and so on.[21]

---

[18] National Catholic Welfare Conference and Donald R. Campion, *Gaudium et Spes*, 27 and quoted in Pope John Paul II, "*Veritatis Splendor*" (Vatican: The Holy See), 80.
[19] Catholic Church, *The Catechism of the Catholic Church*, paragraph 2491.
[20] Much of the criticism surrounding utilitarianism in general (and Singer's utilitarianism in particular) either misunderstands or simply ignores the important place for rules in many such approaches.
[21] Peter Singer, *Practical Ethics*, 2nd edn. (Cambridge; New York: Cambridge University Press, 1993), 78–79.

Singer even claims that the rule-based principle "every person has a right to life" requires our recognition.[22] Though in general we should follow our "well-chosen intuitive principles,"[23] like the Church, Singer claims these rules can be broken in some circumstances. He often considers the rule to 'tell the truth' when making the case; in a situation where following the rule may cause a patient needless suffering, for instance, Singer says that the physician "might be right to lie; and yet the doctor's colleagues may rightly censure him to preserve one standard of truthfulness."[24] So even when Singer allows a rule to be broken, he is still utterly concerned with the principle being respected and nevertheless upheld.

So, in addition to consequence-based reasoning, Peter Singer and the Church share a strong commitment to rule-based reasoning (which admits of rare exceptions) as well. Indeed, if one accepts Singer's claim that we should be seeking a set of well-chosen, intuitive rules based on experience, over centuries, of what produces flourishing for human beings, then I would suggest he or she take a hard look at those principles proposed by a Church that has been doing precisely this in a (more or less) systematic way for the last two thousand years.

A COMMON CONSEQUENTIALIST APPROACH?

But how is the tension highlighted above resolved? Is the Church, at bottom, rules-based or consequence-based? Especially in light of the concept of an intrinsically evil act, many argue that it takes a deontological or rule-based approach. But I want to argue that the Church is actually quite clear that the moral life is ultimately consequentialist in that it is about reaching a goal or destination based on the intrinsic, normative *telos* of various entities – and, indeed, of the whole created order. In explicating why moral rules exist, and doing so under the telling heading *Universal and unchanging moral norms at the service of the person and of society*, Pope John Paul II says the following:

The Church's firmness in defending the universal and unchanging moral norms is not demeaning at all. Its only purpose is to serve [humanity's] true freedom . . . This service is directed to *every man*, considered in the uniqueness and singularity

[22] Peter Singer, *Rethinking Life and Death* (New York: St. Martin's Griffin, 1996), 218.
[23] Singer, *Practical Ethics*, 79. He compares acting morally to "playing percentage tennis" – once in a while one might strike an amazing winner by taking a risky shot, but deviations from the general, time-honored rules of tennis will not work out well in the long run.
[24] Peter Singer, *The Expanding Circle: Ethics and Sociobiology* (New York: Farrar, Straus & Giroux, 1981), 190, 67.

of his being and existence: only by obedience to universal moral norms does man find full confirmation of his personal uniqueness and the possibility of authentic moral growth ... These norms in fact represent the unshakable foundation and solid guarantee of a just and peaceful human coexistence, and hence of genuine democracy, which can come into being and develop only on the basis of the equality of all its members, who possess common rights and duties.[25]

For some Catholics, the idea that even "universal and unchanging" moral rules are at the service of consequentialist considerations (like 'peaceful coexistence' and 'true freedom') coming from the Pope might be a surprise, but John Paul II is quite explicit about the teleological character of the moral life:

Consequently the moral life has an essential *"teleological" character*, since it consists in the deliberate ordering of human acts to God, the supreme good and ultimate end *(telos)* of [humanity].[26]

The *ultimate* goal or end of the human person (at least from a Christian point of view) is of course going to be love of, and ultimate union with, God. But achievement of that ultimate end comes about by uniting our *proximate* ends to conform to the universal common good of persons and the good of the entire created order. We saw above how Thomas connects God's good with the good of the whole universe, and Eric Gregory pointed out at the Oxford conference that Augustine believed Jesus' commands to love God and to love neighbor cannot live without each other.[27]

But who are the serious Christian ethicists who take the teleological approach? Alasdair MacIntyre (who some claim is the most important Christian philosopher of the last several generations, and perhaps even of the last several centuries) is often thought to be arguing *against* a consequence-based ethic, but it is clear that this perception is either mistaken or in need of serious clarification. For he argues that the concepts and judgments through which "human beings express their beliefs and guide their actions when their lives are in good order" can only be adequately grasped "by those who have understood and know how to find application for the concept of an end."[28] For those who have read him carefully, or even for those who know that he takes a Thomistic approach, it will not be news

[25] Pope John Paul II, "*Veritatis Splendor*," 96.   [26] *Ibid.*, 73.
[27] "Peter Singer Conference Archive." McDonald Centre for Theology, Ethics & Public Life. http://mcdonaldcentre.org.uk/resources/peter-singer-conference/ (Accessed July 10, 2011).
[28] Lawrence Cunningham, *Intractable Disputes about the Natural Law: Alasdair MacIntyre and Critics* (Notre Dame, IN: University of Notre Dame Press, 2009), 50.

to read that MacIntyre is a teleologist. But his recent expressions of this fact are striking in what he takes to be the relationship of this approach to utilitarianism:

How then should we formulate the Thomistic and Aristotelian claim that I am advancing? Thomistic Aristoalians [sic] *agree with utilitarians* [emphasis added] that moral rules have to be understood teleologically. They agree with Mill – or rather Mill agreed with them – that there is no inconsistency in asserting of certain kinds of action both that they should be done for their own sake and also for the sake of achieving some further end.[29]

In a fascinating example of theoretical overlap with approaches like that of Singer, MacIntyre claims quite clearly and directly that his ethical theory *agrees with utilitarianism* that moral rules need to be understood teleologically – that is, with a primary focus on the end or ends towards which an act is aimed.[30] And MacIntyre is not some lone voice crying in the wilderness on this topic; in an article written more than three decades ago, the important Roman Catholic ethicist Lisa Cahill made the argument that utilitarianism "is a subset" of teleology and that a Christian teleology, though consequence-based, "can be distinguished" from utilitarianism in various important ways.[31]

Christian teleology

But up to this point we have focused on generalities. What, specifically, does a Christian teleology look like? The Church quite naturally focuses its attention on Jesus' answer to the question, "Which is the greatest commandment?"

You shall love the Lord your God with your whole heart, and with your soul and with your mind. This is the first and greatest commandment. And the second is like it. You shall love your neighbor as yourself. On these two commandments hang all the law and the prophets (Matthew 22: 37–40).

Interestingly, Jesus gives *two* answers to the question. As we saw above, many take the command about 'loving God' to be one's ultimate or

---

[29] *Ibid.*, 49–50.
[30] As we will see below, he argues that once one removes *the metaphysics* supporting the ontological nature of such end or ends, as he takes utilitarians to have done, one's teleology becomes incoherent.
[31] Cahill, "Teleology, Utilitarianism, and Christian Ethics," 601. We will discuss several of these ways below.

formal end and 'loving your neighbor as yourself' to be one's proximate or material end. Consider the *Catechism* on this connection:

The intention is a movement of the will toward the end: it is concerned with the goal of the activity. It aims at the good anticipated from the action undertaken. Intention is not limited to directing individual actions, but can guide several actions toward one and the same purpose; it can orient one's whole life toward its ultimate end. For example, a service done with the end of helping one's neighbor can at the same time be inspired by the love of God as the ultimate end of all our actions.[32]

And a classic way of fleshing out more precisely what this means involves an appeal to humanity's desire for happiness. As Pope John Paul II says:

God alone is worthy of being loved "with all one's heart, and with all one's soul, and with all one's mind" (Matthew 22:37). He is the source of man's happiness. Jesus brings the question about morally good action back to its religious foundations, to the acknowledgement of God, who alone is goodness, fullness of life, the final end of human activity, and perfect happiness.[33]

On this account, while ultimate happiness only comes from final union with God, it is the current flourishing and happiness *of both ourselves and our neighbor* that should be the proximate end of our actions.[34] William Mattison points out that connecting the moral life to happiness is not peculiar to modern Roman Catholicism, but rather

how most Christian thinkers through history have understood the Christian moral life. St. Augustine assumes in his main discussions of morality that the starting point for such reflections is how to live a happy life, and explains why the love of God and neighbor that Christ commands in all four gospels is the true path to happiness. St. Thomas Aquinas follows Aristotle in beginning his most famous discussion of morality with a treatise on happiness, and concludes with Augustine that God alone can fulfill the restlessness and longing that marks all human persons.[35]

Mattison also notes that people are sometimes surprised to hear about this connection between morality and happiness in the Christian tradition,

[32] Catholic Church, *The Catechism of the Catholic Church*, paragraph 1752. This passage is also a nice example of why intention is so important for the teleologist in ways that it is not for the utilitarian.
[33] Pope John Paul II, "*Veritatis Splendor*," 9.
[34] For a nice explication of the relationship between ultimate happiness/good and proximate happiness/goods, see Charles G. Herbermann, *et al.*, (eds.), *The Catholic Encyclopedia: An international work of reference on the constitution, doctrine, discipline, and history of the Catholic Church* (London: Caxton, 1907), 638.
[35] William C. Mattison, *Introducing Moral Theology: True Happiness and the Virtues* (Grand Rapids, MI: Brazos Press, 2008), 429, 25–26.

but the scriptures tell us that Jesus came so that we could "live abundantly" (John 10:10) and follow his commands "so that my joy might be in you and your joy might be complete." (John 15:11, cf. 1 John 1:4) And when Jesus gives the famous Sermon on the Mount he urges us to action by saying, "Happy are those who . . ." (Matthew 5:3–10; cf. Luke 6:20–22)[36]

At first glance this conclusion looks like it sets up quite dramatic common ground between the Church's ethic and Singer-like approaches. After all, many utilitarians also invoke happiness of one kind or another as the measuring stick for maximizing utility. But before making a quick judgment, let us first give careful attention to what one means by the term. As MacIntyre points out, happiness conceived merely "in psychological terms" and "in terms of the passions and inclinations" puts one in the unfortunate position of having to reject "impersonal and universal regard for the persons, interests, and needs of others that moral rules enjoin." The Christian teleologist, however, will understand that there is no such thing as 'happiness' as such. To the contrary:

> To be happy – as contrasted with feeling happy – is always to be happy in virtue of something or other, something done or suffered, something acquired or achieved. When translators have supplied " happiness" as the English translation of *eudaimonia* or *beatitudo*, they have in mind that type of happiness which supervenes upon and is made intelligible by the achievement of a completed and perfected life of worthwhile activity, the achievement of the human end.[37]

MacIntyre seems to assume that a utilitarian will reject this kind of metaphysical understanding of happiness, and most utilitarians have in fact done precisely this and consequently found themselves unable to provide an 'impersonal and universal regard' for persons and interests. But is this *necessarily* the case? Especially in light of the fact that (as we will see in more detail in Chapter 5) Singer also connects happiness to achieving goals in a coherent life plan, I think not. But let us take a more detailed look at Singer's brand of consequentialism.

Singer's two-level preference utilitarianism

Especially if one focuses on the Singer of the last decade, one must tread carefully when attempting to explicate his ethical theory. In addition to

---

[36] *Ibid.*, 26–27. It is worth noting that the word *makarios* has a disputed meaning in this context. Some prefer 'blessed.'

[37] Lawrence Cunningham, *Intractable Disputes about the Natural Law: Alasdair McIntyre and Critics* (Notre Dame, IL: University of Notre Dame Press, 2009), 48–49.

the fact that his theoretical views are currently in flux, we will see in more detail in Chapter 5 how Singer is primarily an applied ethicist who in his more recent writings focuses on making public arguments accessible to those of various traditions and theoretical backgrounds. At any rate, we have already learned that Singer is the kind of preference utilitarian who understands the importance of rules. But lest one get on the wrong track, Singer is quick to say "I have never been a rule utilitarian,"[38] but instead affirms that he holds R.M. Hare's 'two levels' view.[39] It is hardly surprising that Singer took on the theory of his mentor, but understanding two-level preference utilitarianism is absolutely essential for making a comparison of Singer and Christian ethics on ethical theory, and so it is worth quoting Singer on this theory:

> R.M. Hare has suggested a useful distinction between two levels of moral reasoning: the intuitive and the critical. To consider the possible circumstances in which one might maximize utility by secretly killing someone who wants to go on living is to reason at the critical level. Those who are reflective, self-critical or philosophically inclined may find it interesting and helpful to think about such unusual hypothetical cases. In real life, we usually cannot foresee all the complexities of our choices. It is simply not practical to try to calculate the consequences, in advance, of every choice we make ... For all these reasons, Hare suggests, it will be better if we adopt some broad ethical principles for our everyday ethical life and do not deviate from them.[40]

We saw above that these should be well-chosen, intuitive principles that experience has shown, over the centuries, to be generally conducive to producing the best consequences. However, there are rare times where we are called to go against our intuitions and make choices at the critical level which deviate from the usual rules:

> Occasionally, however, we will find ourselves in situations in which we are able to think clearly, calmly, and in a manner sufficiently free from bias, and in which, thinking in this mode, we can see that following the usual moral rules will not have the best consequences.[41]

Unlike rule-utilitarianism, "this two-level model never tells us to follow a rule when we can be sure that breaking the rule will have better consequences." It thus avoids the charge of rule worship: that is, of "putting you in a situation in which your only reason for doing one thing rather

[38] Jeffrey Schaler, *Peter Singer Under Fire*: The Moral Iconoclast Faces His Critics (Chicago, IL: Open Court, 2009), 192.
[39] *Ibid.*, 177. [40] Singer, *Practical Ethics*, 78–79. [41] Schaler, *Peter Singer Under Fire*, 456.

than another is because you are obeying a rule that says you must do it, although disobeying the rule would have better consequences."[42]

Singer, it turns out, shares many of same rules that Christians uphold.[43] We also share the understanding that some of these rules may be broken for a good enough reason. *And* we share much consequentialist reasoning about the universal common good and destination of goods that would determine whether a rule should be followed or broken in a given situation.

CHRISTIAN UTILITARIANISM?

In light of what has just been pointed out above, couldn't Singer simply tell the Christian that she should get on board with his utilitarianism? In addition to the overlap just mentioned, Singer claims that "a consequentialist judgment" is what is actually behind the Church's doctrine of double effect[44] and that "there is an argument, based on the 'Golden Rule,' or the idea of putting yourself in the position of all those affected by your actions, which leads to some version of utilitarianism."[45] Shouldn't Christian ethicists just get over themselves and admit that they should be utilitarians?

Singer would not be the first person to have this view. Despite the telling historical fact that utilitarianism develops, not out of pagan context like ancient Greece or Rome, but out of Christian England, many historians of moral thought neglect to mention that some important Christians have espoused something like 'theological utilitarianism.' Graham Cole suggests that, despite having a significant place in the intellectual landscape of eighteenth-century England, its last great exponent, William Paley, died in 1805.[46] But this is too quick, given that the nineteenth-century Christian legal scholar John Austin was well known in standing for the idea that moral commands which God has not revealed "we must construe by the principle of utility."[47] For a significant part of his career, the great Henry Sidgwick attempted to incorporate both Christianity and utilitarianism. And one would be totally remiss in leaving out the famous Christian utilitarian of the twentieth century, Joseph Fletcher,

---

[42] *Ibid.*

[43] We have already seen that Singer shares the ethical norms against killing persons, lying, abandoning the needy, etc.

[44] Singer, *Practical Ethics*, 184.

[45] Hyun Hochsmann, *On Peter Singer* (Belmont, CA: Wadsworth Publishing, 2002), 85.

[46] Graham Cole, "Theological Utilitarianism and the Eclipse of Theistic Sanction," *Tyndale Bulletin* 42, no. 2 (1991), 226.

[47] John Austin and Robert Campbell, *Lectures on Jurisprudence: Or, the Philosophy of Positive Law* (London: J. Murray, 1920), 2, Lecture IV, page 160.

whose important book *Situation Ethics*[48] is a foundational work for this kind of approach to Christian ethics. He describes his basic thesis as follows: moral obligation "depends on the variables of situations rather than on normative rules of conduct."[49] He claims that "by definition situationists are consequentialists" for "they determine right or wrong practically in terms of gain or loss in human well-being, in actual cases rather than broad generalizations or metaphysical-transcendental presuppositions."[50] What's more, if Fletcher was forced to choose a 'school' for his point of view, he says "situation ethics would be act-utilitarianism." Indeed, he believes that his view puts him very close to those of John Stuart Mill.[51] After all, he has reduced his ethic to

only one duty, namely to act with loving concern. In its Christian form, it seems to me that situationism is a radical *agapism* as to its substantive good and a radical relativism as to its normative obligation. Not doctrines, but data become the all-important consideration.[52]

But ultimately, for Fletcher:

Whether we call it love or "utility," it comes to the same thing. Expressed in nonagapistic language, utility means the greatest possible preponderance of good over evil, calculated for actual situations as to the remote as well as the immediate consequences of whatever choices are open to the moral agent. This is why Mill said, "To do as you would be done by, and to love your neighbor as yourself, constitute the ideal perfection of utilitarian morality."

For Fletcher, "responsible" decision-makers "are concrete and particular" and "do not resort to prefabricated answers" in their moral calculations. Indeed, he refuses to embrace *any* "ideological or doctrinaire approach to any moral problem."[53]

Problems for a Christian utilitarianism

Various utilitarian views are still present today within Christianity. Consider the recent online symposium at *First Things* called "The Truth About Torture? – A Christian Ethics Symposium."[54] Though many Christian

---

[48] Joseph F. Fletcher, *Situation Ethics; the New Morality* (Philadelphia: Westminster Press, 1966), 176.
[49] Joseph F. Fletcher, "Love and Utility," *The Christian Century* (May 31, 1978), 592.
[50] *Ibid.*, 594.   [51] *Ibid.*, 593.
[52] Joseph F. Fletcher, "Responsible Decision Making," *Theology Today* 28:1 (April 1971): 91.
[53] *Ibid.*, 90.
[54] "The Truth About Torture? – A Christian Ethics Symposium," *First Things*, http://firstthings.com/blogs/evangel/the-truth-about-torture – a-christian-ethics-symposium/ (Accessed November 26, 2010).

approaches, including that of the Roman Catholic Church, have ethical doctrines which prohibit torture as intrinsically evil, multiple Christian thinkers participating in this symposium argued that torture could be morally licit in some circumstances. Perhaps the fact that Christians can come to this conclusion might cause one to think that something is amiss with approaches like that of Fletcher which permit the radical reduction of the inherent dignity of persons by torture via a utilitarian calculus.

Indeed, though it remains fashionable in many circles today to follow Fletcher in throwing off the shackles of 'ideology and doctrine,' it is precisely these concepts which avoid what most take to be reprehensible ethical violations. One might point out to Fletcher, for instance, that the Christian God clearly stands for a non-utilitarian concept of justice in many circumstances, but it is difficult to figure out where this concept would fit in his ethic. A classic illustration of this point asks us to consider a judge who is forced to choose between executing ten prisoners she knows to be innocent and causing a mob to riot (at the prisoners not being executed) which she foresees will result in the death of eleven persons. Against the grain of most of our ethical intuitions, and against the demands of justice, the utilitarian appears to be forced to come to the morally questionable conclusion that the judge should indeed execute the innocent prisoners in order to save a greater number of lives. Of course, a two-level or rule utilitarian might object here and claim that the judge should not execute the innocent prisoners because doing so would cause the justice system to break down in the long run and lead to worse consequences, all things considered. But even if the judge decided not to operate on the critical level when she could clearly save more lives, would that be *all* that is wrong with what the judge did?

In order to answer that question we must come to the question of anthropology. What, ultimately, is the human person? If there is nothing wrong 'in principle' with executing the innocent person to save a greater number of persons and thus promote a greater number of interests (i.e., it is wrong only 'derivatively' – because it doesn't maximize utility in the long run), then this presupposes an instrumental and reductionist view of the person as mere placeholder for various interests. As Jean Porter says:

The overarching Christian narrative of salvation further supports the idea that the individual, as such, is irreducibly important; God is seen as acting on behalf of us, not only collectively, but as individuals, who have been alienated from God, whom God wants to redeem, with whom God seeks a personal relationship.[55]

[55] Jean Porter, "Christianity, Divine Law, and Consequentialism," *Scottish Journal of Theology* 48: 4 (1995), 437.

An anthropology which reduces the dignity of the human person to a mere placeholder for a collection of interests (that have value only insofar as they impact a larger or even *universal* calculation of interests) ceases to be authentically Christian.[56]

Indeed, it is precisely this irreducible dignity of the person which leads the Church to claim that some acts are 'intrinsically evil' and can never be licit. Here is *Veritatis Splendor*'s famous passage on this topic:

Reason attests that there are objects of the human act which are by their nature "incapable of being ordered" to God, because they radically contradict the good of the person made in his image.[57]

Interestingly, John Paul II *maintains the teleological language* in explaining why such acts are never permitted. Our proximate goal is happiness (for ourselves and for others), and our ultimate goal is union with God, but there are some acts that simply cannot be ordered either to God or to the flourishing of the human person. Again, what is wrong with enslaving, killing, or torturing a particular person – at least for the Christian – cannot be reduced to the question of 'what happens to interest maximization?' if we were, in fact, to allow slavery, killing, and torture. No, such acts attempt something that is utterly incoherent from the Church's point of view: radical reduction of the irreducible dignity of the person to a mere means to some other end.

But *Veritatis Splendor* attempts to balance a clear understanding and defense of the dignity of the person (and of the nature of certain acts which utterly and radically contradict it) with the fact that, as we saw above, the moral life has an essential teleological character which consists in the deliberate ordering of human acts to God, the supreme good and ultimate end of humanity.[58] But teleology seems consequentialist in its approach, while the concept of absolute moral norms, which valorize and defend irreducible personal dignity and justice, seems deontological. Can the Church have it both ways?

THE PRINCIPLE OF DOUBLE EFFECT

The principle of double effect is often thought to be appropriately invoked only in situations of moral hair-splitting – or in special/extreme

---

[56] In addition, this non-reductionist view of human persons is shared by those of many different kinds of faith and those of no explicit faith at all.
[57] Pope John Paul II, "*Veritatis Splendor*," 80. [58] *Ibid.*, 73.

situations. But I lean in the direction of Peter Knauer who argued that the rule is, in fact, "the fundamental principle of all morality."[59] Though I won't go quite this far, I do believe that it is the principle of double effect which tries to accomplish the delicate but absolutely essential task of negotiating the tension present in a teleological ethic that also contains exceptionless moral norms. Richard McCormick, for instance, claims that the principle of double effect's "understanding of moral norms and exception making has been along teleological lines."[60] And one can even argue, as we will see below, that the fact some acts are understood to be intrinsically evil at all comes directly out of a teleological understanding.

How does the tension work itself out? The principle understands two kinds of effects produced by one's action – those that are intended and those that are unintended but foreseen – to be in significantly different moral categories. One may never *intend* the death of an innocent person (whether, as we have seen, by act or omission), for this would be an intrinsic evil which radically reduces the intrinsic dignity of the human person by using her death as a means to one's end. This kind of act, the Church claims, can never be offered to God or the common good. However, one might licitly act in such a way that *permits* the death of an innocent person as an effect of one's action, so long as that death is *not intended* and one has a *proportionate reason* for doing so.

There are obvious and puzzling complexities inherent in specification and application of the principle, but I agree with Dan Sulmasy's claim that something like the principle of double effect must be true in order for many of our basic moral intuitions to have merit:

> Intention is also obviously important to most people's common sense notions of morality. Harms done intentionally are both bad and wrong. Harms done unintentionally may be bad, but except for special situations like negligence, are not considered wrong.[61]

Of course, it is one thing to point out that there are 'unintentional' effects that one *does not foresee*, and perhaps there is general agreement that these effects are indeed in a different moral category. For instance, one may cause a driving accident that kills an innocent person, and yet, unless one

---

[59] Peter Knauer, "The Hermeneutic Function of the Principle of Double Effect," Hein Online (1967), 132.

[60] Richard A. McCormick and Paul Ramsey, *Doing Evil to Achieve Good: Moral Choice in Conflict Situations* (Chicago, IL: Loyola University Press, 1978), 267, 198.

[61] Daniel Sulmasy, "Double Effect – Intention is the Solution, Not the Problem," *Journal of Law, Medicine and Ethics* 28 (2000), 28. I think perhaps both Singer and I would disagree with Sulmasy about just how 'special' cases of negligence are.

was negligent in some way, be totally blameless. But consider a more interesting case in which one acts in such a way that an innocent person is 'unintentionally' killed, but that this death is, in fact, foreseen. Can the death *really* be said to be unintended such that it is in a different moral category?

I submit that most of us think the answer is yes. What, after all, is the difference between a terrorist who uses the death of innocent civilians as a means to some military or political end, and a bomber pilot who, while taking care to minimize the collateral damage, destroys a military installation – the effect of which (she foresees but does not intend) will also lead to the death of innocent civilians?[62] Something like the principle of double effect must be true if one wishes to claim that the terrorist is in a different moral category from the bomber pilot. In the first case the death of the innocent person is *required* for the terrorist to accomplish her goal, and the life of the human person is reduced to a mere means to the end of the act. But no such reduction takes place in the second scenario. Indeed, if no innocent civilians were killed in the second case, the bomber pilot would be thrilled. But not so in the first case, where the death of the innocent civilians is used precisely to accomplish the end of the act.

The Church explicitly uses this kind of reasoning in two other well-known kinds of cases.[63] It permits, for instance, intentional abortion of pregnancy when it is aimed at something other than the death of the fetus – even when the death of the fetus is a foreseen effect of the procedure:

Deliberately we have always used the expression "direct attempt on the life of an innocent person," "direct killing." Because if, for example, the saving of the life of the future mother, independently of her pregnant condition, should urgently require a surgical act or other therapeutic treatment which would have as an accessory consequence, in no way designed or intended, but inevitable, the death of the fetus, such an act could no longer be called a direct attempt on an innocent human life.

This principle, given the presence of proportionate reason (for instance, the life of the mother being in danger), would allow for hysterectomies, fallopian tube removal, and chemotherapy, even when they

[62] Some, of course, might answer: "nothing." But even if one felt that the pilot did not have a sufficiently serious (proportionate) reason for dropping the bomb (and thus judge the action to be morally wrong), most of our moral intuitions put direct, intentional terrorism in a different moral category.

[63] Both examples are cited in *Medical Ethics: Sources of Catholic Teachings*, 315–316. The first is from Pope Pius XII's "The Attempt on Innocent Human Life," and the second is from his "The Prolongation of Life."

would unintentionally and indirectly lead to the death of the unborn child. For in all these cases the death of the child is not the goal of the act, nor is it the means by which the goal is achieved. In addition, as we have already seen in Chapter 2, this reasoning can be used in making decisions about life-sustaining treatment. Again, given a proportionate reason, one may remove many kinds of life-sustaining medical treatment – from chemotherapy to ventilators – as long as one is not aiming at death.

The principle of double effect, then, does not compromise either on the concept of exceptionless moral norms or on a teleological conception of the moral life. As Lisa Cahill explains, "Good results, even for a majority, cannot be purchased by the sacrifice of moral values, that is, by acts inconsistent with this final *telos*." Indeed, she claims that "prohibitions which are both exceptionless and specific do not vanish" in a Roman Catholic teleology, but that the principle of double effect views the consequences of acts in light of a teleological goal: "the union of all persons in God as the universal common good."[64] Actions which intend certain kinds of morally reprehensible effects will always be incompatible with such a goal, but others which lack such an intention may sometimes licitly permit similar effects, given the presence of a proportionate reason.

Proportionate reasoning

But perhaps at this point we should draw a tighter focus onto something which may appear to be nebulous and evasive: the concept of proportionate reasoning. At an intuitive level one might see how, for instance, permitting the death of one innocent person (a human fetus) is 'proportionate' with saving the life of another human person (her mother). But what precisely is going on in this kind of reasoning – especially when the values at stake are not so easy to compare – is sometimes difficult to articulate. A particularly interesting passage from the Vatican's *Declaration on Euthanasia* might shed some light on this question. In a section entitled "Due Proportion in the Use of Remedies," the following claim is made about comparing the benefits and burdens of a particular kind of medical treatment:

In any case, it will be possible to make a correct judgment as to the means by studying the type of treatment to be used, its degree of complexity or risk, its

---

[64] Cahill, "Teleology, Utilitarianism, and Christian Ethics", 612.

cost and the possibilities of using it, and comparing these elements with the result that can be expected, taking into account the state of the sick person and his or her physical and moral resources.[65]

Here we have a door opened to a kind of proportionate reasoning that goes well beyond 'lives lost vs. lives saved.' Indeed, the Roman Catholic tradition on ordinary and extraordinary means (again, as we saw in Chapter 2) permits removal or refusal of life-sustaining treatment for all kinds of proportionate reasons: excessive pain, lack of expected results, excessive expense, burden on family or community, and even repugnance. The classic historical example of this kind of reasoning comes from battlefield medicine before pain medication. Was a soldier who needed a life-saving amputation required to get one? If the pain and horror at the procedure was such that the solider did not have the "physical or moral resources" to undergo it, the Church was prepared to call this a proportionate reason for refusing the procedure, and did not claim it was an instance of suicide.

THE PLACE OF EXCEPTIONLESS MORAL NORMS

More needs to be said about proportionate reasoning, and we will do so in due course, but at least as it has been described to this point, it might look like a utilitarian calculation. And indeed, this very real similarity is one of the important overlaps between the Church's ethic and that of Peter Singer. But at this point let us say more about the Church's teaching which is primarily responsible for halting a slide into pure utilitarianism: that of the exceptionless moral norm.[66]

Veritatis Splendor recognizes the teleological character of the moral life in claiming that moral choices must be *in conformity with man's true good* and thus express the voluntary ordering of the person towards his ultimate end: God himself, the supreme good in whom man finds his full and perfect happiness.[67] In this document John Paul II recognizes legitimate efforts to have a moral theory that has a focus on the consequences of one's actions, as long as it is not disconnected from this teleological character:

---

[65] Congregation for the Doctrine of the Faith, "Declaration on Euthanasia" (Vatican: The Holy See), www.vatican.va/roman_curia/congregations/cfaith/documents/rc_con_cfaith_doc_19800505_euthanasia_en.html (Accessed December 7, 2010), IV.

[66] A refined understanding of proportionate reasoning, described below, also pushes against the slide.

[67] Pope John Paul II, "*Veritatis Splendor*," 72.

For some, concrete behaviour would be right or wrong according to whether or not it is capable of producing a better state of affairs for all concerned. Right conduct would be the one capable of "maximizing" goods and "minimizing" evils. Many of the Catholic moralists who follow in this direction seek to distance themselves from utilitarianism and pragmatism, where the morality of human acts would be judged without any reference to the man's true ultimate end. They rightly recognize the need to find ever more consistent rational arguments in order to justify the requirements and to provide a foundation for the norms of the moral life. This kind of investigation is legitimate and necessary, since the moral order, as established by the natural law, is in principle accessible to human reason. Furthermore, such investigation is well-suited to meeting the demands of dialogue and cooperation with non-Catholics and non-believers, especially in pluralistic societies.[68]

Indeed, my hope is that this book is an example of precisely what John Paul II has in mind in this passage. But despite the importance of such dialogue and cooperation, the Pope is also understandably concerned that respect for the dignity of the human person will be lost if certain moral norms and precepts are not strongly defended against a slide into utilitarian reasoning:

The *negative precepts* of the natural law are universally valid. They oblige each and every individual, always and in every circumstance. It is a matter of prohibitions which forbid a given action *semper et pro semper*, without exception, because the choice of this kind of behaviour is in no case compatible with the goodness of the will of the acting person, with his vocation to life with God and to communion with his neighbour. It is prohibited – to everyone and in every case – to violate these precepts. They oblige everyone, regardless of the cost, never to offend in anyone, beginning with oneself, the personal dignity common to all.[69]

These precepts highlight actions which can never be ordered to the love of God or the human person and thus are exceptionless:

The reason why a good intention is not itself sufficient, but a correct choice of actions is also needed, is that the human act depends on its object, whether that object is *capable or not of being ordered* to God, to the One who "alone is good", and thus brings about the perfection of the person.[70]

Some actions – rape, torture, murder, etc. – have an object which can *never* be consistent with either the love of God or the irreducible dignity of neighbor. They are intrinsically evil:

If acts are intrinsically evil, a good intention or particular circumstances can diminish their evil, but they cannot remove it. They remain "irremediably"

---

[68] *Ibid.*, 74.   [69] *Ibid.*, 52.   [70] *Ibid.*, 78.

evil acts; *per se* and in themselves they are not capable of being ordered to God and to the good of the person.[71]

So *Veritatis Splendor* is clear: the moral life is teleological, but it supports a teleology that refuses to "deny the existence of negative moral norms regarding specific kinds of behaviour, norms which are valid without exception."[72]

The object of the act

But all of this, so far, might not be too controversial. After all, even many outside the Church also understand the moral norms regarding actions like rape and torture to be exceptionless. The rubber hits the road when we start thinking about other kinds of actions that are more widely debated, and, indeed, when we apply a certain kind of 'action theory' in their moral evaluation. The exceptionless moral norm as articulated above comes from the fact that certain actions have an object that can never be directed towards God or the good of the human person. But what is the 'object' of an action? Here is the *Catechism* on this question:

The *object* chosen is a good toward which the will deliberately directs itself. It is the matter of a human act. The object chosen morally specifies the act of the will, insofar as reason recognizes and judges it to be or not to be in conformity with the true good. Objective norms of morality express the rational order of good and evil, attested to by conscience.[73]

It is also important to understand the object in relation to 'intention' and 'circumstances':

In contrast to the object, the *intention* resides in the acting subject. Because it lies at the voluntary source of an action and determines it by its end, intention is an element essential to the moral evaluation of an action. The end is the first goal of the intention and indicates the purpose pursued in the action. The intention is a movement of the will toward the end: it is concerned with the goal of the activity. It aims at the good anticipated from the action undertaken. Intention is not limited to directing individual actions, but can guide several actions toward one and the same purpose; it can orient one's whole life toward its ultimate end. For example, a service done with the end of helping one's neighbor can at the same time be inspired by the love of God as the ultimate end of all our actions. One and the same action can also be inspired by several intentions, such as performing a service in order to obtain a favor or to boast about it.

[71] *Ibid.*, 81.   [72] *Ibid.*, 90.
[73] Catholic Church, *Catechism of the Catholic Church*, paragraphs 1751, 1752, and 1754.

The *circumstances*, including the consequences, are secondary elements of a moral act. They contribute to increasing or diminishing the moral goodness or evil of human acts (for example, the amount of a theft). They can also diminish or increase the agent's responsibility (such as acting out of a fear of death). Circumstances of themselves cannot change the moral quality of acts themselves; they can make neither good nor right an action that is in itself evil.

And it is the following conclusion, relying heavily on the above framework, which is perhaps the most cited in all of *Veritatis Splendor*:

> *One must therefore reject the thesis*, characteristic of teleological and proportionalist theories, *which holds that it is impossible to qualify as morally evil according to its species – its "object" – the deliberate choice of certain kinds of behaviour or specific acts, apart from a consideration of the intention for which the choice is made or the totality of the foreseeable consequences of that act for all persons concerned.*[74]

This is an important claim – one that deserves close attention given the goals of this chapter. Let us try to unpack it by taking a closer look at the relationship between an act's object and its circumstances and intention.

Jean Porter explicitly supports a significant portion of what John Paul II argues in *Veritatis Splendor*. We have already seen how she resists a Christian consequentialism which radically reduces the value of the human person to a mere means to another end, and she also agrees with the Pope (both cite Thomas Aquinas as their authority[75]) about the morality of an act depending primarily on the object chosen. But Porter points out that determining the object is sometimes a very complex matter, and, at least if Aquinas is correct, it cannot be done in the abstract before making a *moral evaluation* of the act. And moral evaluation depends, at least in part, on discovering the intention and often the circumstances. She says that

> the object of an action is not simply given perspicuously in the description of the act. It certainly cannot be equated with "what is done," described in a simple nonmoral way ... whatever precisely is meant by the object of the action, as understood by Aquinas or by traditional moral theology, this is surely a *moral* concept.[76]

After all, if we were simply to say, without further description, that A killed B, we wouldn't be able to make a moral evaluation of the act

---

[74] Pope John Paul II, "*Veritatis Splendor*," 79.

[75] This is Porter's trajectory in the article cited below, and also John Paul II's in "*Veritatis Splendor*," 78.

[76] Michael E. Allsopp and John J. O'Keefe, *Veritatis Splendor: American Responses* (Kansas City, MO: Sheed & Ward, 1995), 313, 283–284.

and therefore we wouldn't be able to determine the object chosen. If we added the circumstances that A is a public executioner and that B is a justly convicted criminal who cannot be safely incarcerated, then these are essential descriptions of the act which give us insight into whether the object chosen can be ordered to God.

Intention also seems to matter when determining the object of an action. For if A killed B by running into her with her car because A's car accidently slid on some ice, this would likely not be wrong at all. But if A killed B intentionally by running into her with her car because she was angry with her, then this is murder. And if A killed B by running into her with her car because she was late for work and was driving recklessly, then this is yet another kind of moral situation. The second description is of an intrinsically evil act in that it intentionally and radically reduces the dignity of the human person's life to a means to some other end, but the third, while very seriously wrong, is not intrinsically evil given that the death was not intended.

But perhaps we are considering the wrong kind of action. The Church doesn't teach that all killing is intrinsically evil,[77] but it does teach this about rape. If we say that A raped B then surely we don't wish to say that circumstances (A had had two beers or that B was dressed in a certain way) or intention (A was part of a police force attempting to subdue a revolt being led by B's faction) of the act could add anything of import to its moral evaluation, do we? The norm against rape is exceptionless, *full stop*. But let us examine this question a bit more closely: doesn't an act described as 'rape' already have intention and circumstances built into its description? If we were to pull back the description of the act and attempt to determine its object without regard to circumstances and intention, then it would have to be something like 'A *had sex* with B.' Calling it rape already assumes that A was intending to have sex with B in the circumstance where B did not give consent.

It is still possible that we haven't yet landed on the right kind of action. What about torture? Does it have similarly built-in circumstances and intentions? When looking at individual acts of torture, instead of holding the concept in the abstract, it seems the answer must be in the affirmative. Consider the torture involved in the US government's policy of causing someone sleep deprivation and other suffering due to the manipulation of

---

[77] The reference to 'murder' above, of course, simply begs the question given that murder is defined simply as 'wrongful killing.'

temperature. CIA interrogators do this with the intention of causing overwhelming suffering in a prisoner such that his will is weakened to the point where he will give up important information during later questioning. But someone might also cause *exactly the same amount of suffering to someone in exactly the same way* but with a very different intention. Consider instead a landlord, unaware that there is a person squatting in a building which he believes to be empty, who turns off the heat in the dead of winter. Everyone would agree that this act, despite causing exactly the same amount of suffering, has an entirely different object – in light of the intention of the agent and the other circumstances. No, it appears that, regardless of the action considered in the abstract, one at least needs to know the intention (and probably the circumstances) before one can determine its object.

Armed with the insights of this analysis, let us return to the important claim of *Veritatis Splendor* paragraph 79:

> *One must therefore reject the thesis*, characteristic of teleological and proportionalist theories, *which holds that it is impossible to qualify as morally evil according to its species – its "object" – the deliberate choice of certain kinds of behaviour or specific acts, apart from a consideration of the intention for which the choice is made or the totality of the foreseeable consequences of that act for all persons concerned.*

If this statement draws a conclusion about *all* actions, *however described,* then in light of what has just been presented, it is not at all convincing. However, this is not what the text says. The Pope makes the much weaker claim that we must reject a moral theory which claims that *no specific acts* or *kinds of behavior* exist which can be described as having an evil object without further reference to intention or consequences. This claim is actually quite convincing – particularly with regard to the certain specific acts which already have some circumstances and intentions built into their definition: rape, genocide, slavery, torture, etc. Once we have formulated the act sufficiently to get it to this level of description, many would indeed agree that *no other intention or circumstance* could justify, say, torturing someone, even if it could produce a good consequence. These kinds of acts have an intrinsically evil object which cannot be ordered to God or the good of the human person. Indeed, Roman Catholic Christians should be prepared even to accept martyrdom rather than commit one of these acts.[78]

---

[78] Pope John Paul II, "*Veritatis Splendor*," 93.

MORE ON PROPORTIONATE REASONING

But perhaps the weakness of the principle of double effect lies not in its use and application of moral norms, but rather in its use of proportionate reasoning once we agree that an intrinsically evil act is not being considered. I have already pointed out some of the ways in which proportionate reasoning is similar to Singer's utilitarianism. If one is not violating a moral norm that should be respected, then double effect allows one to do something that could even result in the death of another person, as long as one produces something which is 'proportionate' with that great disvalue. So if one allows a fetus to die, for instance, one should do it for a proportionate reason like saving her mother's life rather than a disproportionate one like a desire to continue to lead a certain kind of lifestyle. And if one allows a patient to die, one should do it because the treatment's pain is disproportionate with, say, the small chance it has of actually working rather than the fact that one needs the patient's life insurance money to go on vacation.

Proportionate reasoning also allows many *non*-exceptionless moral norms to be overridden. For instance, one norm of justice requires equal pay for equal work. But Jesus' parable of the vineyard workers is a classic story in which this norm is overruled in favor of the good produced by love, generosity and mercy:

The kingdom of heaven is like a landowner who went out at dawn to hire laborers for his vineyard. After agreeing with them for the usual daily wage, he sent them into his vineyard. Going out about nine o'clock, he saw others standing idle in the marketplace, and he said to them, "You too go into my vineyard, and I will give you what is just."

So they went off. (And) he went out again around noon, and around three o'clock, and did likewise. Going out about five o'clock, he found others standing around, and said to them, "Why do you stand here idle all day?" They answered, "Because no one has hired us." He said to them, "You too go into my vineyard."

When it was evening the owner of the vineyard said to his foreman, "Summon the laborers and give them their pay, beginning with the last and ending with the first." When those who had started about five o'clock came, each received the usual daily wage.

So when the first came, they thought that they would receive more, but each of them also got the usual wage. And on receiving it they grumbled against the landowner, saying, "These last ones worked only one hour, and you have made them equal to us, who bore the day's burden and the heat." He said to one of them in reply, "My friend, I am not cheating you. Did you not agree with me for the usual daily wage? Take what is yours and go. What if I wish to give this last one the same as you? (Or) am I not free to do as I wish with my own money? Are you envious because I am generous?" Thus, the last will be first, and the first will be last.[79] (Matthew 20:1–16)

Indeed, one of the basic themes of the Christian story is that God's love, generosity, and mercy, time and time again, override other norms. In some ways, this is the *entire story* of salvation history: human beings are saved from the just consequences of our sins by the loving mercy of God. This was classically illustrated in the parable of the Prodigal Son in which a father mercifully welcomes his son back into the family with a party after the son left home and squandered his inheritance in immoral ways. When the father's other son points out that he was faithful to his father and never got to have such a party, the father's response indicates that the good of mercy and love is more important than equal treatment (Luke 15:11–32).

We have already seen that Jesus claims "all the law and prophets" are contained in the command to love God totally and utterly and to love one's neighbor as oneself. Indeed, even the sacred laws of the Sabbath could be overruled, given a proportionate reason connected to love of neighbor:

As he was passing through a field of grain on the sabbath, his disciples began to make a path while picking the heads of grain. At this the Pharisees said to him, "Look, why are they doing what is unlawful on the sabbath?"

He said to them, "Have you never read what David did when he was in need and he and his companions were hungry? How he went into the house of God when Abiathar was high priest and ate the bread of offering that only the priests could lawfully eat, and shared it with his companions?"

Then he said to them, "The sabbath was made for man, not man for the sabbath." (Mark 2:23–27)

So the value present in helping a neighbor who is "hungry and in need" is the kind of proportionate reason that makes it legitimate to overrule even the Sabbath laws.

And, in point of fact, this is just how most of us reason about ethics anyway. We of course value the norm (say, that one should not take that which does not belong to us), but we also generally understand that in some extreme situations this norm may be overruled (say, when it is

---

[79] Of course, this is a parable that is likely meant to explain how new converts to the faith could get the same 'reward' as those who had been around a lot longer, but the same principle holds.

the only way to feed one's starving family). While we no doubt value the norm that it is wrong to tell an untruth,[80] most also understand that this norm can be overruled for a proportionate reason – like creating the joy of Christmas presents from Santa for one's children or refusing to damage the feelings of a child after a vocal performance. Non-exceptionless moral norms are at once valued, but also overruled for proportionate reasons, as a matter of course in our everyday moral decision-making.[81]

Problems with proportionate reasoning

While the principle of double effect insists that some moral norms are never to be violated (thus respecting the irreducible value of the human person), and to this extent avoids the critiques traditionally leveled against utilitarianism, one might still argue that proportionate reasoning nevertheless leaves one with important problems. Indeed, assuming that an exceptionless moral norm is not involved, it might appear that proportionate reasoning is not all that different from rule or two-level utilitarianism. If so, then many of the arguments traditionally directed at the latter would also apply to the former. Consider the following criticisms (primarily distilled from the views of John Finnis[82]) that, while traditionally directed against utilitarianism, appear to cause problems for proportionate reasoning as well:

1. There needs to be a *method* by which one can weigh and compare the proportionality of various consequences produced by our actions, including when and/or on what basis to overrule a non-exceptionless moral norm. No such method exists, so 'proportionate reasoning' actually disguises the rationalization of behavior on other grounds.
2. One reason why no method for proportionate reasoning exists is because there is *no objective standard* which one can use to weigh the proportionality of various goods. Many goods are simply incommensurable. On what basis, for instance, can one weigh the good of 'several more weeks of life' against the bad of the 'pain of chemotherapy treatment'? Since there is no scale which exists to compare

---

[80] Though, as anyone who is familiar with the literature on lying can attest, the reasons for believing this – along with what constitutes an 'untruth' in the first place – can be based on very complex arguments.

[81] Perhaps unsurprisingly at this point, this process of reasoning looks much like the 'two-level' approach of Hare and Singer.

[82] John Finnis, *Moral Absolutes: Tradition, Revision and Truth*, (Washington, D.C.: Catholic University Press, 1991).

them, to say that the burden of the treatment is 'disproportionate' with any expected results is meaningless.

3. The value of the lives of persons, for instance, is a particularly important example of a good that cannot be compared with other goods. The lives of persons are of *infinite* value. They cannot be calculated and compared in the way proportionate reason demands.

4. And even if there was some kind of scale to compare goods in the way proportionate reason demands, our human finitude prohibits us from being able to weigh and process the full implications of our actions – especially given virtually unpredictable *future consequences*.

These are very serious critiques, and if they have legs then someone engaging in proportionate reasoning is largely allowing self-deception to replace rational moral inquiry. Can a response be made in defense of proportionate reasoning?

Proportionate reasoning: a defense

Richard McCormick articulates the classic defense against the very broad attack that *any* kind of proportionate reasoning is dubious. Surely an overwhelming majority of (pro-life) people agree with him on what justifies an indirect abortion when, without one, both mother and child will die:

Is it not that we are faced with two alternatives (either abort, or do not abort)? Both alternatives are destructive but one is more destructive than the other. We could allow both mother and child (who will perish under any circumstance) to die; or we could at least salvage one life. Is it not because, *all things considered*, abortion is the lesser evil in this instance? Is it not precisely for this reason, then, that abortion in this instance is proportionate?[83]

Recall that the Vatican's *Declaration on Euthanasia*, in a section appropriately titled "Due Proportion in Use of Remedies," simply asserts both the possibility and value of proportionate reasoning. We also saw that the Church's Just War theory is well known for requiring the use of proportionate reasoning: both in determining whether one has a morally legitimate reason to go to war in the first place, and in determining whether the amount of force used (say, on a particular bombing run) is proportionate with the legitimate military end of the act (so as not to risk more death

---

[83] McCormick and Ramsey, *Doing Evil to Achieve Good*, 27–28.

and destruction than is necessary to accomplish this goal). And far from something that only applies in the extreme situations of abortion, euthanasia, and war, Benedict XVI (both before and after he became Pope) said that proportionate reasoning is a common-sense judgment that is rather routine – even going so far as to claim that it plays a central role in making a choice for whom to vote.[84]

So, perhaps it is too strong to claim that *all* proportionate reasoning is dubious. But wouldn't it be fair to say that *many* instances of proportionate reasoning seem strange or even impossible? Peter Knauer gives us what appears to be a good example:

The good achieved must correspond to the evil accepted in the exchange, and indeed the good must outweigh the evil. But this answer is no advance. Such a quantitative comparison is not possible, as it is a matter of qualitatively different values which cannot be compared with one another. When some years ago in Germany the speed limit was experimentally abolished, the death toll in traffic accidents rose threefold, and therefore the fifty-kilometer limit was very soon restored; but the death toll was still quite high. Could the loss of human life be compared with the advantages which a speedier traffic system brings? The different values which are measurable by themselves are incommensurable with each other. There is no common measure for them.

Knauer claims that the key to proportionate reasoning, at least in this case, would be to try to imagine precisely this common measure between the two alternatives:

A faster traffic causes a loss of more human lives. But if there were no traffic, the preservation of life as a whole surely would not be greater. The preservation of life depends in great part on a sound economy, which, in turn, today depends on the best possible traffic. Thus the complete throttling of traffic would not serve the preservation of human life as a whole.[85]

McCormick claims that while "long-term deleterious effects" certainly might contribute to an act being morally wrong, proportionate reasoning also considers whether "the value I am pursuing is being pursued in a way calculated in human judgment (not without prediscursive elements) to undermine it."[86] Porter's understanding of Thomas Aquinas on these

---

[84] "When a Catholic does not share a candidate's stand in favour of abortion and/or euthanasia, but votes for that candidate for other reasons, it is considered remote material cooperation, which can be permitted in the presence of proportionate reasons." Cardinal Joseph Ratzinger, "Worthiness to Receive Holy Communion," Teachings of the Catholic Church on Abortion, www.priestsforlife. org/magisterium/bishops/04-07ratzingercommunion.htm (Accessed December 12, 2010).
[85] Knauer, "The Hermeneutical Function of the Principle of Double Effect," 142.
[86] McCormick and Ramsey, *Doing Evil to Achieve Good,* 264–265.

matters uncovers very similar reasoning. For Thomas "clarifies and extends the meaning of basic moral concepts, such as murder or theft, through an extended reflection on the point of the prohibitions or injunctions connected with them."[87] If, for instance, someone takes what belongs to another in order to sustain her life (or that of her family), then that act is not wrong because it does not violate 'the (teleological) point' of the institution of property: namely, to provide the necessities of life to all persons.[88] All three, however, would claim that while this narrow case might be one of justified stealing because there is proportionate relationship between the value sought and the way it is achieved, most examples of taking another's property involve a disproportionate relationship and would therefore be properly described as theft.

But even if there are situations where the two values can be re-described in such a way that they are comparable, don't there remain some values that are simply unable to be compared in any meaningful way? Aren't there times where we just can't tell whether 'the point' of a norm is being violated or whether the value being pursued is being undermined by the act itself? Consider a Roman Catholic who vigorously opposes both abortion and ecological destruction, takes the Pope's earlier point about voting seriously, and attempts to determine whether she may ethically vote for a pro-choice candidate. Can she really use proportionate reasoning to determine whether, say, the evils present in the radical destruction of the ecological world are proportionate to the evils present in abortion? Wouldn't someone who accepts the kind of reasoning above be forced to claim that these are simply unable to be compared? Sure, a common measure might be found between the two (the number of human lives destroyed or otherwise harmed, perhaps) but because ecological destruction involves harming the value of non-human entities, it presents values incommensurate with those at stake in abortion. How, then, does proportionate reasoning help someone determine whether she can vote for a pro-ecology candidate who is pro-choice, over a pro-life candidate who has a terrible ecological record?

Perhaps, despite appearances, values and concepts that at first seem to be obviously incommensurable become less so after some reflection. Consider the concepts of 'being cold' and 'being lonely.' On the one

---

[87] Jean Porter, "Christianity, Divine Law, and Consequentialism," *Scottish Journal of Theology* 48: 4 (1995), 285.

[88] One might recall here the position of Catholic Social Teaching described in Chapter 4 that all private property, while a 'right,' is under a social mortgage for the common good.

hand they are *prima facie* incommensurable concepts – especially when considered in the abstract. After all, it is difficult to imagine on what basis one could possibly compare coldness with loneliness. But what happens if one gets out of the realm of abstractions and instead thinks about these concepts in a specific and 'thick' set of circumstances? Suppose, for instance, that soon after being rescued from the experience of spending several weeks in isolation after the collapse of a mine shaft, a miner is asked whether he got lonely during his time underground. Suppose he responds by saying, "Well, I did miss my family, but I got to see video of them and I had faith that I was going to get out soon. I was actually more cold than lonely." Is this person just confused? Irrational? Engaging in self-deception? Doesn't he know that there exists no scale or basis for comparing his 'being cold' with 'being lonely'?

No, it is simply a brute fact that in a good number of *specified* situations, our intuitive or common-sense judgments can make the kind of comparisons that seem difficult or even impossible in the abstract.[89] In the abstract it may seem hopeless to compare massive ecological devastation with an overwhelming number of abortions. But in another example of why starting with the practical is so important, when one compares specific candidates and their relative voting records, their ability to affect change on a particular topic, etc., an intuitive and prudential judgment becomes possible. In point of fact, these kinds of judgments are made by human persons, as Pope Benedict observes, on a rather routine basis. And though it is undoubtedly the case that perhaps even a significant number of them are made on the basis of self-deception, and are therefore misguided, this need not necessarily be the case.

But isn't there another serious problem for proportionate reasoning? Exceptionless moral norms protect the individual dignity of human persons. Indeed, it is sometimes claimed in this line of thinking that each human person's life is of *infinite* value. If we take that anthropological claim seriously, then it makes little sense to compare the value of one life against that of another life – or even against that of many other lives. But aren't there other times where proportionate reasoning asks us to do precisely this? Consider the Just War theory: what is the basis for claiming that bombing runs which disproportionately endanger the lives of innocent civilians are immoral? Implicit in this claim is the principle that the death of 'many' civilians is a worse state of affairs than the death of 'few'

---

[89] Indeed, as we saw above, examination of practical issues and specified cases can help us overcome abstract theoretical problems in ethics.

civilians. But if every person is of 'infinite' value then how can this judgment be made? Sets containing 'many' persons and sets containing 'few' persons have exactly the same value: an infinite amount.[90]

From a perspective of a moral anthropology which understands the value of a human person as infinite, such reasoning is indeed flawed. But we need not accept this understanding of the value of the human person. It is one thing to say that the value of a human person's life is *irreducible* and not subject to radical reduction as a mere means to someone else's end. But it is quite another to say that the life of a human being has *infinite* value. From a Christian perspective at least, it would seem that only God has such value. Indeed, would it not be idolatry to make any value other than union with God the source of one's ultimate concern? And as we saw in Chapter 2, the Church's teaching of ordinary and extraordinary means of medical treatment attempts to reflect just this understanding. One may never directly attack the irreducible value of human life by using it as a mere means to one's end through something like euthanasia, but other values can trump preservation of human life which would make it acceptable to forego life-sustaining treatment. So while our intuition that 'few deaths are better than many'[91] is indeed inconsistent with the questionable claim that each human life has *infinite* value, it is perfectly consistent with the claim that each human life has *irreducible* value.

But perhaps another anthropological point hasn't been sufficiently explored. Human nature is finite and flawed, and we will therefore fail in our proportionate reasoning quite often. Even on the occasions in which we somehow manage to avoid a mistake, our reasoning nevertheless always retains the important limitations of space and time. We simply cannot see anywhere close to the *total* effect that our actions have: either in the short term (and especially in a globalized, interconnected world) or in the long term where one is trying to think about future generations. We might think, for instance, that the joy produced by telling our child that there is a Santa Claus easily outweighs the harm in telling him a small white lie, but how can we know what this will do to the relationship with our child down the road? How will it inform our child's understanding of his own duty to tell the truth – especially when it is difficult to do so? Furthermore, what will establishing the principle 'one may lie to

---

[90] As many of us learned in math class, ∞ multiplied by 'x' (when x = any natural number) is still ∞.

[91] And this intuition is not only important for many claims made as part of Just War Theory, but it is a central and underlying principle of triage medicine as well.

produce a good result' do over time and through the centuries? These are questions, given our finite natures, for which we cannot have acceptably accurate answers. Perhaps if we *could* see into the future, what looks like a proportionate reason for lying about Santa Claus to our child might end up being outweighed by other considerations. But because we are limited by space and time, the whole concept of proportionate reasoning seems hopelessly limited.

Like all things human, proportionate reasoning does indeed have important limits which need to be carefully considered. That said, there are good reasons to avoid using the adjective 'hopeless' to describe such limits. For other kinds of reasoning is limited by space and time, but this is no argument for abandoning reasoning itself as hopelessly limited. We simply need to be carefully, prayerfully, and prudentially provisional with regard to any judgments made on the basis of proportionate reasoning. Critical theory, history, and other social sciences available to the contemporary world provide data which can and should inform and shape the prudential judgments of proportionate reason, but abandoning the concept altogether because of our limitations is throwing the baby out with the bathwater. Furthermore, the Church's tradition (which has wrestled with many of these moral questions for two millennia, gathering insights from the untold number of cultures with which it has interacted) is a wonderful source of data and wisdom for making the judgments of proportionate reason. Indeed, many of the non-exceptionless moral norms that the Church proposes are similar to the rules Singer would support which, given the wisdom of the ages past, tend to produce the best consequences. A significant amount of the work has already been done for us, especially (but not only) if one believes that the Church's tradition has the Holy Spirit working in and through it.

CONCLUSION

Once again we have seen dramatic overlap between Singer and the Church. Both approaches, for instance, value consequence-based reasoning while at the same time having an important place for moral rules. Both also believe that many of these rules can be overruled for a sufficiently serious reason. The two approaches obviously differ in their moral anthropologies and specifically on whether the value of individual human persons may be reduced to their relevant interests in a broader, even universal calculation of interests. This in turn leads to important and substantial disagreement about the status and applicability of some moral norms involving the intentional reduction of human persons as mere means to some other end. But despite these differences, the overlap remains substantial. Obviously Singer will reject the Church's claims about a person's ultimate end consisting in union with God, but we have seen that he shares much with what the Church's describes as our proximate end.

Some might reasonably believe that fundamental disagreements, like the nature of the human person described above, are simply non-starters in any exchange between Peter Singer and Christian ethics. And given the theory articulated by Singer for most of his career, the two approaches do seem as if they will simply run into a theoretical brick wall on those kinds of issues. But Singer is in the process of fundamentally rethinking his preference utilitarianism. And as we will see in the next and final chapter, he is now open to objective moral concepts in ways which allow for even more points of contact with Christian ethics.

CHAPTER 6

Singer's shift?

I no longer hold Hume's view of practical reason.
> Peter Singer, 'Christian Ethics Engages Peter Singer' (May, 2011)

I am now more ready to entertain – although not yet embrace – the idea that there are objective ethical truths that are independent of what anyone desires.
> Peter Singer, *Practical Ethics* (2011)

INTRODUCTION

One might expect a 65-year-old philosopher who has espoused preference utilitarianism for virtually his entire career to be pretty set in his ways. Indeed, many consider Peter Singer to be the kind of ideologue and extremist who would never reconsider arguments against his long-standing positions. It might be surprising to some, then, that Singer is undergoing a major shift in his thought at this late stage of his career – one which may even end up challenging the very foundations of his views. He hints at this shift in the new edition of *Practical Ethics*, but it was at the aforementioned 'Christian Ethics Engages Peter Singer' May 2011 conference in Oxford where he revealed many more details about it.

Part of the shift appears to have been facilitated by the ongoing work of the philosopher Derek Parfit who has apparently convinced Singer to become more open to objectivity in his moral theory.[1] But attentive readings of Singer's corpus reveal that, for some time now, he has become less and less interested in defending his utilitarianism as a detailed moral theory, and has instead become more concerned with

---

[1] Although those who take a more narrative and contextual approach to ethics are right to highlight the role each of these often plays in our moral lives, Singer's shift shows that sometimes people do make major shifts based simply on the strength of the arguments with which they are confronted.

engaging a diverse readership on the practical implications of taking a generalized, other-centered point of view:

> One could argue endlessly about the merits of each of these characterizations of the ethical, but what they have in common is more important than their differences. They agree that the justification of an ethical principle cannot be in terms of any partial or sectional group. Ethics takes a universal point of view.[2]

We also saw this most clearly in the chapter on duties to the poor, when he says that this first and most important orientation shift "is encapsulated by the Golden Rule" – a principle that has wide support across a number of traditions. He makes a similar consensus-building move in his updated version of *Practical Ethics*:

> A plausible principle that would support the judgment that I ought to pull the child out is this: if it is in our power to prevent something very bad happening, without thereby sacrificing anything of comparable moral significance, we ought to do it. This principle seems uncontroversial. It will obviously win the assent of consequentialists; but non-consequentialists should accept it too, because the injunction to prevent what is bad applies only when nothing comparably significant is at stake ... Most non-consequentialists hold that we ought to prevent what is bad and promote what is good. Their dispute with consequentialists lies in their insistence that this is not the sole ultimate ethical principle: that it is *an* ethical principle is not denied by any plausible ethical theory.[3]

And perhaps related to this focus on convincing his readers of various practical implications involved when one accepts these general, or 'thin,' ethical principles, Singer has also become increasingly forthright about the challenges a 'thick' preference utilitarianism faces – especially from those who espouse objective moral value.

This creates yet another fascinating opening for interaction between Peter Singer and Christian ethics. In this final chapter, I will detail the kind objectivity that, having been convinced by Parfit's arguments, Singer is now explicitly willing to embrace: namely, the objectivity of practical reason. But despite being "open" to making an even more dramatic shift toward objectivity in his moral theory, Singer is not yet willing to go further than this. The next part of this chapter will challenge Singer to push beyond his current position by exploring several proposed tensions in his theory which will remain if he does not find a more substantial place for objective moral value. I will then detail a Christian attempt to

---

[2] Peter Singer, *Practical Ethics*, 3rd edn. (New York: Cambridge University Press, 2011), 11.
[3] Singer, *Ibid.*, 199–200.

ground certain objective values in the flourishing and happiness of human persons, try to align it with Singer's understanding of happiness, and then show that there is good reason to think fruitful conversation could take place on these topics. The chapter will conclude by exploring whether Singer could accept the kinds of metaphysical claims that some believe are necessary for his theory to be coherent.

OBJECTIVITY AND PREFERENCE UTILITARIANISM

Derek Parfit has had a major book in the works for two decades. Having circulated drafts among many of his peers and colleagues during that time, the finished work (which thanked more than 250 people for their comments in the acknowledgements) finally came out in May 2011 to great acclaim. Singer reviewed the book, ultimately titled *On What Matters*,[4] in *The Times Literary Supplement* and called it, "The most significant work in ethics since 1873."[5] For most of his career, Singer has accepted David Hume's view that reason, because it applies to means and not ends, cannot move us to moral action. What we happen to desire is neither rational nor irrational, it just is. Indeed, Hume famously said that it was not irrational even to prefer the destruction of the world to the scratching of one's finger.

But at the Oxford conference, Singer revealed that Parfit's ongoing work has convinced him that this view is mistaken, and that, despite many decades of defending it, he no longer holds Hume's view of practical reason.[6] One of Parfit's classic arguments asks us to consider someone who, on normal days, prefers not to be in severe pain, but discounts such pain if happens on Tuesdays. Such a person, if given a choice between slight pain on Monday and severe pain on Tuesday, prefers the latter to the former. Parfit appears to have convinced Singer, *contra* Hume, that this is an objectively irrational preference. For some this might not sound like a major shift, but, especially because he now needs to find a way to *ground* such objectivity, this is a major shift for Peter Singer. Currently unwilling to commit to theological or even metaphysical claims about the good or flourishing of human persons, he instead seems to side with Parfit in claiming that such judgments are justified by rational intuition.

---

[4] Derek Parfit. *On What Matters* (Oxford University Press, 2011).
[5] Peter Singer, "The Most Significant Work in Ethics Since 1873," *Times Literary Supplement* (May 20, 2011).
[6] "Peter Singer Conference Archive," McDonald Centre for Theology, Ethics & Public Life. http://mcdonaldcentre.org.uk/resources/peter-singer-conference/ (Accessed July 10, 2011).

We come to see certain objective ethical truths, says Singer, "in something like the way in which we come to see that two plus two equals four." Indeed, "insofar as we are rational beings, we will respond to the reasons that morality offers."[7] But once one opens the door to objectivity in one's moral theory, it is quite difficult to limit its place. And Singer appears on the verge of accepting theoretical claims about objective moral value in ways that were unthinkable just a few years ago.

Singer on objective goods

In the closing session of the Oxford conference, Singer said that perhaps his new openness to objectivity could still be consistent with preference utilitarianism by claiming that there is *only one* objective value: preference maximization from the point of view of the universe. However, he then immediately hinted at problems that would make this move unlikely to succeed. The problems posed by speculating about future people and future preferences are, in particular, "very difficult to deal with just on the basis of preference utilitarianism." One way to deal with such problems, he said, is to consider the possibility of "values independent of preferences." Indeed, in a stunning moment for those familiar with his work, Singer admitted that he has been doing "some rethinking about the idea that preference utilitarian alone is the right understanding of what are the things we should value."[8] Let us now move to consider three different kinds of problems that preference utilitarianism struggles to address.

The first kind of problem is one about which Singer is quite explicit in the latest version of *Practical Ethics*. Of the complex questions surrounding whether bringing into existence a new human being or non-human animal could ever replace the preferences lost with the death of a similar being, he says, "I have found myself unable to maintain with any confidence that the position I took in the previous edition – based solely on preference utilitarianism – offers a satisfactory answer to these quandaries."[9] He points out that we don't consider it a good thing to deliberately make ourselves thirsty simply because we know that there is sufficient water to satisfy our preference to no longer be thirsty, and that this implies the creation and satisfaction of preferences is neither good nor bad.[10] And in response to those who claim that, from a preference utilitarian perspective, the world would be

---

[7] Singer, "The Most Significant Work in Ethics Since 1873."
[8] "Peter Singer Conference Archive" (Accessed July 10, 2011).
[9] Singer, *Practical Ethics*, x.   [10] Singer, *Ibid.*, 113.

better off if no future people existed at all, Singer says that it "seems obvious" that a peopled universe is better than one without people.[11] Why? Because the peopled universe contains beings who

> lead rich and full lives, experiencing the joys of love and friendship, of fulfilling and meaningful work, and of bringing up children. They seek knowledge, successfully adding to their understanding of themselves and the universe they inhabit. They respond to the beauties of nature, cherish the forests and animals that pre-date their own existence, and create literature and music on a par with the works of Shakespeare and Mozart.

If one didn't know from which book they were reading, one could be excused if they confused this passage for a list of 'basic goods' written by a Christian natural-law ethicist like John Finnis or Robert George. And indeed, Singer admits his view that a peopled universe is better "requires an appeal to a notion of value that goes beyond the minimalist basis for preference utilitarianism" for which he had previously argued.[12] However, in overcoming the charge that a universe without people is a better one, Singer is aware that he has created a new problem for himself. For

> this combination of preference utilitarianism and an idea of intrinsic value that is not dependent on preference sacrifices one of the great advantages of any form of utilitarianism that is based on just one value, which is that there is no need to explain how different values are to be traded off against one another. Instead, because this view suggests that there are two kinds of values, one personal and based on preferences and the other impersonal, it isn't easy to see how we are to proceed when the two kinds of values clash.[13]

But, of course, if one actually and independently believes that a universe with persons is better than one without, then the fact that this implies greater difficulty in moral reasoning, while interesting and important to note, should not be a decisive consideration.

The good of future people?

Tim Mulgan, a utilitarian with a secular approach to ethics, suggested at the Oxford conference that worries about "controversial foundational

---

[11] Some hold this view, in part, because rational and self-aware creatures find it much more difficult to have their preferences satisfied that other kinds of creatures.
[12] Singer, *Practical Ethics*, 116–117. Singer might get himself off the hook here by saying that the preference of persons are stronger, but perhaps he doesn't say this because it just isn't clear that the preference of a person to listen to music is stronger than the preference of, say, a non-human animal to satisfy her hunger.
[13] Singer, *Ibid.*, 119.

questions" might drive preference utilitarians away from considering
objective goods.[14] But he also argued that a preference utilitarian not
only struggles in the way Singer acknowledges above, but also with
regard to an even more basic question: what constitutes acting in the
best interests of distant future people at all? Especially in light of
ecological devastation, both Christians and utilitarians have thought
long and hard about what we owe distant future generations.[15] When
thinking about how we should change behavior in light of the interests
of distant future people, preference utilitarians will argue that we
should give them what they want. But Singer asks, "Can we be sure
that future generations will appreciate wilderness? Not really; perhaps they
will be happier playing electronic video games more sophisticated
than any we can imagine."[16] Though Singer goes on to say that we
shouldn't give this possibility much weight, Mulgan reminds us that
people have wanted things in the past that we now find difficult to
understand and suggests it is highly likely the same will be true of
future people. Mulgan also asks us to consider *adaptive* preferences; for
if "distant future people have no experiences of diverse ecosystems or a
stable climate – if they cannot even imagine such things – how can they
prefer them?"[17] And even if we can somehow know what future people
will want, he asks Singer, how do I know "how strongly they will want
it?"[18] After all, without knowing how strongly they will desire something, we have no idea how to compare the strength of their preferences
with the strength of ours.

   Mulgan notes that the preference utilitarian struggles with these questions despite the fact that they must maximize utility in a way that is
temporally disinterested. The utilitarian dogma that each person "counts
as one, and none more than one" is true of people whether they are living

---

[14] "Peter Singer Conference Archive," McDonald Centre for Theology, Ethics & Public Life. Talk by
    Tim Mulgan entitled "The Impact of Climate Change on Utilitarianism and Christian Ethics."
    http://mcdonaldcentre.org.uk/resources/peter-singer-conference/ (Accessed July 10, 2011). As we
    will see below, Mulgan also suggests that concerns about how to ground such goods also play an
    important role.
[15] For instance, Pope Benedict says, "Human beings interpret and shape the natural environment
    through culture, which in turn is given direction by the responsible use of freedom, in accordance
    with the dictates of the moral law. Consequently, projects for integral human development cannot
    ignore coming generations, but need to be *marked by solidarity and inter-generational justice*, while
    taking into account a variety of contexts: ecological, juridical, economic, political and cultural."
    ("*Caritas in Veritate*," 48)
[16] Singer, *Practical Ethics*, 243.
[17] Mulgan, "The Impact of Climate Change on Utilitarianism and Christian Ethics."
[18] *Ibid.*

now or 500 years from now. But objectivists, Mulgan says, have answers to the above questions that the preference utilitarian does not:

We ought to ensure that distant future people have access to desirable things – drinkable water, breathable air, stable climate, ecological diversity. If the natural world is intrinsically valuable, then human lives go better (and perhaps can only go well) when they are appropriately related to that value.[19]

We have already seen that Singer hesitates to accept multiple objective goods, but could he accept the general thrust of Mulgan's argument? Given that their practical intuitions match up so well, I think the answer is yes. Singer says, "It may nevertheless be true that this appreciation of nature will not be shared by people living a century or two hence. If wilderness can be the source of such deep joy and satisfaction, that would be a great loss."[20] But assuming that distant future people are fully informed and are capable of rational thought, and they nevertheless prefer video games to walks in the woods, on what basis could one say that this a great loss? Singer must go beyond preference utilitarianism to lament this state of affairs.

Future preferences in an already-existing being

Another problem for preference utilitarianism arises when we think about how to morally evaluate actions which affect, not the preferences of some future being, but the future preferences of beings that already exist. For if the only objective good is to maximize preference satisfaction, then there appears to be no way to evaluate which of many available preferences to satisfy and even create. G.F. Schueler presses this point with regard to the preference utilitarianism of R.M. Hare, Singer's mentor. Universalizability requires that we acquire the hypothetical preference that, were we in the other person's situation, x should happen (where x is what the other person prefers to happen). This is because, "universalizability requires that I understand the other person's situation in such a way that if I were in his situation I would prefer what he in fact prefers."[21] But a serious problem arises in situations where "one might perfectly well know that if one were in a certain situation one would have a certain preference without its being the case that one now prefers

---

[19] *Ibid.*   [20] Singer, *Practical Ethics*, 244.
[21] G.F. Schueler, "Some Reasoning About Preferences," *Ethics* 95:1 (Oct. 1984), 78.

that if one were in that situation that this thing would happen."[22] Indeed, he asks us to consider cases like the following:

A reformed alcoholic, now sober, might know that if he were on a binge he would prefer another drink. At the same time he clearly sees the consequences of his drinking and so does not now prefer that if he were on a binge he should take another drink.

Odysseus, before hearing the song of the Sirens, knows that if he hears their song he would prefer his companions to release him. At the same time he clearly sees the consequences of his being so released (their ship will be wrecked) and so does not now prefer that if the Sirens start singing he be released.

Hare's response to the second case attempts to navigate this prickly problem. He claims that although Odysseus will then prefer that his sailors should set him free, "he does not now *prefer overall* [emphasis added] that they then should."[23] Hare also refers to the concepts of 'fully representing one's situation to oneself' and 'fully representing to oneself *another's* situation with another's preferences.'[24]

But to what do concepts like "preferring overall" and "fully representing" refer? Perhaps they refer to an objective understanding of the good of human persons and that Hare is willing to ignore certain preferences that are obviously counter to that good in favor of the 'overall' and 'full' flourishing of such persons. But let us table that answer for just a moment and explore another possibility. Perhaps what Hare means instead is that the current preferences of the alcoholic and Odysseus are to be satisfied because they are taking a more broad overview of what they would prefer in the long run, fully informed. But this can't be right, for if one asks Odysseus as he listened to the Sirens' song, or the alcoholic while on a binge, they would say that – even while taking a fully informed and broad point of view – they would still prefer something different to what they did earlier. Why should one accept the current perspective over the future one? If one cannot appeal to some objective sense of what is good for the flourishing of human persons, it seems arbitrary to give higher weight to broadly considered and informed preferences at one point in time over another point in time.

But preference utilitarianism has an even more serious problem when one's actions permit or create preferences in someone's future – something every good parent at least attempts to do. Consider the following example:

[22] *Ibid.*
[23] R.M. Hare, "Some Reasoning About Preferences: A Response to Essays by Persson, Feldman, and Schueler," *Ethics* 95:1 (Oct. 1984): 82.
[24] *Ibid.*

A father's 12-year-old daughter now prefers not to go to school and asks him to drop her off at the mall for the rest of the school year instead. At the same time, the father clearly sees the consequences of failing out of school and, putting himself in the place of her future self, prefers that she be forced to go to school – against her current preferences.

Without some objective sense of the good of education for the 'overall' or 'full' flourishing of human persons, how can the father come to the conclusion that, when he puts himself into the position of his future daughter, he would prefer that he be forced to go to school? One could say that this allows her to achieve more preferences in the long run, but suppose she becomes convinced that she can go shopping all day at the mall for the rest of the year, drop out of school, and then go on to become a successful buyer for a retail company. If this comes to pass, then not only would his decision to let her skip school have helped to shape her future preferences, but also *achieve* them as well. Without appealing to goods independent of preferences, it is difficult to argue that he should force her to stay in school.[25]

We can also see that preference utilitarianism seems to allow the father to create some preferences for his daughter even if they seem, not just misguided, but diabolically evil. Consider a situation where some believe that the best chance for a young woman to make a living is via prostitution. Suppose that the father not only lets his daughter skip school, but raises her, from a young age, to be in the best position possible to be an excellent and successful prostitute. Suppose she grows up thinking that this is what is best for her, and at every step of the way while becoming a prostitute – and in her life *as* a prostitute – she is satisfying these preferences instilled in her by her father. Unless there is a way to show that this somehow violates the objective good of human persons, it looks as if the father maximized preference satisfaction with regard to how he raised his daughter. That the overwhelming majority of us (I hope) react with moral outrage at such a scenario is evidence that the way to think about what someone 'prefers overall' and how to 'fully represent' their

---

[25] The preference utilitarian might still push the claim that what is really going on here is an experienced parent forcing his inexperienced daughter to conform to behavior that, based on *percentages*, will maximize her preferences over time. He might explain to her that the chances of her becoming a successful buyer without a degree from high school are quite small, etc. But it isn't clear why the preference utilitarian should accept this reasoning – given that the daughter could simply say that, overall, her preferences are maximized if she is free to do what she wants now, and then simply has a reasonable shot at being a buyer later. She might weigh her current preferences for fun and shopping as far more important than her future preferences. Indeed, many of us know people who live by this "I could get hit by a truck tomorrow" philosophy.

preferences, is by referring to something objective about the good and flourishing of human persons.

Comparing and ordering preferences

Perhaps one could argue that there is nothing objectively bad about being a prostitute, but rather what the father did was wrong because he brought into existence preferences which are worse than those if he had forced his daughter to go to school and encouraged her to have another kind of career. Of course, given that in her career as a prostitute she is having her preferences satisfied, and that in his judgment she would have been less likely to have her preferences satisfied if she had had a different career, the preference utilitarian cannot appeal to preferences maximization to make this claim. It looks as if something like an objective *order* of preferences – relative to an objective concept of human good and flourishing – needs to be invoked to raise this challenge.

In a co-interview they did for *Standpoint* magazine after the Oxford conference, Singer and Nigel Biggar continued a discussion they were having in the conference's final session.[26] Biggar was pressing Singer on what basis we should consider a Jewish person's preference to live to be of more worth than a Nazi's preference to kill her. Singer's initial response in the interview is to say that it is stronger, not because of any "outside objective values," but because he just thinks it is obvious that the desire to live is the stronger preference. But Biggar doesn't think it's that obvious:

I have no idea how on earth you can determine which is the stronger. If you want to make a judgment that the Nazi desire to cleanse the world of Jews is wrong and the Jews' desire to live is right, then I'm with you there, but that has to be in terms of some appeal to what's objectively valuable in the world and what's immoral. I know that you want to avoid that but I don't think you have succeeded in doing it.

And here is Singer's rejoinder:

I agree it could be done in the way that you are suggesting if you were to have this independent standard of objective values, which you then need to ground in some way. What I'm suggesting is that it's enough to try to put yourself in the position of both the Jewish person who's going to be killed, and then to put yourself in the position of the Nazi and see whether they are comparable desires.

---

[26] "Putting A Value On Human And Animal Life," *Standpoint*, http://standpointmag.co.uk/node/3990/full (Accessed July 11, 2011).

One way of putting it would be to say if you were the Nazi, to think about your own life, and think about whether if you had the choice of saying, "So the Jew will be killed but you will also be killed," will you accept that choice? Or alternatively saying, "The Jew will live and you will live," then I'm sure that 99.9 percent of Nazis would have said, "Oh well, if that's the choice, then yes, I will let the Jew live." That is a way of indicating that for the Nazi himself the desire to live is more important than the desire to satisfy his racist or ideological preference that there not be Jews in the world.

The interview then moved on to other topics, but in continuing the debate Singer should now be asked why this is the best way to compare the strength of the preferences. To do a better job of actually getting at the strength of the Nazi's *specific* preference, which seems to be missed in the example Singer gives above, we would have the Nazi compare the strength of his preference to live if he were the Jewish person versus the strength of his own preference to have a racially pure, and (in his view) flourishing, German state. I think the Nazi could easily come to the conclusion that, if he were the Jewish person, his desire to live should be overridden for the common good of the Third Reich. And this conclusion, according to the method that Singer has set up, would indicate that it isn't obvious at all that the desire to live is *de facto* stronger than the Nazi's desire for racial purity. Indeed, it is fairly common to hold the view that individual lives – and perhaps even one's own life – must be sacrificed for the common good in certain circumstances. In fact, the Nazi might claim that, if he himself found out he had Jewish blood, he should voluntarily accept extermination for the sake of the common good of the German community. No, it is necessary to find some objective way of ordering the preferences that doesn't rely on the relative strength with which they are held.

So let's quickly review those contexts in which preference utilitarianism alone fails to give satisfactory answers, the first three of which Singer himself admits are problematic:

1. Deciding whether or not to bring a new being into the world to replace another
2. Deciding if the world is better off with people or without
3. Discovering our moral duties to distant future people
4. Resolving a conflict between satisfying current preferences and future preferences
5. Deciding which kinds of future preferences to permit or create in someone
6. Finding a basis for ordering preferences such that one preference trumps another preference

Now, as Singer mentioned in a response to Biggar above, one problem that goes beyond even the wildly complex and difficult task of reasoning morally about multiple objective goods, is that it looks like we need to ground the objective status of such goods. Many atheist utilitarians are loath to even think about this question because it looks like it moves us in the direction of a metaphysics, and even theology, which does not cohere with their world view. But in the next section of the chapter we will explore an attempt to ground objective goods that may avoid some of their concerns.

OBJECTIVITY AND CHRISTIAN ETHICS

At least if they accept the kind of teleology discussed in the previous chapter, Christians will attempt to ground their belief in objective goods in an objective understanding of the flourishing of the human person – and, indeed, all of creation. Biggar, for instance, claims

> that there is a form of flourishing that is given in and with the nature of the human being; that reflection on human nature can achieve an understanding of that flourishing and its component basic goods; that reflection on human experience can produce a grasp of kinds of disposition and action that respect and promote those goods; that all human beings are, despite their sinfulness, somewhat capable of an accurate grasp of basic goods and their practical requirements; and that, therefore, there are sometimes areas of ethical agreement between Christians and others.[27]

But to many people it isn't at all obvious that objective goods are, in fact, available to us simply by reflecting on human nature. Let us test this reaction by exploring the attempt of Jean Porter to ground objective goods and flourishing in the nature of human beings in her important book *Nature as Reason*.

Porter on the flourishing of the human beings

There is a lot of push-back against the idea that objective goods or flourishing can be inferred from what we know of human nature. After all, isn't it the case that modern science and biology – with everything we now know about evolution – fly in the face of any kind of teleological

---

[27] Nigel Biggar, *Behaving in Public: How to Do Christian Ethics* (Grand Rapids, MI: William B. Eerdmans Publishing, Co., 2011), 41–42.

approach that would speak of 'the' good or flourishing of the human being? Jean Porter, however, takes issue with this received wisdom:

Recently, however, a number of biologists and philosophers of science, most of whom have no allegiance to theological perspectives on human life, have begun to argue for the legitimacy and indeed the necessity of incorporating certain kinds of teleological analysis into the biological sciences.[28]

Indeed, this fact paves the way for Porter to bring the substantial resources of a Christian scholastic teleology (focusing in particular on that of Thomas Aquinas) to bear on the question of human flourishing. Such objective approaches have been dismissed in the past, according to Porter, because of the view

not only that species emerge and develop over time, but also that the natural kinds which emerge out of this process have no real existence independently of the particular creatures that instantiate them. In other words, because the processes of evolution are construed as random interactions of chance events, therefore the products of evolution, namely species, are likewise to be seen as sheerly contingent groupings. And this view would of course rule out any kind of appeal to the norms of flourishing intrinsic to a kind of creature, for the simple reason that it denies that there are kinds of creatures, existing as such apart from our system of classification.[29]

Porter, along with many who have no stake in the argument about teleology, begins by making the seemingly obvious point that "natural kinds of living creatures" do in fact "seem to exist in nature."[30] But then she goes further and argues that the existence of such natural kinds

implies that recognizable kinds of creatures exhibit intelligible similarities, and relate to one another in orderly ways. Moreover, these ordered interactions take place not only within species, but between members of different species – diverse kinds of creatures are related to one another over time by relations of descent, and synchronously by a multitude of relations of competition and interdependence, in accordance with the capacities and limitations proper to their kinds. If this is so, then the diverse kinds of living creatures are not just a set of random groupings – they constitute an *ordered* set of natural kinds. And it is difficult to see how this ordering can be entirely the result of random chance.

But isn't this just sneaking in God through the backdoor of a scientific argument? Porter thinks not – and claims that her conclusion need not

[28] Jean Porter, *Nature as Reason: A Thomistic Theory of the Natural Law* (Grand Rapids, MI: William B. Eerdmans Publishing Co., 2005), 420, 82.
[29] *Ibid.*, 89.   [30] *Ibid.*, 90.

invoke a power directing the process "from above" but rather that "the order reflected in living creatures reflects causal forces intrinsic to the creatures themselves which operate in directed and intelligible ways."[31]

But the conventional wisdom is that evolution is a random process. Is Porter denying evolution? No, she is instead denying that one can conclude something about evolution's randomness merely from random interactions of genetic material, or even from such interactions at a lower level of molecular and atomic interactions. She claims that many modern biologists – led by figures like Richard Lewontin, author of *The Triple Helix*[32] – point out that "the genes by themselves do not even determine their expression in an individual creature" and cannot account for "the processes through which kinds of creatures develop and evolve."[33] Instead, "the relevant processes should be understood as occurring most frequently through the expression and development of potentialities already existing with the genotype, rather than through changes which alter the phenotype in some stable way." This leads Porter to argue that

this process presupposes ongoing interactions among creatures of a given kind in a changing environment, in which the potentialities of the kind of creature, expressed most immediately through its phenotype, provide it with a range of responses through which it can adapt to changing conditions. For this reason, explanations for the adaptive development of a given kind of creature cannot proceed without some reference to the kind of creature in question.[34]

Does this mean we can reason teleologically about 'kinds of creatures' – including human persons – based on the considerations presented above? Porter cites philosopher of biology Michael Ruse in defense of both the use of "design language" and the claim that while no serious biologist interprets such language in terms of externally imposed design, "it is clear that it does carry connotations of purpose and function."[35] Porter's teleology fits nicely with this understanding of design:

Thus understood, teleological language does not imply any reference to externally imposed purposes, whether ours, those of some demiurge or creator, or a generalized nature or evolutionary process. Rather, in this context the language of purpose functions in such a way as to render the different components of a living creature intelligible, in terms of the contributions to the life processes of the creature . . . Interpreted this way, the observation that the eye is meant for seeing

---

[31] *Ibid.*, 93.
[32] Richard C. Lewontin, *The Triple Helix: Gene, Organism, and Environment* (Cambridge, MA: Harvard University Press, 2000), 136.
[33] Porter, *Nature As Reason*, 94.   [34] *Ibid.*, 95.   [35] *Ibid.*, 99.

does not presuppose a story about the way the physical mechanism of the eye reflects the contrivance of an omnipotent designer ... Rather, it presupposes a more straightforward account of the role the eye plays in promoting the overall well-being of the creature by means of providing an organ for sight, which will include a further account of what sight itself is good for, given an overall orientation toward life, growth, and reproduction shared (in some way) by all living creatures.[36]

She claims that this understanding of teleology fits well with many of our attitudes and intuitions about the living things around us. We have an intuitive sense, for instance, which allows us to discern "what it means to be a healthy, functioning, flourishing creature of a certain kind" – indeed, all of us "can tell a scrawny puppy from a robust puppy, a sick horse from a healthy horse, a dying ficus from a happy ficus." She even goes so far as to say that these kinds of judgments are "fundamental to functioning in the world" and that "it would be absurd to consider them to be arbitrary or wholly the product of cultural construction."[37]

Porter's account wants to make room for judgments about a specific kind of flourishing: that of human beings. But are we entitled to move from the flourishing of a ficus tree to that of humans? One might think that the human person is just too complex or too distinctive to make this move. After all, isn't it the case that our "capacities for rational reflection, self-determin-ation, and historical change place the human agent outside the constraints of nature more generally considered?" And even if we could somehow arrive at a determinate natural end for human beings that the concept of objective flourishing requires, she asks how we could free ourselves of "our own cultural and even personal suppositions" in doing so.[38]

Porter's response to this challenge is a sympathetic rejoinder. She is perfectly comfortable with the idea that our knowledge of human nature is not comprehensive, but it is nevertheless the case that "a few philoso-phers and not a few scientists have been prepared to say that we do indeed know something about the characteristic constitution of human nature, and by implication, we do know what it means to enjoy a distinctively human form of flourishing."[39] She claims that whatever we say about the human person's self-transcending capacities, we are "first of all and most obviously part of a natural order, animals among other animals, creatures among other creatures." Even this knowledge, she admits, is mediated through "some cultural form or another," but this means that we will need to be "particularly careful not to generalize about our own particular

---

[36] *Ibid.*, 100.   [37] *Ibid.*, 101–102.   [38] *Ibid.*, 104.   [39] *Ibid.*, 115.

customs and preferences into general characteristics of humanity."[40] Done correctly, an investigation into human nature can give us limited but genuine knowledge about ourselves that has significant moral import.

Porter also claims that we cannot even begin to understand what it means to be a human person unless we have some idea of what it means to *do well* as a human person. Building on a Thomistic framework, she claims that human beings can flourish on three different levels: (1) as living things with a desire to continue to live, (2) as animals with a desire to eat, drink, stay warm, reproduce, live socially, etc., and (3) as rational animals who self-consciously seek proximate and ultimate truth.[41] And in order to give the concept of flourishing moral content, Porter refers to it as "well-being" when speaking of a general normative ideal, and as "happiness" when specifying and qualifying it in a moral sense. This former includes "all the components of a humanly desirable life, including life itself, health, security, and participation in a network of family and social relations," while the latter specifies "the best or most appropriate way in which men and women can attain and enjoy the activities constitutive of well-being."[42] By reasoning analogously in light of what constitutes well-being with other kinds of animals, says Porter, it is "not difficult to come up with a persuasive account of human well-being."[43] And specifying happiness in light of these objective goods pushes Porter away from thinking merely about subjective preferences and desires, and instead about activities objectively proper to the human person.[44] In other words, she rejects the subjective 'preference' model in favor of a teleological model which attempts to understand those things that objectively contribute to the best interests and flourishing of human beings.

SINGER ON PREFERENCES, INTERESTS, AND HAPPINESS

How does Porter's argument inform our examination of Singer? In addition to the fact that it uses a 'thin' metaphysics which Singerites might find palatable, to a certain extent both of them are after the same

---

[40] *Ibid.*, 117–118.

[41] This last level is the one in which human beings flourish distinctively as persons – through certain kinds of self-reflective, reasoned activities, aimed at pursuing and enjoying the natural values of our existence in appropriate ways. Porter believes that this allows for a plurality of ways in which we can achieve this distinctively human kind of flourishing.

[42] *Ibid.*, 142–143.   [43] *Ibid.*, 145.

[44] Porter has an extended discussion of what these activities consist of, and following Thomas Aquinas she focuses on the virtues, but that complex discussion is not necessary for our purposes in this chapter.

thing: human flourishing and happiness.[45] In the final chapter of *Practical Ethics*, when Singer is asking why anyone should act morally at all, he appears to agree with Henry Sidgwick that "we could show that it is rational to act morally by showing that it is in our long-term interests to do so."[46] But it turns out that our long-term interests consist in *being happy*. Singer locates himself firmly in a philosophical tradition (encompassing, he says, Aristotle, Aquinas, Spinoza, Butler, Hegel, and Bradley[47]) arguing that happiness and the moral life are connected. He also cites a "growing body of modern research" that explores happiness in human persons and from where it comes:

Americans who give to charity were, in one large survey, 43 percent more likely to say that they were "very happy" about their lives than those who did not give. Those who did voluntary work for charities were similarly more likely to say that they were happy than those who did not. In a separate study, those who give were 68 percent less likely to have felt "hopeless" and 34 percent less likely to say that they felt "so sad that nothing could cheer them up." Giving blood, another altruistic act, also makes people feel good about themselves. Volunteering actually seems to improve the health of elderly people and helps them live longer. Jonathan Haidt, a professor of psychology and author of *The Happiness Hypothesis*, comments, "At least for older people, it really is more blessed to give than to receive."[48]

What makes human beings happy increasingly appears to be something objective that can be measured and studied.

But, like Porter, Singer asks whether human nature "is so diverse that one may doubt if any generalization about the kind of character that leads to happiness could hold for all human beings."[49] Consider psychopaths: these individuals often act contrary to ethical norms, but do not appear to suffer from their condition and even often report being quite happy and fulfilled with their lives. But Singer asks:

Must we accept psychopaths' own evaluations of their happiness? They are, after all, notorious liars. Moreover, even if they are telling the truth as they see it, are they qualified to say that they are really happy when they seem unable to

---

[45] Certain philosophers will have trouble going from an 'is' to an 'ought' even if the 'is' about human beings can be shown to be objective. But Singer doesn't appear to fall into this category, both because (1) he believes human happiness and flourishing is the reason to be moral in the first place, and (2) he is considering making a place in his consequentialism for the kind of objective value for which Porter argues.
[46] Singer, *Practical Ethics*, 284.
[47] Though, of course, this tradition is diverse in that not all of these thinkers have the same understanding of happiness.
[48] Singer, *Practical Ethics*, 287–288.   [49] *Ibid.*, 288.

experience the emotional states that play such a large part in the happiness and fulfillment of others? Admittedly, a psychopath could use the same argument against us: how can we say that we are truly happy when we have not experienced the excitement and freedom that comes from complete irresponsibility? We cannot enter into the subjective states of psychopathic people, nor they into ours, so the dispute is not easy to resolve.

Cleckley suggests that the behaviour of psychopaths can be explained as a response to the meaninglessness of their lives. It is characteristic of psychopaths to work for a while at a job and then, just when their ability and charm have taken them to the crest of success, commit some petty and easily detectable crime. A similar pattern occurs in their personal relationships. They live largely in the present and lack any coherent life plan.[50]

And it is in response to this insight that Singer begins to reveal what is essential in his understanding of happiness. It does not consist of mere feelings of 'excitement and freedom' that could come from failing to see oneself as a person existing over time, with the present being "merely one among other times one will live through."[51] No, for Singer, happiness consists of choosing *a coherent life of meaning* which goes beyond merely the subjective satisfying of preferences and desires in the present moment, however enjoyable it might be.[52] Especially given that Singer connects this understanding of happiness with the reason one should be ethical in the first place, this is similar to the Christian teleology described above. Consider the following set of claims:

Human beings survive and reproduce themselves through purposive action. We obtain happiness and fulfillment by working towards and achieving our goals. In evolutionary terms, we could say that happiness functions as an internal reward for our achievements. Subjectively, we regard achieving the goal (or progressing towards it) as a reason for happiness. Our own happiness, therefore, is a by-product of aiming at something else and is not to be obtained by setting our sights on happiness alone.[53]

But there might be one more objection to consider: Singer is speaking here about happiness for *the agent* – but what about the happiness of others? Is he a pure egoist? A Christian who upholds the absolutely central

---

[50] *Ibid.*, 289–290.   [51] *Ibid.*, 290.

[52] Notice that Singer's claim here goes beyond simply subjectively experiencing our lives as coherent and meaningful. This could apply to the psychopath who says, "Yeah, my life is coherent: I live in the present moment and that gives it all the meaning I need." Singer is apparently willing to say that this subjective understanding of the good life is objectively mistaken about in what true happiness consists.

[53] Singer, *Practical Ethics*, 292.

command of Jesus to "love our neighbors as we love ourselves" will always connect love of self with love of another and, of course, reject pure egoism. Happily, and not surprisingly, so does Singer:

Most of us would not be able to find full satisfaction by deliberately setting out to enjoy ourselves without caring about anyone or anything else. The pleasures we obtained in that way would seem empty and soon pall. We seek a meaning for our lives beyond our own pleasures and find fulfillment and happiness in doing what we see to be meaningful. If our life has no meaning other than our own happiness, we are likely to find that when we have obtained what we think we need to be happy, happiness itself still eludes us.[54]

Indeed, the way to escape the "cycle of accumulation and ruin" of the life of a pure egoist is to look for "a purpose broader than our own interests" and for "something that will allow us to see our lives as possessing significance beyond the narrow confines of our wealth or even our own pleasurable states of consciousness."[55] Happiness comes when we transcend our inward-looking concerns and instead identify ourselves with "the most objective point of view possible": the point of view of the universe.[56] And this requires taking the 'long-term view' of happiness for others when we evaluate their preferences:

People have very strong preferences for winning lotteries, although researchers have shown that those who win major lotteries are not, once the initial elation has passed, significantly happier than they were before.[57]

Concern for the objective flourishing and happiness of the self and of the other are, for Peter Singer, inextricably connected.

A CHRISTIAN UNDERSTANDING: LOVING YOUR NEIGHBOR AS YOURSELF

Moral theories that focus on happiness tend to follow either the classic *eudaimonia* perspective of Aristotle, focused on the flourishing of the moral agent, or the modern utilitarian position focused on producing happiness for others. However, a Christian understanding, as we saw in the previous chapter, will refuse this false choice. Jesus' command to love

---

[54] *Ibid.*, 291. Though he does admit that those who focus on themselves (in the case of those who focus their lives on, say, collecting stamps or their favorite football team – rather than taking the point of view of the universe) are not irrational. But implied in Singer's view is that those who have such things as their source of ultimate concern are not leading the best or most flourishing life possible.
[55] *Ibid.*, 293.   [56] *Ibid.*   [57] *Ibid.*, 14.

our neighbor as our self also inextricably connects the two ideas in the Christian tradition. We saw in Chapter 4 that Thomas Aquinas, in line with much contemporary psychology, sees love of self as the primary and foundational partial preference, necessary for all other loves. But the tradition is also clear that, as Singer claims above, it is through care and concern for others that human beings flourish. Sidney Callahan has just completed a book on happiness which points this out:

> The near unbelievable news of Christianity is that a nurturing God plays a win-win game. In the creation, giving and loving is also receiving – and this mutuality and union brings happiness. As in the description of the love generated in the Trinity, giving, loving and receiving produce joy. This ultimate template for all reality is reproduced and instanced in the way human happiness is engendered by giving in friendship, sexual love, family nurturing and creative engaged work. In losing self for love you find yourself, and in giving you receive – so frequently receiving back tenfold of the gift.[58]

Indeed, conventional wisdom is turned on its head in this way time and time again in the Christian tradition: the last shall be first, the leader is to be a servant, the humble will be exalted, and dying brings new life. One of the implications of the intrinsic connection between love of self and love of neighbor is that, as I have argued elsewhere, what is in one's own interest cannot easily be separated from what is in others' interests – and *vice versa*. Indeed, this seems to follow from a Christian understanding of the human person. For

> it is not only an empirical fact that human persons are *fundamentally and intrinsically* social, but this is backed up theologically by the triune, relational image of God that exists in each person. This sociality is so fundamental that one cannot speak of the 'dignity' or 'best interests' or 'quality of life' of a human person except with reference to some kinds of social considerations.[59]

Christian ethics, then, like Peter Singer, strongly and mutually connect the flourishing of others with the flourishing of the moral agent. One difference between the two approaches, however, might be that Singer appears to see aiming at one's own flourishing as a consideration and goal that stands outside of ethics proper. For him, one's own happiness is the answer to the *meta*-ethical question, "Why be moral?" But for the Christian tradition, this distinction will not do justice to the command of

---

[58] Sidney Cornelia Callahan, *Called to Happiness: Where Faith and Psychology Meet* (Maryknoll, NY: Orbis Books, 2011), 46.
[59] Charles Camosy, *Too Expensive to Treat? – Finitude, Tragedy and the Neonatal ICU*, 114.

Jesus. Both loves are so strongly connected that the ethical/meta-ethical distinction does not easily hold. In authentically pursuing our own flourishing we pursue the flourishing of others and *vice versa*. Love of self is every bit as much of an ethical duty as is love of neighbor.

We saw above that Singer understands happiness as something that goes beyond fleeting feelings of pleasure; for him, happiness is instead something that comes about over time with living a coherent life of meaning. Notice how similar this is to Alisdair MacIntyre's view, which we encountered in the previous chapter:

To be happy – as contrasted with feeling happy – is always to be happy in virtue of something or other, something done or suffered, something acquired or achieved. When translators have supplied "happiness" as the English translation of *eudaimonia* or *beatitudo*, they have in mind that type of happiness which supervenes upon and is made intelligible by the achievement of a completed and perfected life of worthwhile activity, the achievement of the human end.[60]

And Callahan agrees:

Happiness is also relating rightly to myself as a whole and feeling congruent or together. Therefore the philosophers are right when they say happiness includes the kind of good feeling I get when my life is going well . . . Happiness is present when my positive good feelings are embedded within a life that seems valuable. This robust definition of happiness covers a lot of territory and allows for being happy during difficult hard times if they are part of a meaningful life.[61]

Indeed, sometimes this kind of happiness has almost nothing to do with feeling pleasure in the sense we normally use the term. On the contrary, a significant number of people have claimed

that they are intensely happy while undergoing dreadful experiences in awful circumstances. Individuals have reported themselves to be happy and joyful while incarcerated in the Gulag, or suffering from debilitating and painful diseases, or while being persecuted and tortured as missionaries or reformers. In the most extreme cases martyrs have gone singing to their deaths, displaying joy in the midst of pain and distress. Indian warriors engaged in triumphant death songs while being flayed alive. In less violent instances, stoic philosophers, saints and sages have serenely accepted their unjust imprisonment and executions.[62]

For both Christians and Singerites, then, an understanding of happiness will be far more complex than attempting to determine a particular

---

[60] Lawrence Cunningham, *Intractable Disputes about the Natural Law: Alasdair MacIntyre and Critics* (Notre Dame, IN: University of Notre Dame Press, 2009), 48–49.
[61] Callahan, *Called to Happiness*, 16–17.   [62] *Ibid.*, 30.

psychological state at a particular time. Rather, happiness is a concept that transcends feelings of present moment to instead connect to an authentic life of meaning in service to others.

TELEOLOGY AND THE POSSIBILITY OF CONVERSATION

If Singer can accept that his method needs an objective understanding of human flourishing and happiness – which comes from living a coherent life of meaning – then it looks as if both the Church and Singer have very similar understandings of the ethical life as teleological.[63] And now things get very interesting. For we have already seen that in certain cases Singer and the Church disagree about what rule or ethical principle to apply, and many ethicists believe that this is simply a hopeless, intractable situation in which no productive conversation can take place. But recall Singer's claim that the moral life should make space for well-chosen, intuitive principles that experience has shown, over the centuries, to be generally conducive to producing the best consequences. Since both approaches agree at least at a certain level about what consequences should be produced – the happiness and flourishing of the agent and the common good of affected others – then why can't Singer and the Church have productive exchange about which principles are doing the best job at producing these consequences? Indeed, the Church often claims that the vast experience which comes with a 2,000-year-old tradition of thinking systematically about the flourishing of human beings gives it an expertise in humanity.[64] This long experience, and the insights about what produces human happiness and flourishing gained from it, should be respected and (critically) engaged as a source of moral wisdom whether or not one accepts the Church's claims to special revelation.

Fortunately, we are now living in an exciting time when we are beginning to find a way of appealing to science to help determine which principles are best for producing happiness and human flourishing. We saw above that Singer himself points with interest to a growing academic

---

[63] As Gerard Maguiness notes, this may seem strange given that Singer appears to have "no interest in a teleological scheme for his philosophical ethics," but Singer nevertheless repeatedly "resorts to the very purposeful and wider ethical vision he abhors." (122).

[64] "As an expert in humanity, she is able to understand man in his vocation and aspirations, in his limits and misgivings, in his rights and duties, and to speak a word of life that reverberates in the historical and social circumstances of human existence." Catholic Church, *Compendium of the Social Doctrine of the Church*, 71.

literature on what makes the human person happy, and Callahan high-lights this exploding research in some detail:

> In more specialized academic circles another flood of publications, books and hundreds of research articles and studies are devoted to happiness. Newly founded journals, and professional conferences appear along with an innovative field known as the "science of happiness." At least one international center has been established in the Netherlands to provide a data base for happiness studies serving up fat bibliographies and a huge number of published resources from around the globe.[65]

And far from a kind of study limited to happiness for individuals,

> impressive and large-scaled studies are taking place focused on the happiness or subjective well-being of populations and groups. Much of this research includes economic and political variables. Multi-disciplined, multi-method research studies now focus on the comparative happiness of different nations and populations. Such research is useful in the work of policy analysts and government decision makers whose interest lies in increasing a society's general levels of subjective well-being, or "Gross National Happiness."

As John Hare warns below, it is often a dicey proposition to determine how a particular moral principle is affecting the happiness of any one person. But these large studies of populations and groups – and particu-larly the ones geared toward public policy – could be an interesting tool to use in an exchange between Singer and Christian ethics. We saw Singer cite studies which show that, generally speaking, those who live with generosity and altruism are happier than hyper-autonomous, self-centered consumers. But what else can we learn about various moral principles and their relationship to the happiness and flourishing of a culture on a broad scale? Of course, many variables would have to be controlled in these studies to give us valuable data, but we could certainly investigate the relationship between happiness and several key issues examined in this book: abortion rights, euthanasia, and meat-eating, for example. And obviously we could go beyond these now familiar issues to examine the relationships between happiness and, say, the retributive punishment of the death penalty, or various sexual practices, or the many different kinds of social welfare and safety net programs. The sky appears to be the limit. Perhaps the explosion of the academic study of happiness, combined with a common teleological approach to ethics, indicates that many future debates between Singerites and Christians could be hashed out in the *Journal of Happiness Studies.*

[65] Callahan, *Called to Happiness*, 46.

Further grounding of objective value

Broad and large-scale happiness trends are easier to interpret and accept than are investigations into and claims about the happiness of an individual. Furthermore, even Jean Porter's teleology gives us a way of discovering and thinking about human flourishing only on a limited basis. But what if we want to go beyond this? Many of us, for instance, would want to condemn the aforementioned father for raising his daughter as a prostitute. But why? Recall that she is getting many of her preferences satisfied and she might even report being very happy with her life. If we as a community are to restrict this father's actions, and in the process make arguments against those who can't see anything wrong with them, we need more than just rational intuition. After all, one person's justified intuition is another's absurdity. We must ground ourselves in fairly descriptive understandings of the good of the human person which are at variance with raising one's child to be a prostitute. We must heed the warning of Tim Mulgan who asks whether we can speak of objective values without digging deeper and asking *why* these things are valuable and what grounds their value. Can we really ground objective moral value in the tough cases, he asks, without asking what the human story is for and what our place in the cosmos is?[66]

These questions get us into deep metaphysical waters. Could Singer ever swim out this far? Until recently, one might have argued that, while claiming to be advocating a metaphysically neutral, universal ethic for application in a pluralistic world, Singer actually snuck his metaphysics in through the backdoor.[67] But perhaps not surprisingly in light of his turn toward objectivity, I think we can now see some cracks beginning to form in the wall that he has tried to use to separate his method from metaphysics. This is especially true when he speaks about the wilderness and ecological concern. Singer suggests, for instance, that his own experiences of nature's beauty rise "to an almost spiritual intensity" and he even describes the value of the wilderness as "timeless and priceless."[68]

---

[66] Tim Mulgan, "The Impact of Climate Change on Utilitarianism and Christian Ethics."

[67] There are several metaphysical claims operating in much of his corpus: that persons are merely bundles of preferences, that preferences matter morally, that preferences are the only thing that matter morally, that future people count the same as present people, etc. Singer and others worry that invoking objective value will remove their discourse from a metaphysically neutral place and hurt their chances of succeeding in a pluralistic culture, but it should be clear that even without explicitly accepting such goods, they were never in this neutral place to begin with.

[68] Singer, *Practical Ethics*, 243–244.

Also consider his fascinating response to those wishing to locate moral value in non-sentient beings:

> Nevertheless, in the case of both plants and machines, *it is possible to give a purely physical explanation of what the organism or machine is doing* [emphasis added]; and in the absence of consciousness, there is no good reason why we should have greater respect for the physical processes that govern the growth and decay of living things than we have for those that govern non-living things.[69]

The clear implication of this claim is that it is at least possible, and perhaps likely, that we *cannot* give "a purely physical explanation" of what a conscious being is doing. One wonders what the non-physical explanation might be.

And we have already seen that he values the wilderness such that it would be a "great loss" if future generations no longer valued it. That he is willing to take a view of objective value which so clearly goes beyond his preference utilitarianism is strong evidence for which value actually has the more fundamental place in his method. Furthermore, we saw above that he thinks a world without people is worse than one with people because it lacks things like love, friendship, fulfilling and meaningful work, bringing up children, seeking knowledge, appreciating the beauties of nature, and creating literature and music. Interestingly, at the end of *Pushing Time Away* he personally adds the following two points to his grandfather's list of things which constitute the good life:

- Close personal relationships, in particular living in loving companionship with someone who understands you and with whom you can enjoy an intellectual as well as an emotional and physical relationship
- Understanding, defending, and passing on to others the highest and most humane ideas of wisdom, goodness, and beauty that can be gathered from thousands of years of human literature, philosophy, and art[70]

Such conceptions of a good life (and a good world), at least as they are articulated here, go well beyond what preference utilitarianism can give us.

And accepting objective value in these ways might just be the beginning. Singer, I believe, needs to invoke specific and normative metaphysical claims about the flourishing and happiness of human beings in order to rank various preferences, decide which future preferences

---

[69] *Ibid.*, 250.
[70] Peter Singer, *Pushing Time Away: My Grandfather and the Tragedy of Jewish Vienna* (New York: Ecco, 2003), 242.

to permit or create, and in trying to discover what will promote the
well-being of distant future people. And, indeed, he appears to be on
the metaphysical path to facing these difficult problems. It is likely to
be a path that will force him to rethink many things – including his
understanding of the human person. If one needs to consider something
beyond preferences when determining what is in the best interests
of a person, then one must of necessity reject a moral anthropology
which understands the human person as merely a placeholder for a
particular bundle of preferences. And if there are objective goods
required for the flourishing and happiness of a human person, and we
are required to evaluate these goods over time within his understanding
of a 'coherent life of meaning,' then how far away are we from talking
about a person as a 'kind of thing' – as a *substance with a nature* – that
persists through time? If Singer could consider incorporating substance
metaphysics into his ethical theory, a possibility that seemed inconcei-
vable before this shift began, then the potential overlap and room for
conversation between his views and those of the Church becomes simply
extraordinary.[71]

A need for God?

Of course, one reason why Singerites are loath to venture into these deep
metaphysical waters is that they seem pretty close to going off the
deep end into theism. And indeed, Mulgan claims that the best kind
of utilitarianism, one that promotes objective value, "both supports and
requires an unconventional form of theism."[72] John Hare also argued at
the Oxford conference that Singer's views require a kind of theism. Both
he and Singer agree that Henry Sidgwick was greatest of the utilitarians,
but, according to Hare, Sidgwick demonstrates a problem for Singer's
linking morality and individual happiness. And the problem arises when
trying to figure out how the following views, both of which seem self-
evident, could be true:

---

[71] This might eliminate the differences in the important and foundational arguments over moral
status and personhood in abortion and end-of-life issues – which we saw came down to an
argument about substance metaphysics. But we could also begin to talk about what metaphysical
relationships (perhaps understood as 'vocations') might mean for partial preferences and also what
they might mean for treating another person as a mere means to an end. Perhaps a Singerian
metaphysics could even be open to 'kinds of acts,' in addition to kinds of beings.
[72] Tim Mulgan, "The Impact of Climate Change on Utilitarianism and Christian Ethics." Mulgan
makes this argument in some detail in *Purpose in the Universe*, which is forthcoming from Oxford
University Press.

Egoistic Hedonism (the view that an individual ought to aim at a maximum balance of happiness for herself, where this is understood as the greatest balance of pleasure over pain), and Utilitarianism, or Universalistic Hedonism (the view that she ought to aim at the maximum balance of happiness for all sentient beings present and future, whatever the cost to herself).[73]

The psychological solution – that sympathy for others gives individuals happiness – was rejected by Sidgwick because such sympathy is inevitably limited in its range, and we feel it most towards those closest to us. But the other solution proposed was to

bring in a god who desires the greatest total good of all living things and will reward and punish in accordance with this desire ... Sidgwick recognized this as a return to the utilitarianism of William Paley's *The Principles of Moral and Political Philosophy*, in which Paley argues that God being just and benevolent must have so ordered the world that Happiness will in the long-run be distributed in proportion to Virtue. Sidgwick thought this solution was both necessary and sufficient to remove the contradiction in ethics.[74]

Can Singer claim that morality and happiness are linked without dealing with the problem Sidgwick faced? Some might think that the idea of Singer accepting a god, and especially the God of traditional theism, is absurd. But at the opening session of the Oxford conference, Singer admitted that he "regrets" not having a god to ground an answer to the question, "Why be moral?" And as John Hare has pointed out in his other work, utilitarianism might actually *require* a belief in something like traditional theism. For if we decide to reject the level of the principle and norm in favor of the "critical level" of moral reasoning (so named by his father), this "requires complete information and complete impartiality."[75] Indeed, R.M. Hare tries to talk about the human person at this level of reasoning as taking the perspective of an archangel, a being "who has the unlimited impartiality and unlimited information necessary to carry out critical thinking successfully."[76] Recall that Singer requires that, in order to reason at the critical level, we need to think clearly, calmly, and

---

[73] "Peter Singer Conference Archive," McDonald Centre for Theology, Ethics & Public Life. Talk by John Hare, 'Morality, Happiness, and Peter Singer,' http://mcdonaldcentre.org.uk/resources/peter-singer-conference/ (Accessed July 10, 2011).
[74] *Ibid.*
[75] J.E. Hare, *The Moral Gap: Kantian Ethics, Human Limits, and God's Assistance* (Oxford; New York: Clarendon Press; Oxford University Press, 1997), 19. As John Hare pointed out at the Oxford conference, the archangel is really just a substitute for God here.
[76] *Ibid.*, 22.

in a manner sufficiently free from bias. But our finite, flawed, and (in the Christian tradition) sinful natures appear to prohibit us from ever having anything approaching this capacity. Our finitude limits us such that we cannot predict the total impact of our actions on the flourishing of others, especially when we consider the effects over hundreds or thousands of years. In addition, contemporary critical theory gives us all good reason to think that we have deep-seated biases and blinders which, as John Hare points out, make it practically impossible to take the point view of the universe without aid:

> For example, I may magnify the intensity of my own preferences, so that they outweigh the preferences of others in the moral calculus; or I may cloak self-interest in the disguise of normative principles with the appearance of objectivity.[77]

If John Hare is correct, then something like God's providence and grace are necessary to jump the 'moral gap' that exists between what many like Singer claim we ought to do and what we actually can do in light of our finite and flawed human nature. Indeed, if 'ought' implies 'can,' then non-theists who argue that we ought to take the point of view of the universe should provide an explanation for how it is possible for human persons to take such a view.[78] In what many would no doubt consider to be an ironic twist, it may turn out that one must hold something like traditional theism in order to accept even the practical possibility of utilitarianism in the first place.[79]

CONCLUSION

From what we have learned from each of the previous two chapters, both Peter Singer and the Church can accept the following theoretical principles:

---

[77] *Ibid.*, 25.

[78] The atheist utilitarian might respond by saying that we "should just try to do the best we can," but especially if we owe the same moral consideration to distant future people that we owe to people currently alive, this response cannot defeat Hare's argument. In addition to not knowing what they will prefer, as we saw above, we have virtually no idea how our current decisions will affect them. Just to give one example: we can't even predict how social welfare programs will affect the most vulnerable, even just a few years down the road (they often end up hurting the very populations they are supposed to help, for instance). How could we ever meaningfully take into account the effect our actions will have on people living centuries or even millennia into the future?

[79] Hare also notes that utilitarianism, because of its near perfectionist moral standard, must also build in a way for human persons to be forgiven when they consistently fail to meet the standard.

1. The moral life is about directing one's choices toward the universal common good and flourishing of one's self and that of others. It is in this sense consequentialist.
2. The good and flourishing of others consists of something that can be studied in a biological and academic sense and is therefore something about which we can know objective facts. It is in this sense teleological.
3. Generally speaking, at least, concern for the flourishing of others is a prerequisite for, and mutually connected with, one's own flourishing.
4. Generally speaking, at least, following moral rules is important for the long-term flourishing of others and for one's own flourishing.
5. In relatively rare situations, some moral rules may be broken in the interest of promoting the flourishing of others and, again, for one's own flourishing.
6. The flourishing of others and of ourselves is indicated primarily by happiness.
7. Happiness is not indicated merely by 'feeling happy' but rather the long-term fulfillment which comes from achieving goals in a coherent life of meaning.
8. A life of meaning is constituted by various objective goods like friendship, raising of children, expanding one's knowledge, appreciation of music and art, etc.

This is a remarkable list. The fact that such overlap exists might help us recall Pope John Paul II's claim in *Veritatis Splendor* that the Christian teleological method described in the previous chapter is well suited for meeting the demands of dialogue and cooperation with non-Catholics and non-believers, especially in pluralistic societies. With the rise of happiness studies as a serious academic discipline, both Singerites and Christians could engage in productive debate both about which principles and norms are best for producing happiness and flourishing, and in which situations it might be acceptable to violate such principles and norms. Not every moral dispute could be adjudicated this way, of course. Porter, recall, points out that not everything that is true about human flourishing is objectively clear to everyone (hence its limitations as a tool for dialogue in moral debate). But many of us can agree about some things related to the flourishing and happiness of human beings, and this provides a basis for testing the viability of various moral norms and principles.

Conclusion

> One could argue endlessly about the merits of each of these characterizations of the ethical; but what they have in common is more important than their differences.
>
> Peter Singer, *Practical Ethics*

> Fruitful dialogue between faith and reason cannot but render the work of charity more effective within society, and it constitutes the most appropriate framework for promoting *fraternal collaboration between believers and non-believers* in their shared commitment to working for justice and the peace of the human family.
>
> Pope Benedict XVI, *"Caritas in Veritate"*

The previous six chapters have shown us in specific detail both how Peter Singer and Christian ethics can mutually push each other, and also how much they have in common. Indeed, it is precisely because of how much they have in common that the arguments are so interesting and productive. But in concluding this book let me pull back from these details and make some 'big picture' observations and suggestions.

HOW PETER SINGER HELPS PUSH CHRISTIAN ETHICS

Perhaps Singer's most important gift to Christians, and indeed to all who care about ethics, is his formidable and authentic push *to think and act consistently* with regard to one's ethical beliefs. He does this with his own crowd (the classic example being his insistence that one must support infanticide for the same reasons one supports abortion), but he of course calls out his opponents for their inconsistencies as well. As we saw in Chapter 3, he argues that when anti-abortionists claim to support and defend life, they almost never mean what they say. And while he is certainly correct that most self-described pro-lifers inconsistently limit their concerns to topics related to abortion and euthanasia, this unfortunate situation has been in the process of changing.

The feminist and progressive writer Mary Meehan wrote the following words back in 1980:

> Some of us who went through the anti-war struggles of the 1960s and early 1970s are now active in the right-to-life movement. We do not enjoy opposing our old friends on the abortion issue, but we feel that we have no choice. We are moved by what pro-life feminists call the "consistency thing" – the belief that respect for human life demands opposition to abortion, capital punishment, euthanasia, and war.[1]

Just three years later the Roman Catholic Archbishop Joseph Cardinal Bernardin would deliver his now famous Gannon Lecture at Fordham University in New York City, entitled "A Consistent Ethic of Life: an American–Catholic Dialogue." This ground-breaking talk began his defense of an ethic, discussed briefly in Chapter 4, which requires consistent reasoning across the issues of genetics, abortion, capital punishment, modern warfare, and the care of the terminally ill.[2] Bernardin would go on to refine his view and, as Sidney Callahan notes, add poverty and welfare reform, healthcare, and civil rights to what he called the "seamless garment" of concern for life.[3] The Consistent Ethic, Callahan claims, "frames the Christian love commandment as well as reason's requirement of logical consistency in the application of principle." Indeed, she pushes Bernardin's ethic further and says that those who support consistent application of Jesus' command to love one's neighbor will

> do no harm; relieve human suffering of every kind by appropriate works of mercy; affirm the equal moral value and dignity of each human life regardless of race, gender, class, health, wealth, power, or moral condition; strive for the development and flourishing of the human community to achieve a "civilization of love" and "a culture of life" as proclaimed in Church social doctrine.[4]

And this is no mere academic or obscure ivory-tower approach. The far and powerful reach of groups like Feminists for Life and Democrats for Life, even into the incredibly difficult struggle over US healthcare reform,[5]

---

[1] Mary Meehan, "Abortion: The Left Has Betrayed the Sanctity of Life," *The Progressive* 44 (Sept. 1980).

[2] Joseph Cardinal Bernadin and Thomas G. Fuechtmann, *Consistent Ethic of Life* (Kansas City, MO: Sheed & Ward, 1988).

[3] Sidney Callahan, "The Consistent Ethic of Life," *University of St. Thomas Law Journal* 2:2 (Spring 2005): 272–273.

[4] Callahan, *Ibid.*, 275–276.

[5] Pro-life Democrats like Rep. Bart Stupak (D-MI) were able to change the whole trajectory of the debate by connecting their support of basic healthcare for all to a concern for the protection of the human fetus. Pete Winn, "Rep. Stupak: White House Pressuring Me to Keep Quiet on

is evidence of the fault lines shifting in a way which reveals that many are beginning to apply pro-life principles more consistently.

But, particularly in light of engagement with Singer's thought, Christians need to push a pro-life ethic beyond even where Callahan ends up. Here are four principles that combine the insights of Bernardin and Callahan with those of this book. Those who adhere to a consistent ethic of life, I argue, should do the following:

1. Acknowledge the moral value of *all* life: persons (both human and non-human), non-human animals, and the broader ecological world.
2. Have a presumption against using violence and especially aiming at death.[6]
3. Have a presumption *for* aiding those in need and especially those who will die without aid.[7]
4. Foster a special concern for the most vulnerable (especially persons, but not excluding any entities which have interests) regardless of *species, age, condition of dependency, net contribution to the economy,* race, gender, class, health, wealth, power, or moral condition.

Those who uphold a consistent ethic of life will be especially skeptical, then, not only of violent practices like abortion and euthanasia, but also the death penalty, war, and factory farming – all of which involve aiming at the death of the vulnerable. They will also understand the grave moral responsibility one has for the violence one does to the vulnerable global poor when, because of greed, one violently abandons them to misery and even death.[8] Finally, they will understand the serious moral obligation to curb the violence done to the whole of creation more generally.

Indeed, Christians who hold this ethic may invoke Isaiah's prophecy cited in Chapter 3: "They will neither harm nor destroy on all my holy mountain, for the earth will be full of the knowledge of the LORD as the

Abortion Language in Senate Health Bill," CNS News, http://cnsnews.com/news/article/58921 (Accessed March 19, 2011). It should be noted that the US Bishops, supporting a consistent ethic, also supported universal healthcare while insisting that it did not support abortion.
[6] This is especially true if one takes seriously both the Church's 'Just War' tradition (which only permits violence in defense of another against a non-innocent aggressor) and Jesus' well-known prohibitions against violence and killing.
[7] This principle might recall the *Catechism* connecting abandonment of poor (especially when due to greed) to a violation of the fifth commandment, "Thou Shalt Not Kill."
[8] Recall from Chapter 5 that Gratian and St. Ambrose of Milan claim that consuming more than we need is "violence" against the poor – and that the *Catechism* speaks about abandoning the poor in the context of the fifth commandment against killing.

waters cover the sea." In that same chapter we saw Stanley Hauerwas build on this eschatological vision and call Christians to "witness to the world that God's creation is not meant to be at war with itself," and that "our lives are not captured by the old order" of violence. Indeed, in *Caritas in Veritate*, Pope Benedict issues a special call to "contemporary society to a serious review of its life-style, which, in many parts of the world, is prone to hedonism and consumerism, regardless of their harmful consequences."[9] The radical lifestyle changes necessary to live out the Consistent Ethic of Life, as we shall see below, will have much in common with the kinds of changes for which Singer calls. But this should not be surprising given that his insights and challenges give Christians important tools to shape and live an even more consistent ethic of life.

HOW CHRISTIAN ETHICS PUSH PETER SINGER

At various points in this book we saw just how negative a view Singer has had of Christianity in particular, but also of religious thought more generally. But today's post-modern world has revealed an important fact: we cannot find the kind of objective meaning and ethical principles Singer wishes to enjoin upon us without standing on the firm foundation of some faith-based first principles that come from a narrative or tradition. And the first principles he has in mind (like 'we should do the greatest good for the greatest number' or 'one person counts as one and none more than one') are, in fact, faith-based claims for which there cannot be arguments. They simply 'claim' or 'grab' one as being true via some authority. Furthermore, Singer's ethic comes out of a well-developed utilitarian tradition with its own authoritative figures, texts, and principles which define it. Utilitarianism deserves a fair hearing in the public debate, of course, but Christian ethics push secularists like Singer to consider the claims of religious traditions in the public debate without (what at times appears to be) dismissive prejudice. To a very real extent, anyone who makes claims which are thought to have normative weight outside of a particular tradition – whether explicitly religious or not – is engaging in the same kind of practice. From this perspective, then, the Christian ethicist and Peter Singer are doing the same kind of thing and should not be held to different standards when it comes to engaging in public debate.

The Christian ethicist will also be quite interested in Singer's important new revelation that he is now willing to entertain the idea that there are

[9] Pope Benedict XVI, *"Caritas in Veritate"* (Vatican: The Holy See), 51.

objective ethical truths that are independent of what anyone desires. Christians will push Singer to clarify this new and important shift in his thinking. Is he willing to admit that there are objective goods and interests for persons? In what would the metaphysical grounding of such objectivity consist? How he ends up answering these questions could dramatically impact some of the arguments about issues to which he has given sustained attention: the moral status of the fetus and of the mentally disabled, partial preferences for our family and friends, etc.

And if Singer admits that there are, in fact, certain goods and interests which objectively contribute to the flourishing of human persons, then Christians should certainly push him to apply this consistently to other ethical issues which he has not addressed in sufficient detail. In particular, he should be pushed to justify the following claim:

Decisions about sex may involve considerations of honesty, concern for others, prudence, avoidance of harm to others and so on, but the same could be said of decisions about driving a car. (In fact, the moral issues raised by driving a car, both from an environmental and from a safety point of view, are much more serious than those raised by safe sex.) Accordingly this book contains no discussion of sexual morality. There are more important ethical issues to be considered.[10]

Singer is right to point out that there was a time when concern for sexual morality seemed to drown out other important concerns, but the above claim is nevertheless astounding given what we know both about the flourishing and happiness that good sexual choices produce, and the suffering and misery produced by poor choices. The dramatic and ongoing rise in STD rates[11] (despite the wide availability of contraception and the practice of 'safe' sex) and widespread sexual violence are hard data which would challenge Singer's claim all by themselves,[12] but we also have 'soft' data which suggest that sexual behavior can dramatically affect human flourishing and happiness. One need only think for a short time about the hook-up culture of young people and our culture more generally (which promotes and valorizes the use of another's body merely for sexual gratification), or the rate of adultery and divorce

[10] Peter Singer, *Practical Ethics*, 2nd edn. (Cambridge; New York: Cambridge University Press, 1993), 2.
[11] Over one-quarter of all New Yorkers, for instance, has a sexually transmitted disease (STD). And rates continue to rise.
[12] This is especially true if we define sexual violence as an encounter where a person cannot give consent. This would apply not only to physical violence, but also violence directed at minors and those who cannot consent because of the influence of alcohol or other drugs.

(and the miserable and broken households it has produced), or the sexual objectification of women (and, increasingly, of men) and their bodies by profit-hungry corporations via various media, to see the dramatic harm that unethical sexual practices can bring. Add the radically important fact that sexual behavior produces children, and you've got one of the most important ethical issues one could possibly imagine.[13] Singer, especially if he is interested in flourishing and happiness, should be pushed to engage sexual ethics as a major part of his broader ethical project.

MOVING FORWARD TOGETHER

The Church speaks of "the necessity" of our culture seeking "in common the rules for living together in justice and peace."[14] With that strong claim in mind, I am convinced that the common ground between Singer and the Church is far more important than the disagreements. Recall that Singer says that what characterizations of the ethical have in common is more important than their differences.[15] The Pontifical Council *Cor Unum* also says that its spirit is not based on any particular ideology.[16] Realizing that both approaches are not wed to ideological polarization helps create the conceptual space necessary for Peter Singer and Christian ethics to engage in the spirit of intellectual solidarity; an attitude and practice which, as we saw David Hollenbach claim, regards differences among traditions as stimuli to intellectual engagement across religious and cultural boundaries.

And if a genuine attempt at unified engagement between the two approaches is made, we will find that not only is there intellectual common ground, but also that the ethical concerns of each approach come from a similar *emotional* place as well: that of loving compassion for others. Singer's foundational moral concern comes from the genuinely good place of an empathetic desire to reduce suffering. The prophet Ezekiel (36:26)

---

[13] This is especially true as our culture attempts to further disconnect sex from procreation – and re-*production* (interestingly, a consumerist word used to talk about having children) is thought of more and more as something that begins in a laboratory rather than with the loving sexual relationship of two people permanently committed to each other and to any future children that might be created. The consequences of thinking about our children as products of a consumer culture, and as tools of our will more generally, have yet to be fully understood.

[14] The International Theological Commission, 113.

[15] Singer, *Practical Ethics*, 11.

[16] Pontifical Council *Cor Unum*, WORLD HUNGER, A Challenge for All: Development in Solidarity, Preface.

and Pope Benedict in *Caritas in Veritate* (paragraph 79) both speak about the need to have one's heart be of "flesh" rather than "stone," but the Vatican's International Theological Commission discusses this concept precisely in the context of the kind of dialogue that is a focus of this book:

> The search for a common ethical language is inseparable from a hope of conversion, with which individuals and the community detach themselves from the forces that seek to imprison the human being in indifference or drive him to raise walls against others or against foreigners. The heart of stone – cold, inert, and indifferent to the lot of one's neighbour or of the human race – must be transformed, under the action of the Spirit, into a heart of flesh, sensible to the calls of wisdom, to compassion, to the desire for peace and to hope for all. This conversion is the condition for a true dialogue.[17]

Peter Singer, I believe, has precisely this kind of heart and thus this necessary condition for true dialogue. It is in light of his person, then, and not just his ideas, that he is an ideal candidate for Pope Benedict's important goal of fostering: "*fraternal collaboration between believers and non-believers* in their shared commitment to working for justice and the peace of the human family."[18]

At various times, some Christian thinkers give the impression that they aren't ready for what Pope Benedict asks of us here. Among certain ethicists there appears to be a push and even a need to be fundamentally distinctive from those who are doing ethics in other traditions, and even define Christianity specifically against the secular culture. Tristram Engelhardt, for instance, claims traditional Christian and secular approaches are "radically disparate moral perspectives."[19] Christopher Tollefsen believes not only that the gap between Christian and secular ethics is *inevitably* widening, but that the Christian ethicist must "expect to suffer" as a result.[20] But Nigel Biggar reminds us that Christian distinctiveness is an accident of history and that it is no measure at all of what really matters: theological *integrity*.[21] Attempts to be distinctive limit the common ground that Biggar claims Christians should have theological reason to

---

[17] The International Theological Commission, "The Search of a Universal Ethic: a New Look at Natural Law", 4. Translation by Joseph Bolin www.pathsoflove.com/universal-ethics-natural-law.html (Accessed March 27, 2011).

[18] Pope Benedict XVI, "*Caritas in Veritate,*" 57.

[19] H. Tristram Engelhardt, Jr., "The Culture Wars in Bioethics Revisited," *Christian Bioethics* 17:1 (2011), 1.

[20] Christopher Tollefsen, "Mind the Gap: Charting the Distance Between Christian and Secular Bioethics," *Christian Bioethics* Advanced Access: May 16 (2011), 6.

[21] Nigel Biggar, *Behaving in Public: How to Do Christian Ethics* (Grand Rapids, MI: William B. Eerdmans Publishing, Co., 2011), 8.

expect to find with others. The world's unified created order is "comprehensible by rational creatures, especially humans, who reflect God's image.
And since the created world is ordered for good, what is comprehensible
includes goods or forms of flourishing."[22] The increasing influence of
the Roman Catholic 'Focolare' movement, which has made a name for
itself bridging polarized gaps by practicing a "spirituality of unity,"[23] is an
important example of what can happen when Christians engage as Biggar
suggests. Indeed, the legal scholar and Focolare leader Amy Uelmen suggests that for those who practice a spirituality of unity, sincere engagement
with the other is not merely "an added dimension" of what it means for
them to practice the Christian faith, but it is instead at "the very core
of their way of being."[24]

If those who take Singer's approach are united in the spirit of
intellectual solidarity with the Church, and *vice versa*, both will see that
we have a fundamental trajectory in common. We will agree that there is
a need for a Copernican revolution, but rather than reacting primarily
against a disproportionate focus on the human person as a member of
the species *Homo sapiens*, the revolution should instead react against our
culture's disproportionate focus on the human person *as a consuming,
private, supposedly autonomous individual*. Both Singer and the Church
can and should move together against this understanding of the secular
Enlightenment[25] – especially as it runs counter to the other-centeredness
which both Singer and the Church believe is essential to leading an
ethical life. Both can and should join their efforts to create *new lifestyles*
which run counter to our culture's obsession with hyper-autonomy
and consumerism. These two values (far more than God, love, or even
maximizing preference satisfaction), sadly, appear to form the sources of
our ultimate concern in the secular West.

This general ethical stance could then play out in several instances
of public policy – including especially (though obviously not limited to)
the four main applied ethical issues considered in this book. The most
obvious concern of this new Copernican revolution would be for the
vulnerable global poor. As mentioned in Chapter 4, we live in a unique

---

[22] *Ibid.*, 26.
[23] They have been particularly strong, for instance, in leading Muslim– and Jewish–Christian
dialogue.
[24] Thomas Masters and Amy Uelmen, *Focolare: Living the Spirituality of Unity in the United States*
(Hyde Park, NY: New City Press, 2011), 196.
[25] Recall that Singer faults the Enlightenment's move away from Roman Catholicism for our
culture's attitude of indifference toward the global poor.

the proof further [handwritten marginalia]

moment in which the eradication of absolute poverty is within our grasp. Singerites and Christians have a moral obligation to work together to achieve this goal. Both could think and strategize, for instance, not only about how best to motivate individuals to move past appeals to autonomy, privacy, and consumerism to meet their ethical duties in this regard, but also how businesses, governments, and economic theory can meet their duties to the most vulnerable as well.[26] The torture and slaughter of non-human animals in our factory farms, one of the most odious and reprehensible practices in the developed world, should also be attacked in light of the attitude that makes them possible: consumerism and a self-obsessed autonomy which fails to see the value and interests of these vulnerable creatures. While concluding his thoughts at the Oxford conference, Singer himself mentioned that these two issues, along with ecological concern, provided genuine ways that he and Christian ethics could make common cause.

I also have hope that a consistent suspicion of hyper-autonomy and consumerism will lead Singerites to rethink abortion and euthanasia as well.[27] The 1.2 million abortions of vulnerable prenatal human beings done every year in the United States are permitted and driven by a disproportionate focus on autonomy and choice, and we saw in Chapter 1 that Peter Singer rejects this as an ethical justification for the practice.[28] Furthermore, courageous and counter-cultural groups like Feminists for Life highlight the consumerist reasons why abortion continues to be seen as necessary in many communities. The consumerism-driven standard of living to which one is now expected to attain in the developed world is often based on a work schedule with which having and raising children often seems incompatible. Short-term profit maximization is also a main

---

[26] Pope Benedict XVI valorizes another Focolare concept, the 'economy of communion,' which attempts to rid ourselves of the "distinction between profit-based companies and non-profit organizations" which "can no longer do full justice to reality, or offer practical direction for the future" ("*Caritas in Veritate*," 46). For more on the economy of communion, see www.edc-online. org/index.php/en.html (Accessed March 22, 2011).

[27] Some might think that, in light of Singer's commitments, this hope is simply naiveté. But my research has revealed a man who is primarily interested in mitigating suffering – especially with regard to the poor and non-human animals. Many of his other positions have simply followed logically from the way he has decided to do that. But Christians can show him, for instance, that one may strongly condemn unethical treatment of other animals without downgrading the value of vulnerable human beings. Singer could indeed stand against abortion and euthanasia without giving up his core practical ethical concerns.

[28] Peter Singer currently supports abortion rights, but the first chapter showed that those who hold views like his are not that far away from an anti-abortion position – especially if one is willing to accept a substance metaphysics.

reason why most companies and other institutions do not provide their employees (and especially women) with legitimate opportunities to be both parents and workers, even on a part-time basis. Indeed, such companies tend to look at the very possibility of child-rearing as reason to discriminate against female employees.[29] Finally, an obsession with privacy and autonomy also takes support of euthanasia from an often understandable empathetic response to circumstances of extreme suffering, to a major push for the right to be killed simply because one is "tired of life." Add a consumerist and youth-obsessed culture which locates one's value primarily in what one can contribute to the economy while living a (supposedly) autonomous life, and it is easy to understand how those who are vulnerable and needy because of age or sickness might come to the conclusion that their lives are burdensome (for their community, family, and even themselves) and no longer worth living – especially when they are pushed away from the cultural mainstream and into a nursing home.

Those who are interested in making practical change will be happy to know that Singer, despite being a chaired professor at Princeton University, is no ivory-tower academic. Much like his grandfather before him, and from the beginning of his career, "he was determined to drag philosophy from the academic talking shops into the real world, and prove that it had relevance for how people should act."[30] Indeed, Singer is very explicit in his goal of going beyond his professional circle:

I want to change people's views, and their actions, on issues like obligations of the rich to the poor, or what we eat, but I also expect that learning to think rigorously and critically will bring more general benefits. Too many of my colleagues write only for other philosophers. That's understandable, because it is the opinions of other philosophers that will determine whether they get jobs, or tenure, or promotion. But it's also regrettable because it means that the most intelligent, educated people who pick up a philosophy book or journal will get little from it.[31]

Both able and unafraid to write and speak in non-academic venues, his body of work has gone a long way toward justifying his bold claim in 1974 that "Philosophers are Back on the Job."[32] Indeed, he has become the world's most influential living philosopher as a result of this approach.

[29] Pushing for abstractions like 'choice' within this kind of social reality, without challenging the structural injustice, actually ends up producing something very different from authentic freedom.
[30] Gerard Maguiness, "Assisted Suicide, Self-Love, and a Life Worth Living," 103.
[31] Jeffrey Schaler, *Peter Singer Under Fire: The Moral Iconoclast Faces His Critics* (Chicago, IL: Open Court, 2009), 65.
[32] Peter Singer, "Philosophers are Back on the Job," *New York Sunday Times Magazine* (July 7, 1974).

Christian ethics have a 'pastoral' bent that, like Singer's, is designed to have relevance for those outside the academic discipline of theology. However, like Singer's colleagues, some academic theologians often get caught in the trap of focusing their efforts only on an academic audience. The renowned Christian ethicist, James Keenan, SJ, had the following response to this phenomenon during his address to the Catholic Theological Society of America in 2009:

In the first phase of the promotion of solidarity and justice, church leaders and theologians developed inter-departmental bonds so as to fix the agenda of solidarity. Now, however, we must move beyond the chancery and beyond the academy. I believe we need better rhetorical strategies so as to prompt others to stand in solidarity and to promote justice for the alienated ... What happens when we do not resonate with the public audience and when this audience shows little interest in our positions: as for instance, immigration reform, prison reform, or in solidarity with the poor throughout the world?[33]

Indeed, Keenan calls for an approach that is much like Singer's:

If we want to talk with more than ourselves, then we must develop more embodied, relational, practical, and narrative-based arguments to offer effective ways of addressing impasse in the world, the church and the academy today. We need to develop strategies that are more affectively evident, more emotionally resonant, more imaginatively developed, and more liberating for both the marginalized and the isolationist. We must therefore be suspicious when as academics we think that concepts and good critical thinking are rhetorically sufficient for addressing the challenges of the day.[34]

One of those imaginative strategies, it seems to me, would be Singerites and Christians working together on issues of practical ethics: both the world of ideas and also the world of public policy and service. Not only would it unleash the tremendous power and influence of each approach, united in combating some of the most important injustices of our time, but it would also create 'hearts of flesh' through the embodied relationships and even friendships that would no doubt be formed as a result.[35]

---

[33] James Keenan, "Impasse and Solidarity in Theological Ethics," *CTSA Proceedings* 64 (2009), 53–54.
[34] *Ibid.*, 55. Keenan goes on to lament the fact that the very (privileged and isolated) structure of academic life inhibits the kind of virtues necessary to be in true solidarity with the vulnerable. Theologians who share Keenan's view here share this in common with Singerites as well.
[35] As my friend and colleague John Perry pointed out to me some years ago, "bare philosophical argument" is only the shadow or ghost of genuine exchange. Some kind of personal encounter is almost always required for the real thing to take place. As mentioned above, this insight has deep theological resonances for Christians who believe that God became human in the person of Jesus of Nazareth, and not a mere abstract proposition, for precisely this reason.

As this book goes to press, plans are already in the pipeline for Singer and other philosophers to engage with theologians and religious leaders to address the structural evil of factory-farming non-human animals. My hope is that this is just the beginning of much more collaboration to come.

But despite the power and promise of these two approaches uniting in the ways I have suggested they might, the overwhelmingly powerful and entrenched sinful social structures (which make possible horrific practices like factory farming, millions of birth-control abortions, and marginalization of the global poor) might drive us to despair of making any significant change. While I understand this sentiment, and at times even share it, I find comfort in the following two responses. The first is perhaps best told in the classic 'starfish story':

One night, on a sandy beach, a terrible storm started. It rained. The wind blew so hard that it shook the houses along the beach. The next morning was foggy and gloomy. Many thousands of starfish had washed up on the beach. A man named Buck walked out on the beach to look around. Peering into the mist he saw a young man walking along the beach. He was tall and slender. Buck saw him throwing starfish back into the ocean. Buck walked up to him and said, "Why are you throwing a few starfish back into the ocean? You'll never get them all back in the water. It doesn't matter." Without a word the young man bent over, picked up a starfish, and threw it with all his might. It went way out in the ocean. The young man turned to Buck and said, "It mattered to that one."[36]

The second comes from the great Roman Catholic fantasy author, J.R.R. Tolkien, which he puts in the mouth of Gandalf the White:

It is not our part to master all the tides of the world, but to do what is in us for the succour of those years wherein we are set, uprooting the evil in the fields that we know, so that those who live after may have clean earth to till. What weather they shall have is not ours to rule.[37]

Let's get to work.

---

[36] This basic story has been told in many forms, but all have been adapted from Loren C. Eiseley, *The Star Thrower* (New York: Times Books, 1978).
[37] J.R.R. Tolkien, *The Lord of the Rings* (London: Harper Collins, 1974), Book V, Chapter 9. I owe this example to Maura Ryan.

Appendix

General moral principles	Peter Singer	Christian ethics
Are there non-human persons?	YES	YES
Are there human non-persons?	YES	NO
Logical possibility of human non-persons?	YES	YES
Rationality as a basis for personhood	YES	YES
Personhood grounded in membership in *Homo sapiens*?	NO	NO
Is taking the life of a person worse than taking the life of some other being?	YES	YES
Morally and legally wrong to kill a person?	YES	YES
Is Church teaching speciesist?	YES	NO
Significant moral value outside *Homo sapiens*?	YES	YES
Should "potential" count when determining moral status?	NO	YES
Is pain morally significant?	YES	YES
Is there a hierarchical ordering of beings?	YES	YES
Moral responsibility for what one does *and* what one fails to do?	YES	YES
Accepts Golden Rule	YES	YES
Partial preferences can and should foster impartial preferences	YES	YES
Ethics relative to society in which one lives?	NO	NO
Can there be intrinsically evil acts?	NO	YES
Objective concept of human flourishing	MAYBE	YES

General moral principles	Peter Singer	Christian ethics
Preservation of lives of persons can be trumped by other values in certain situations	YES	YES
Objective concept of "happiness"	YES	YES
Flourishing of others and ourselves is indicated primarily by happiness	YES	YES
Happiness determined not by "feeling happy" but by fulfilling long-term goals in a life of meaning	YES	YES
The flourishing and happiness of various living things can be studied academically and known objectively?	YES	YES
Concern for flourishing and happiness of self and others inextricably connected	YES	YES

Abortion	Peter Singer	Christian ethics
Is the fetus a person?	NO	YES
Decisions on abortion should be private choice	NO	NO
In support of *Roe* v. *Wade*	NO	NO
Does the "unintended consequences" argument against making abortion illegal hold?	NO	NO
Is abortion a fundamental human right?	NO	NO
Is it morally wrong to kill a fetus acknowledged to be a person?	YES	YES
Is it morally wrong to refuse to sustain a fetus acknowledged to be a person?	YES	YES
Is a human infant a person?	NO	YES
Is there a logical link between abortion and infanticide?	YES	YES
Is the human embryo a person?	NO	MAYBE (should treat as a person)
Reject viability as a morally significant indicator of moral status personhood	YES	YES

Euthanasia and the end of life	Peter Singer	Christian ethics
Brain death is the death of a human organism	NO	Growing skepticism
Acceptability of pain medication that hastens death	YES	YES
Intent to kill permissible	YES	NO
Moral permissibility to forego life-sustaining treatment	YES	YES
Intrinsic moral difference between killing and allowing to die	NO	NO
Extrinsic moral difference between killing and allowing to die	NO (consequence is the same)	YES (intention of agent is morally significant)
Intrinsic moral value of human beings indicated by species membership	NO (requires actualization of rationality and self-awareness to articulate preferences)	YES (based on potentiality for possessing morally significant traits)
Public policy: slippery-slope concerns in legalizing voluntary active euthanasia	NO	YES

Non-human animals	Peter Singer	Christian ethics
Focus on sentience as an ethical concern	YES	YES
Morally wrong to cause needless suffering to non-human animals	YES	YES
Non-human animals have moral value independent of human beings	YES	YES
God created non-human animals to be the companions of human animals?	NO	YES
Moral duty to be kind to non-human animals?	YES	YES
Logical possibility of non-human animal personhood?	YES	YES

Non-human animals	Peter Singer	Christian ethics
Non-human animals have their own teleological sense of flourishing?	NO	YES
Covenant between human and non-human animals?	NO	YES
Concern for the effect of violent killing of non-human animals on the moral agent?	NO	YES

Duties to the poor	Peter Singer	Christian ethics
Moral duty to aid poor	YES	YES
Stronger duty to those in closer relationships to us	NO	YES (all things being equal)
Certain amount of our resources are *owed* to the poor	YES	YES
Right to private property	YES	YES
Refusal to aid is akin to homicide	YES	YES
We are in part responsible for existence of structural poverty	YES	YES
Emphasis on aid to combat unjust structures rather than mere charity	YES	YES
Re-allocate resources rather than control population	YES	YES
Every act of consumption ethically significant	YES	YES
Objective to personalize the poor by connection	YES	YES
Support the creation of culture of giving through peer pressure	YES	YES
We should be thinking of ourselves as a world community	YES	YES

Ethical theory and method	Peter Singer	Christian ethics
Is the intention of the agent relevant?	NO	YES
Common good of all people is central moral consideration	YES	YES
Rule-based reasoning	YES	YES
Consequence-based reasoning	YES	YES
Teleological method	YES	YES
Exceptionless rules?	NO	YES
Proportionate reasoning	YES	YES
Do all interests have equal moral weight?	NO	NO
Some interests are objectively morally valuable	YES	YES
Rules help us on a teleological path for ourselves and others	YES	YES
The concept of a human being is merely a placeholder for a particular bundle of preferences	YES	NO
Potential reduction of human beings as means to some other ends?	YES	NO
Following rules is important for the long-term flourishing of the self and others	YES	YES
Moral rules may be broken in the interests of promoting human flourishing	YES (in certain cases)	YES (in certain cases)
Objectivity in practical reasoning?	YES	YES
Focus moral concern on future generations?	YES	YES
Objective goods need to be metaphysically grounded	MAYBE	YES
Accepts objective goods	MAYBE	YES

Bibliography

Abend, Lisa. "In Spain, Human Rights for Apes." TIME.com. www.time.com/time/world/article/0,8599,1824206,00.html (Accessed May 1, 2010).

Allen, John L. *The Future Church: How Ten Trends are Revolutionizing the Catholic Church* (New York: Doubleday, 2009).

Alleyne, Richard. "Chimpanzees grieve for loved ones." *Telegraph* online. www.telegraph.co.uk/science/science-news/7634918/Chimpanzees-grieve-for-loved-ones.html (Accessed February 5, 2011).

Allsopp, Michael E., and John J. O'Keefe. *Veritatis Splendor: American Responses* (Kansas City, MO: Sheed & Ward, 1995).

Alvare, Helen. "An Anthropology for the Family Law of Indis/solubility," *Ave Maria Law Review* 4, no. 2 (June 2006): 497.

American Foreign Press. "Vatican searches for extra-terrestrial life." Google. www.google.com/hostednews/afp/article/ALeqM5iXaUKFhkbVieQAqtllc-sCKsba9w (Accessed April 24, 2010).

Angier, Natalie. "The Most Compassionate Conservative." *The New York Times.* www.nytimes.com/2002/10/27/books/the-most-compassionate-conservative.html?pagewanted=1 (Accessed April 2, 2010).

Aquinas, Saint Thomas. *Sentencia Libri de Anima.* Commentary on Aristotle's De Anima. English. Translated by Kenelm Foster and Silvester Humphries (Notre Dame, IN: Dumb Ox Books, 1994).

    Summa Contra Gentiles, Translated by Anton C. Pegis (Notre Dame, IN: University of Notre Dame Press, 2005).

Associated Press. "Russia Marks Day of Conception." MSNBC.com. www.msnbc.msn.com/id/20730526 (Accessed May 9, 2009).

Austin, John, and Robert Campbell. *Lectures on Jurisprudence: Or, the Philosophy of Positive Law* (London: J. Murray, 1920).

Barnes, Michael Horace and College Theology Society. Meeting. *An Ecology of the Spirit: Religious Reflection and Environmental Consciousness.* The Annual Publication of the College Theology Society. Vol. 1990, v. 36 (Lanham, MD: University Press of America: College Theology Society, 1994).

Benedict XVI, Pope. "*Caritas in Veritate*" (Vatican: The Holy See), www.vatican.va/holy_father/benedict_xvi/encyclicals/documents/hf_ben-xvi_enc_20090629_caritas-in-veritate_en.html (Accessed February 14, 2010).

Address to participants at an International Congress organized by the Pontifical Academy for Life (Vatican: The Holy See), www.vatican.va/holy_father/benedict_xvi/speeches/2008/november/documents/hf_ben-xvi_spe_20081107_acdlife_en.html (Accessed June 29, 2011).

Ben-Shahar, Tal. *Happier: Learn the Secrets to Daily Joy and Lasting Fulfillment* (New York: McGraw-Hill, 2007). www.loc.gov/catdir/enhancements/fy0642/2006103344-b.html; www.loc.gov/catdir/enhancements/fy0642/2006103344-d.html.

Bernardin, Joseph Cardinal and Thomas G. Fuechtmann, *Consistent Ethic of Life* (Kansas City, MO: Sheed & Ward, 1988).

Bettenson, Henry (trans.), *Concerning the City of God Against the Pagans*. 2003 edn. (New York: Penguin Books, 1972).

Biggar, Nigel. *Aiming to Kill: The Ethics of Suicide and Euthanasia.* (Cleveland, OH: Pilgrim Press, 2004).
Behaving in Public: How to Do Christian Ethics (Grand Rapids, MI: William B. Eerdmans Publishing, Co., 2011).

Bliss, William Dwight Porter, and Rudolph Michael Binder. *The New Encyclopedia of Social Reform, Including all Social Reform Movements and Activities, and the Economic, Industrial, and Sociological Facts and Statistics of all Countries and all Social Objects*. New edn. (New York: Funk & Wagnalls Company, 1908).

Boethius, H. F. Stewart, and Edward Kennard Rand. *The Theological Tractates.* The Loeb Classical Library (London; New York: W. Heinemann; G.P. Putnam's Sons, 1918).

Boyle, Joseph. "A Case for Sometimes Tube-Feeding Patients in Persistent Vegetative State" in John Keown (ed.), *Euthanasia Examined* (Cambridge University Press, 1995).

Brugger, E. Christian. "Transplants From Murder Victims." *ZENIT – The World Seen From Rome*. www.zenit.org/article-31647?l=english (Accessed June 29, 2011).

Cahill, Lisa. "Teleology, Utilitarianism, and Christian Ethics," *Theological Studies* 42: no. 4 (1981): 601–629.

Calderone, M.D. Mary S. "Illegal Abortion as a Public Health Problem," *American Journal of Public Health* no. 50: (1960) 948.

Callahan, Daniel. *Abortion: Law, Choice and Morality*, 3rd print edn. (New York: Macmillan Publishing Co., 1972).

Callahan, Sidney. "The Consistent Ethic of Life," *University of St. Thomas Law Journal* 2, no. 2 (Spring 2005): 272–273.

Callahan, Sidney Cornelia. *Called to Happiness: Where Faith and Psychology Meet* (Maryknoll, NY: Orbis Books, 2011).

Camosy, Charles C. "Common Ground on Surgical Abortion? – Engaging Peter Singer on the Moral Status of Potential Persons," *The Journal of Medicine and Philosophy* (January 2009) 33(6).
Too Expensive to Treat? Finitude, Tragedy, and the Neonatal ICU (Grand Rapids, MI: William B. Eerdmans Publishing Co., 2010).

Carey, Benedict. "Study Finds Activity in Brain That Seems to Be Shut Down." *The New York Times.* www.nytimes.com/2010/02/04/health/04brain.html (Accessed February 4, 2010).

"Caritas Launches Zero Poverty Campaign." *ZENIT – The World Seen From Rome.* www.zenit.org/article-28176?l=english (Accessed July 28, 2011).

Catholic Church. *Catechism of the Catholic Church* [Catechismus Ecclesiae Catholicae], 2nd edn., Vol. 5–109 (Citta del Vaticano; Washington, D.C.: Libreria Editrice Vaticana; distributed by United States Catholic Conference, 2000).

National Conference of Catholic Bishops and Catholic Church. National Conference of Catholic Bishops. *Economic Justice for All: Pastoral Letter on Catholic Social Teaching and the U.S. Economy.* Office of Publishing and Promotion Services. Vol. 101 (Washington, D.C.: Office of Publishing and Promotion Services, United States Catholic Conference, 1986).

On the Hundredth Anniversary of Rerum Novarum = Centesimus Annus [Centesimus annus.]. Vol. 436–8 (Washington, D.C.: Office for Publishing and Promotion Services, United States Catholic Conference, 1991).

Pontifical Council for the Pastoral Care of Migrant and Itinerant People and United States Catholic Conference. *Refugees: A Challenge to Solidarity.* Vol. 576–3 (Washington, D.C.: United States Catholic Conference, 1992).

Pontificium Consilium de Iustitia et Pace. *Compendium of the Social Doctrine of the Church* (Dublin: Veritas, 2005).

Pope (1958–1963: John XXIII) and William Joseph Gibbons. *Mater Et Magistra: Encyclical Letter: Christianity and Social Progress* [Mater et magistra.] (New York: Paulist Press, 1961).

Pope (1978–2005: John Paul II). *Encyclical Letter Sollicitudo Rei Socialis of the Supreme Pontiff, John Paul II, to the Bishops, Priests, Religious Families, Sons and Daughters of the Church and all People of Good Will for the Twentieth Anniversary of Populorum Progressio* [Sollicitudo rei socialis.]. Vol. 205–5 (Washington, D.C.: Office of Publishing and Promotion Services, United States Catholic Conference, 1988).

Pope (1963–1978: Paul VI) and Barbara Ward. *Encyclical Letter of His Holiness Pope Paul VI, on the Development of Peoples* [Populorum progressio.] (New York: Paulist Press, 1967).

"The Celestial Hierarchy-Dionysius the Areopagite." Esoterica. www.esoteric.msu.edu/VolumeII/CelestialHierarchy.html (Accessed April 23, 2010).

"Chimps may be aware of others' deaths." ScienceNews. www.sciencenews.org/view/generic/id/58652/title/Chimps_may_be_aware_of_others'_deaths (Accessed February 5, 2011).

Clough, David and Celia Deane-Drummond (eds.), *Creaturely Theology* (Norwich, UK: SCM Press, 2009).

Cohen, Andrew I., and Christopher Heath Wellman. *Contemporary Debates in Applied Ethics.* Contemporary Debates in Philosophy. Vol. 3 (Malden,

MA: Blackwell Publishing, 2005). www.loc.gov/catdir/toc/ecip0420/2004016921.html.

Cole, Graham. "Theological Utilitarianism and the Eclipse of Theistic Sanction," *Tyndale Bulletin* 42, no.2 (1991): 226.

Congregation for the Doctrine of the Faith. "Commentary" (Vatican: The Holy See). www.vatican.va/roman_curia/congregations/cfaith/documents/rc_con_cfaith_doc_20070801_nota-commento_en.html (Accessed December 3, 2009).

"Declaration on Euthanasia" (Vatican: The Holy See). www.vatican.va/roman_curia/congregations/cfaith/documents/rc_con_cfaith_doc_19800505_euthanasia_en.html (Accessed December 7, 2010).

Declaration on Procured Abortion (Vatican: The Holy See), November 18, 1974. www.vatican.va/roman_curia/congregations/cfaith/documents/rc_con_ cfaith_ doc_19741118_declaration-abortion_en.html (Accessed July 31st, 2011).

"*Donum Vitae*. Instruction on respect for human life in its origin and on the dignity of procreation: replies to certain questions of the day" (Vatican: The Holy See). February 22, 1987 (Accessed July 31st, 2011).

Instruction Dignitas Personae on Certain Bioethical Questions (Vatican: The Holy See). June 20, 2008. www.vatican.va/roman_curia/congregations/cfaith/documents/rc_con_cfaith_doc_20081208_dignitas-personae_en.html (Accessed May 10, 2011).

"Responses to Certain Questions Concerning Artificial Nutrition and Hydration" (Vatican: The Holy See). www.vatican.va/roman_curia/congregations/cfaith/documents/rc_con_cfaith_doc_20070801_risposte-usa_en.html (Accessed December 10, 2009).

Coonan, Terry. "There Are No Strangers Among Us: Catholic Social Teachings and U.S. Immigration Law," 40 *Catholic Lawyer* 105, n. 62 (2000).

Cunningham, Lawrence. *Intractable Disputes about the Natural Law: Alasdair MacIntyre and Critics* (Notre Dame, IN: University of Notre Dame Press, 2009).

Dombrowski, Daniel A. and Robert Deltete, "A Brief, Liberal, Catholic Defense of Abortion," *American Journal of Theology and Philosophy* 22, no. 3 (S, 2000): 78.

DuBois, James M. "Brain Death and Organ Donation." *America Magazine*, www.americamagazine.org/content/article.cfm?article_id=11369 (Accessed December 6, 2009).

Durant, Will. *Caesar and Christ: A History of Roman Civilization and of Christianity from their Beginnings to A.D. 325. The Story of Civilization.* Vol. 3 (New York: Simon and Schuster, 1944).

"Dutch activists planning euthanasia clinic." Free Republic, www.freerepublic.com/focus/f-news/2665426/posts (Accessed June 30, 2011).

Dworkin, Ronald. *Life's Dominion: An Argument about Abortion, Euthanasia and Individual Freedom* (New York: Alfred A. Knopf, 1993).

Eberstadt, Mary. "Pro-Animal, Pro-Life." First Things, www.firstthings.com/article/2009/05/pro-animal-pro-life-1243228870 (Accessed April 2, 2010).

Eiseley, Loren C. *The Star Thrower* (New York: Times Books, 1978).

Engelhardt, Jr., H. Tristram. "The Culture Wars in Bioethics Revisited," *Christian Bioethics* 17: 1 (2011).

"The EU's baby blues." BBC News, http://news.bbc.co.uk/2/hi/europe/4768644. stm (Accessed May 9, 2009).

Finnis, John. *Moral Absolutes: Tradition, Revision, and Truth* (Washington, D.C.: Catholic University Press, 1991).

    Response to Singer's 'Brain Death and the Sanctity of Life Ethic'. Response paper given at a meeting with the Philosophy Society, University of Oxford: May 14, 1998.

Fletcher, Joseph F. "Love and Utility," *The Christian Century* (May 31, 1978), 592.

    "Responsible Decision Making," *Theology Today* 28:1 (April 1971), 91.

    Situation Ethics: The New Morality (Philadelphia, PA: Westminster Press, 1966).

Foley, Kathleen M., Herbert Hendin, and Inc Ebrary. *The Case Against Assisted Suicide* (Baltimore: Johns Hopkins University Press, 2002). http://avoserv. library.fordham.edu/login?url=http://site.ebrary.com/lib/fordham/Doc?id= 10021569.

Gentleman, Amelia. "Inside the Dignitas House." *The Guardian*. www.guardian. co.uk/society/2009/nov/18/assisted-suicide-dignitas-house (Accessed June 28, 2011).

Goodway, Nick. "Mobile Rivals Set for India Battle." *Daily Mail* Online. www.dailymail.co.uk/money/markets/article-1605698/Mobile-rivals-set-for-India-battle.html (Accessed December 10, 2009).

Gregory, Eric. "Agape and Special Relations in a Global Economy: Theological Sources," in Douglas Hicks and Mark Valarie (eds.), *Global Neighbors: Christian Faith and Moral Obligation in Today's Economy* (Grand Rapids, MI: William B. Eerdmans Publishing Co., 2008).

Grisez, Germain Gabriel. *The Way of the Lord Jesus* (Chicago, IL: Franciscan Herald Press, 1983).

Hallett, Garth. *Priorities and Christian Ethics*. New Studies in Christian Ethics (Cambridge; New York: Cambridge University Press, 1998).

Hanke, Lewis. *The Spanish Struggle for Justice in the Conquest of America* (Boston, MA: Little, Brown, 1965).

Hardwig, John. "Is there a Duty to Die?" *Hastings Center Report* 27:2 (1997), 36.

Hare, J. E. *The Moral Gap: Kantian Ethics, Human Limits, and God's Assistance*. Oxford Studies in Theological Ethics (Oxford; New York: Clarendon Press; Oxford University Press, 1997).

Hare, R. M. *Essays on Bioethics* (Oxford; New York: Clarendon Press; Oxford University Press, 1993).

    "A Philosophical Autobiography," *Utilitas* 14:3 (November 2002), 295.

    Moral Thinking: Its Levels, Method, and Point (Oxford, UK: Clarendon Press, 1981).

    "Some Reasoning About Preferences: A Response to Essays by Persson, Feldman, and Schueler," *Ethics* 95:1 (Oct. 1984), 82.

Hartman, Steve. "On Elephant Sanctuary, Unlikely Friends." CBS News. www.cbsnews.com/stories/2009/01/02/assignment_america/main4696340. shtml?tag=currentVideoInfo;videoMetaInfo (Accessed April 25, 2010).

Hauerwas, Stanley, and John Berkman. "The Chief End of All Flesh." *Theology Today* Vol 49: No. 2 (July 1992), 196–208.

Herbermann, Charles G., *et al.* (eds.). *The Catholic Encyclopedia: An international work of reference on the constitution, doctrine, discipline, and history of the Catholic Church* (London, UK: Caxton, 1907).

Himes, Kenneth R. *Responses to 101 Questions on Catholic Social Teaching* (New York: Paulist Press, 2001).

Himes, Michael J., and Kenneth R. Himes. *Fullness of Faith: The Public Significance of Theology.* Isaac Hecker Studies in Religion and American Culture (New York: Paulist Press, 1993).

Hollenbach, David. *The Common Good and Christian Ethics.* New Studies in Christian Ethics. Vol. 22 (Cambridge, UK; New York: Cambridge University Press, 2002), www.loc.gov/catdir/description/cam0210/2002073786.html.

The International Theological Commission. "The Search of a Universal Ethic: A New Look at Natural Law," 9. Translation by Joseph Bolin, www.pathsoflove.com/universal-ethics-natural-law.html (Accessed March 27, 2011).

Jamieson, Dale. *Singer and His Critics.* Philosophers and their Critics. Vol. 8 (Oxford, UK; Malden, MA: Blackwell Publishers, 1999).

Jochemsen, Henk, and John Keown. "Voluntary Euthanasia Under Control? More Empirical Evidence from the Netherlands." *Journal of Medical Ethics* (1999) 25: 16–21.

John Paul II, Pope. *Address of the Holy Father John Paul II, to the 18th International Congress of the Transplantation Society* (Vatican: The Holy See), www.vatican.va/holy_father/john_paul_ii/speeches/2000/jul-sep/documents/hf_jp-ii_spe_20000829_transplants_en.html (Accessed December 6, 2009).

Evangelium Vitae. Issues in Law & Medicine 11, no. 4 (Spring, 1996): 443–453.

Evangelium Vitae (Vatican: The Holy See), www.vatican.va/holy_father/john_paul_ii/encyclicals/documents/hf_jp-ii_enc_25031995_evangelium-vitae_en.html (Accessed July 31, 2011).

Veritatis Splendor (Vatican: The Holy See), August 6, 1993, www.vatican.va/holy_father/john_paul_ii/encyclicals/documents/hf_jp-ii_enc_06081993_veritatis-splendor_en.html (Accessed July 31, 2011).

Jones, David Albert. "Nagging Doubts About Brain-Death." *Catholic Medical Quarterly* (Feb. 1995). Available online at: www.catholicdoctors.org.uk/CMQ/Feb_1995/nagging_doubts_about_brain_death.htm (Accessed December 7, 2009).

Jonsen, Albert and Stephen Toulmin. *The Abuse of Casuistry: A History of Moral Reasoning* (Berkeley, CA: University of California Press, 1988).

Kamm, F. M. *Creation and Abortion: A Study in Moral and Legal Philosophy* (New York: Oxford University Press, 1992).

Keenan, James. "Impasse and Solidarity in Theological Ethics," *CTSA Proceedings* 64 (2009): 53–54.

Knauer, Peter. "The Hermeneutic Function of the Principle of Double Effect." Hein Online (1967).

Konenig-Bricker, Woodeene. *Ten Commandments for the Environment: Pope Benedict Speaks Out for Creation and Justice* (Notre Dame, IN: Ave Maria Press, 2009).

Lauritzen, Paul. *Cloning and the Future of Human Embryo Research* (Oxford; New York: Oxford University Press, 2001).

Lewis, C. S. "The Pains of Animals: A Problem in Theology" in *God in the Dock: Essays on Theology and Ethics* (Grand Rapids, MI: William B. Eerdmans Publishing, Co., 1994).

    The Problem of Pain. 1 Touchone edn. (New York: Simon & Schuster, 1996).

    Vivisection. New England Anti-Vivisection Society, 1947.

Lewontin, Richard C. *The Triple Helix: Gene, Organism, and Environment* (Cambridge, MA: Harvard University Press, 2000).

Lincoln, Abraham, and Stephen A. Douglas. *Political Debates between Hon. Abraham Lincoln and Hon. Stephen A. Douglas, in the Celebrated Campaign of 1858 in Illinois: Including the Preceding Speeches of each at Chicago, Springfield, etc., also the Two Great Speeches of Mr. Lincoln in Ohio, in 1859, as Carefully Prepared by the Reporter of each Party and Published at the Times of their Delivery* (Columbus, OH: Follett, Foster and Company, 1860).

Lindsay, Jack. *The Ancient World: Manners and Morals* (London, UK: Weidenfeld & Nicolson, 1968).

Linzey, Andrew. "C.S. Lewis's Theology of Animals," *Anglican Theological Review* (Winter 1998).

Lyubomirsky, Sonja. *The How of Happiness: A Scientific Approach to Getting the Life You Want* (New York: Penguin Press, 2008).

Magister, Sandro. "Transplants and Brain Death. 'L'Osservatore Romano' Has Broken the Taboo." *Chiesa: Notizie, analisi, documenti sulla Chiesa cattolica, a cura di Sandro Magister.* http://chiesa.espresso.repubblica.it/articolo/206476?eng=y (Accessed December 6, 2009).

Maguiness, Gerard H. "Assisted Suicide, Self-Love, and a Life Worth Living." Dissertation (Rome, 2002).

Marquis, Don. "Why Abortion is Immoral," *Journal of Philosophy* 86 (AP: 1989): 189.

Masters, Thomas, and Amy Uelmen. *Focolare: Living the Spirituality of Unity in the United States* (Hyde Park, NY: New City Press, 2011).

Mattison, William C. *Introducing Moral Theology: True Happiness and the Virtues* (Grand Rapids, MI: Brazos Press, 2008).

McCormick, Richard A., and Paul Ramsey. *Doing Evil to Achieve Good: Moral Choice in Conflict Situations* (Chicago, IL: Loyola University Press, 1978).

Meehan, Mary. "Abortion: The Left Has Betrayed the Sanctity of Life," The Progressive 44 (Sept. 1980).

Milhaven, John G. "Moral Absolutes and Thomas Aquinas," in Charles Curran (ed.), *Absolutes in Moral Theology?* (Westport, CT: Greenwood Press, 1975).

National Catholic Welfare Conference and Donald R. Campion. *Pastoral Constitution on the Church in the Modern World: Gaudium et Spes, December 7, 1965* (Washington, D.C.: National Catholic Welfare Conference, 1976).

Noe, Alva. *Out of Our Heads: Why You are Not Your Brain and Other Lessons from the Biology of Consciousness* (New York: Hill and Wang, 2010).

Nuland, Sherwin B. "The Principle of Hope," *Human Life Review* (July 1, 2002).

Oderberg, David S. "The Illusion of Animal Rights," *Human Life Review* (Spring-Summer 2000): 42.

O'Meara, Thomas. "Christian Theology and Extraterrestrial Intelligent Life," *Theological Studies* 60 (1999): 5–6.

Open Hearts, Open Minds, Fair-Minded Words: A Conference on Life and Choice in the Abortion Debate. "Abortion in America: Should it be a Constitutional Question?" (October 15, 2010) http://uchv.princeton.edu/Life_Choice/program.html (Accessed January 22, 2011).

O'Rourke, OP, Kevin D., and Philip J. Boyle. *Medical Ethics: Sources of Catholic Teaching* (Washington, D.C.: Georgetown University Press, 1999).

Panicola, Michael R. "Quality of Life and the Critically Ill Newborn: Life and Death Decision Making in the Neonatal Context." Ph.D., Saint Louis University, 2000, http://proquest.umi.com/pqdweb?did=732237101&Fmt=7&clientId=65345&RQT=309&VName=PQD.

Panicola, Michael R., David M. Belde, John Paul Slosar, and Mark F. Repenshak. *An Introduction to Healthcare Ethics: Theological Foundations, Contemporary Issues, and Controversial Cases* (Winona, MN: Saint Mary's Press, 2007).

Parfit, Derek, and Samuel Scheffler. *On What Matters* (Oxford University Press, 2009).

Parks, Brian D. "The Natural-Artificial Distinction and Conjoined Twins: A Response to Judith Thomson's Argument for Abortion Rights." *National Catholic Bioethics Quarterly* 6, no. 4 (Winter 2006).

Paul VI, Pope. "Dogmatic Constitution on the Church – *Lumen Gentium*" (Vatican: The Holy See), www.vatican.va/archive/hist_councils/ii_vatican_council/documents/vat-ii_const_19641121_lumen-gentium_en.html (Accessed July 31, 2011).

Perrett, Roy W. "Taking Life and the Argument from Potentiality," *Midwest Studies in Philosophy* 24 (2000): 189.

"Peter Singer Conference Archive." McDonald Centre for Theology, Ethics & Public Life. http://mcdonaldcentre.org.uk/resources/peter-singer-conference/ (Accessed July 10, 2011).

Pinches, Charles, and Jay B. McDaniel (eds.). *Good News for Animals? Christian Approaches to Animal Well-Being* (New York: Orbis, 1993).

Pius XII, Pope. *The Prolongation of Life: Allocution to the International Congress of Anesthesiologists* (November 24, 1957) in "*The Pope Speaks*" 4 (1958).

Pontifical Council *Cor Unum, WORLD HUNGER, A Challenge for All: Development in Solidarity* (Vatican: The Holy See), www.vatican.va/roman_curia/pontifical_councils/corunum/documents/rc_pc_corunum_doc_04101996_world-hunger_en.html (Accessed July 31, 2011).

Pope, Stephen J. *The Evolution of Altruism and the Ordering of Love* (Washington, D.C.: Georgetown University Press, 1994).

"Pope Benedict XVI Continues Tradition of Papal Concern for Animals." *People for the Ethical Treatment of Animals (PETA)*, www.peta.org/features/pope-benedict-xvi.aspx (Accessed February 14, 2010).

"Pope Benedict XVI: Save the Earth." *People for the Ethical Treatment of Animals (PETA)*, www.peta.org/b/thepetafiles/archive/2007/09/04/pope-benedict-xvi-save-the-earth.aspx (Accessed February 12, 2010).

Porter, Jean. "Christianity, Divine Law, and Consequentialism," *Scottish Journal of Theology* 48: 4 (1995), 437.

Nature as Reason: A Thomistic Theory of the Natural Law (Grand Rapids, MI: William B. Eerdmans Publishing Co., 2005).

Preece, Gordon R. *Rethinking Peter Singer: A Christian Critique* (Downers Grove, IL: InterVarsity Press, 2002).

The President's Council on Bioethics. *Controversies in the Determination of Death* (Washington, D.C.: The President's Council on Bioethics, 2008). www.thenewatlantis.com/docLib/20091130_determination_of_death.pdf (Accessed May 9, 2010).

"Putting A Value On Human And Animal Life." Standpoint. http://standpointmag.co.uk/node/3990/full (Accessed July 11, 2011).

Putz, Oliver. "Moral Apes, Human Uniqueness, and the Image of God," *Zygon* 44:3 (September 2009): 615 and 617.

Ratzinger, Joseph Cardinal. *God and the World: A Conversation with Peter Seewald* (San Francisco, CA: Ignatius Press, 2002), 78–79.

"Worthiness to Receive Holy Communion." Teachings of the Catholic Church on Abortion. www.priestsforlife.org/magisterium/bishops/04–07ratzingercommunion.htm (Accessed December 12, 2010).

Rawstorne, Tom. "The chilling truth about the city where they pay people to die." *Daily Mail,* www.dailymail.co.uk/debate/article-1205138/The-chilling-truth-city-pay-people-die.html (Accessed January 24, 2010).

Reichlin, Massimo. "The Argument from Potential: A Reappraisal." *Bioethics* 11: no. 1 (January 1997): 1.

Reinhartz, Adele. "Philo on Infanticide." *Studia Philonica Annual* 4 (1992): 46–47.

Roberts, Holly R. *Vegetarian Christian Saints* (Anjeli Press, 2004).

Robinson, J. Armitage (trans. and ed.). "Didache." *Barnabas, Hermas and the Didache, D.ii.2c* (New York: The MacMillan Co., 1920).

Schaler, Jeffrey A. *Peter Singer Under Fire: The Moral Iconoclast Faces His Critics.* The Under Fire Series. Vol. 3 (Chicago, IL: Open Court, 2009).

Schueler, G. F. "Some Reasoning About Preferences," *Ethics* 95:1 (Oct. 1984).

Scully, Matthew. *Dominion: The Power of Man, the Suffering of Animals, and the Call to Mercy.* 1st edn. (New York: St. Martin's Press, 2002).

Seed, Patricia. "'Are These Not Also Men?': The Indians' Humanity and Capacity for Spanish Civilisation." *Journal of Latin American Studies* Vol. 25: No. 3 (Oct. 1993): 642.

Seligman, Martin E. P. *Authentic Happiness: Using the New Positive Psychology to Realize Your Potential for Lasting Fulfillment. 1 Free Press trade paperback* edn. (New York: Free Press, 2004), www.loc.gov/catdir/description/simon032/2002069288.html.

Selling, Joseph A., and Jan Jans. *The Splendor of Accuracy: An Examination of the Assertions made by Veritatis Splendor.* Grand Rapids, MI: William B. Eerdmans Publishing Co., 1995.

Shewmon, D. Alan. "Recovery from 'Brain Death': A Neurologist's Apologia," *Linacre Q.* 64 (1997): 30–96.

Singer, Peter. *Animal Liberation. New rev. edn.* (New York: Avon Books, 1990).

   A Darwinian Left: Politics, Evolution and Cooperation. Darwinism Today (New Haven, CT: Yale University Press, 2000).

   The Expanding Circle: Ethics and Sociobiology. 1st edn. (New York: Farrar, Straus & Giroux, 1981).

   How Are We to Live? Ethics in an Age of Self-Interest (Amherst, NY: Prometheus Books, 1995).

   In Defense of Animals: The Second Wave (Malden, MA: Blackwell Publishing, 2006). www.loc.gov/catdir/toc/ecip0510/2005009479.html.

   The Life You Can Save: Acting Now to End World Poverty. 1st edn. (New York: Random House, 2009).

   "The Most Significant Work in Ethics Since 1873," *Times Literary Supplement* (May 20, 2011).

   One World: The Ethics of Globalization. Terry Lectures (New Haven, CT: Yale University Press, 2002).

   "Philosophers are Back on the Job," *New York Sunday Times Magazine* (July 7, 1974).

   Practical Ethics. 2nd edn. (Cambridge; New York: Cambridge University Press, 1993).

   Practical Ethics. 3rd edn. (New York: Cambridge University Press, 2011).

   Pushing Time Away: My Grandfather and the Tragedy of Jewish Vienna. 1st edn. (New York: Ecco, 2003).

   Rethinking Life and Death: The Collapse of Our Traditional Ethics (New York: St. Martin's Griffin, 1996).

   "R.M. Hare's Achievements in Moral Philosophy: A Talk for the Memorial Service at St. Mary's Church, Oxford, 25 May, 2002," *Utilitas* 14:3 (November 2002): 309.

Singer, Peter, and Jim Mason. *The Way We Eat: Why Our Food Choices Matter* (Emmaus, PA; New York: Rodale; Distributed to the trade by Holtzbrinck Publishers, 2006), www.loc.gov/catdir/enhancements/

fy0629/2006002899-b.html; www.loc.gov/catdir/enhancements/fy0629/
2006002899-d.html.

Smith, Wesley J. "At the Bottom of the Slippery Slope." *The Weekly Standard*,
www.weeklystandard.com/articles/bottom-slippery-slope_575552.html (Accessed
June 28, 2011).

Specter, Michael. "The Dangerous Philosopher." *The New Yorker*. www.newyorker.
com/archive/1999/09/06/1999_09_06_046_TNY_LIBRY_000018991 (Accessed
December 3, 2009).

Stark, Rodney. *The Rise of Christianity: A Sociologist Reconsiders History*
(Princeton University Press, 1996).

Steel, Karl. "Cynocephali, Animal Savagery, and Terror." In the Middle,
www.inthemedievalmiddle.com/2007/07/cynocephali-animal-savagery-and-
terror.html (Accessed April 24, 2010).

Stefanatos, Joanne. *Animals and Man: a State of Blessedness* (Minneapolis,
MN: Light and Life Publishing Company, 1992).

Steinbock, Bonnie. *The Oxford Handbook of Bioethics*. Oxford Handbooks
(Oxford; New York: Oxford University Press, 2007).

Suárez, Francisco, and Jean Malou. *Opera Omnia* (Venetiis: Balleoni, 1745).

Sulmasy, Daniel. "Double Effect – Intention is the Solution, Not the Problem,"
Journal of Law, Medicine and Ethics 28 (2000): 28.

"Re-inventing the Rule of Double Effect," in *The Oxford Handbook of
Bioethics*, B. Steinbock (ed.) (Oxford University Press, 2007), 114–149.

Tacitus, Cornelius, and D. S. Levene. *The Histories*. *The World's Classics* (Oxford;
New York: Oxford University Press, 1997).

Thomas and Dominicans. English Province. *Summa Theologica*. Complete
English edn. (Allen, TX: Christian Classics, 1981).

Thomson, Judith Jarvis. "A Defense of Abortion," *Philosophy and Public Affairs* 1:
no. 1 (Autumn, 1971): 47–66, www.jstor.org/stable/2265091.

Tierney, Brian. *The Idea of Natural Rights: Studies on Natural Rights, Natural
Law, and Church Law, 1150–1625*. Emory University Studies in Law and
Religion. Vol. 5 (Atlanta, GA: Scholars Press, 1997).

"Tired of life? Group calls for assisted suicide." *DutchNews*. www.dutchnews.nl/news/
archives/2010/02/tired_of_life_group_calls_for.php (Accessed May 9, 2010).

Tolkien, J. R. R. *The Lord of the Rings* (London: Harper Collins, 1974).

Tollefsen, Christopher. "Mind the Gap: Charting the Distance Between
Christian and Secular Bioethics." *Christian Bioethics* Advanced Access:
May 16 (2011).

Tomkins, Stephen. *William Wilberforce: A Biography* (Grand Rapids, MI:
William B. Eerdmans Publishing Co., 2007). www.loc.gov/catdir/toc/
ecip0710/2007004652.html.

Tonti-Filippini, Nicholas. "Religious and Secular Death: A Parting of the Ways,"
Bioethics (forthcoming), 5.

Tooley, Michael. *Abortion and Infanticide* (Oxford; New York: Clarendon Press;
Oxford University Press, 1983).

"The Truth About Torture? – A Christian Ethics Symposium," *First Things*, http://firstthings.com/blogs/evangel/the-truth-about-torture – a-christian-ethics-symposium/ (Accessed November 26, 2010).

Turvey, Jacaranda. *Thesis:* "Natural Law and the Environment: A Critical Engagement with Grisez School Ethics and Theology of Creation." Work in progress at University of Chester.

United States Conference of Catholic Bishops. "*Catholics Confront Global Poverty.*" USCCB website, www.usccb.org/sdwp/globalpoverty/ccgp_index.shtml (Accessed April 13, 2009).

Van der Heide, Agnes, *et al.* "End-of-Life Practices in the Netherlands under the Euthanasia Act," *New England Journal of Medicine* 356: no. 19 (May 10, 2007).

"Vatican Observatory examines theological implications of finding alien life." *Catholic News Agency*, www.catholicnewsagency.com/news/vatican_observatory_examines_theological_implications_of_finding_alien_life/ (Accessed April 24, 2010).

"Vick Suffers the Wrath of the Hypocrites," *Experience Project*, www.experienceproject.com/stories/Hate-Michael-Vick/50226 (Accessed February 13, 2010).

Walters, Kerry S., and Lisa Portmess. *Religious Vegetarianism: From Hesiod to the Dalai Lama* (Albany, NY: State University of New York Press, 2001).

Webb, Clement Charles Julian. *God and Personality: Being the Gifford Lectures Delivered in the University of Aberdeen in the Years 1918 & 1919, First Course.* Gifford Lectures. Vol. 1918–19 (London; New York: Allen & Unwin; Macmillan, 1918).

Wennberg, Robert N. *God, Humans, and Animals: An Invitation to Enlarge Our Moral Universe* (Grand Rapids, MI: William B. Eerdmans Publishing Co., 2003).

Whitmore, Todd. "Catholic Social Teaching: Starting with the Common Good" in Kathleen Maas Weigert and Alexia K. Kelley, *Living the Catholic Social Tradition: Cases and Commentary* (Lanham, MD: Rowman & Littlefield Publishers, 2005).

Wiedemann, Thomas E. J. *Emperors and Gladiators* (London; New York: Routledge, 1992).

Wiest, Michael. "Faith, Justice and Solidarity in the 21st Century." Talk at Fordham University. April 2009.

Willard, Dallas (ed.). *A Place for Truth: Leading Thinkers Explore Life's Hardest Questions* (Madison, WI: InterVarsity Press, 2010).

Williams, Thomas D. "Francisco de Vitoria and the Pre-Hobbesian Roots of Natural Rights Theory," 57, www.upra.org/archivio_pdf/a07103-williams.pdf (Accessed April 23, 2010).

Wilpert, P. (ed.). *De docta ignorantia* 2.12, in *Nikolaus von Kues, Werke* (Berlin: de Gruyter, 1967).

Winn, Pete. "Rep. Stupak: White House Pressuring Me to Keep Quiet on Abortion Language in Senate Health Bill." CNS News, http://cnsnews.com/news/article/58921 (Accessed March 19, 2011).

Woods, Thomas E. *How the Catholic Church Built Western Civilization.* Washington, D.C.; Lanham, MD: Regnery Publishing; Distributed to the trade by National Book Network, 2005, www.loc.gov/catdir/toc/ecip059/ 2005007380.html.

"World Population in 2300." *Welcome to the United Nations: It's Your World,* www.un.org/esa/population/publications/longrange2/longrange2.htm (Accessed July 30, 2011).

Index